IBM SPSS Essentials

IBM SPSS Essentials

Managing and Analyzing Social Sciences Data

Second Edition

John Kulas
Northern Illinois University

Renata Garcia Prieto Palacios Roji
Montclair State University

Adam Smith
Auburn University

Edition History
Jossey-Bass (1e, 2018)

The right of John Kulas, Renata Garcia Prieto Palacios Roji, and Adam Smith to be identified as the authors of this work has been asserted in accordance with law.

Registered Office
John Wiley & Sons, Inc., 111 River Street, Hoboken, NJ 07030, USA

Editorial Office
111 River Street, Hoboken, NJ 07030, USA

For details of our global editorial offices, customer services, and more information about Wiley products visit us at www.wiley.com.

Wiley also publishes its books in a variety of electronic formats and by print-on-demand. Some content that appears in standard print versions of this book may not be available in other formats.

Library of Congress Cataloging-in-Publication Data

Names: Kulas, John T., author.
Title: IBM SPSS essentials : managing and analyzing social sciences data /
    John Kulas, Northern Illinois University, Renata Garcia Prieto Palacios Roji, Montclair State University,
    Adam Smith, Auburn University.
Other titles: SPSS essentials
Description: Third edition. | Hoboken, NJ : John Wiley & Sons, Inc., [2020]
    | Earlier editions published as: SPSS essentials : managing and
    analyzing social sciences data.
Identifiers: LCCN 2020025372 (print) | LCCN 2020025373 (ebook) | ISBN
    9781119417422 (paperback) | ISBN 9781119417439 (adobe pdf) | ISBN
    9781119417446 (epub)
Subjects: LCSH: SPSS (Computer file) | Social sciences – Computer programs.
Classification: LCC HA32 .K85 2020 (print) | LCC HA32 (ebook) | DDC
    300.285/555 – dc23
LC record available at https://lccn.loc.gov/2020025372
LC ebook record available at https://lccn.loc.gov/2020025373

Cover Design: Wiley
Cover Image: © sesame/Getty Images

Set in 9.5/12.5pt STIXTwoText by SPi Global, Chennai, India

SKY10025085_022221

We would like to dedicate this book to those who have brought happiness, love, and fun into our lives – Judy Kulas, Zak Kulas, Yvan Vazquez, Ricardo Garcia Prieto, Connie Palacios Roji, Steven Boomhower, and Lee & Phyllis Smith.

Contents

Preface

This book represents a summarized compilation of problem-solving successes that we collectively gleaned while working for various academic and private organizations. These are all institutions at which we've held jobs and at which at least a portion of our duties included minimizing errors in various applications (including SPSS).

This is a "how to" book. We present a *system* for using a software program known by the ubiquitous anagram: SPSS. You are not expected to know anything about SPSS at the beginning of the book – however, by the time you get to the end of the book, you are expected to know enough about SPSS to comfortably use the program. The intended audience of this second edition is undergraduate students who are learning SPSS in classroom environments (whether the delivery of the class content is "in person" or online). This differs in focus from the first edition, which was intended to be a bookshelf reference – a guide for practitioners who are using SPSS with real-world data (which is almost always "messy"). The information found in this book should not become outdated with future versions of SPSS – the basic premise will be useful with SPSS version ∞.

Regardless of slight shifting of organization and emphasis, the purpose of both versions of this book is to teach you **how you should use SPSS**. The goal throughout is to minimize errors. Errors can occur in data entry, analysis interpretation, and even the choice of which dataset to use for analysis. This last error, sadly, has increased in probability with the most recently released versions of SPSS. If you follow the "how to"s of this book, you will greatly decrease your likelihood of introducing errors into your research/analyses. Essentially, the book is a template for how you should organize your SPSS life. Generally speaking, you will learn to organize through keeping "diaries" of what you: (1) plan to do, (2) actually do, and (3) (perhaps regrettably) did.

The initial title of this book, when it was only used in the first author's personal statistics classes, was "Use syntax or I'll bonk you over the head with this book … and other cheerful stories from an SPSS practitioner". When it was decided that the material in that book should be made more widely available, the title was changed but the basic message of the initial book is the same – our intent is to build your skill not only using SPSS, but also in using it in a manner that keeps a record of what you've done and increases your chances of finding and correcting errors. This is accomplished via "using syntax".

Students will find this text helpful as a supportive framework while learning statistics – knowing how to properly use SPSS will ideally parallel your increasing knowledge of statistical procedures (e.g. SPSS can confirm or disconfirm, for example, exercises that may also be calculated "by hand"). Instructors should find this text a useful step-off point for instruction (i.e. you should be able to focus on SPSS's relevance to classroom material instead of database set-up, variable identification, etc.). Practitioners will likely find the previous edition of this text a more useful reference and guide with real-world data, so we recommend searching for a first edition if you intend to use SPSS in your work (e.g. outside of a classroom setting).

Preview of the book's organization:

Part I: Introduction

This section of the book introduces the reader to the "concept" of SPSS and provides a framework for how SPSS should be approached and used. While there is a lot of flexibility in how SPSS can be used, there is very little flexibility in how SPSS *should* be used. Part I introduces a fairly rigid framework that takes away some of the flexibility in the use of SPSS through introducing a "syntax diary" method of interfacing with SPSS. This is very important, because expert-level SPSS users **all** use this "syntax diary" method. Novice users typically resist using this method when they first encounter SPSS. The main purpose of Part I is to convince you, the SPSS novice, that the method used by SPSS experts is an approach you should adopt sooner (before you've made catastrophic mistakes) rather than later (after you've made catastrophic mistakes).

In addition to an introduction to the program and a listing of reasons why you should adopt the syntax diary method, Part I also covers basic concepts that will help you get your data/information into SPSS format: (1) conceptualizing your data (numbers versus words), (2) actually *creating* empty SPSS datashells that conform to your data, (3) defining variables and possible variable values, (4) entering data, and (5) accessing and organizing the datafiles. Chapters that cover these concepts include:

- Introduction to Data
- Getting Your Data into SPSS

- Accessing Your Data
- Defining Your Data

Part II: Statistics

SPSS has two primary functions – data manager and data analyst. Although Parts I and III focus on the first stated SPSS function, Part II covers the most common analytical applications of SPSS. Here we focus not only on how to perform computer-assisted analyses, but also how to navigate the sometimes voluminous and confusing output received from these analyses. This is important because the output that SPSS provides for requested analyses tends to look quite different from the output generated "by hand" (the output you may calculate, for instance, in your statistics class). Part II chapters walk you through syntax specification and output interpretation for common descriptive (mean, standard deviation, frequency distribution) and inferential (t-test, ANOVA, correlation, regression) analyses. We do so with a focus on the important shared elements provided by the six-step hypothesis testing process and SPSS output:

- Descriptive Statistics
- Hypothesis Testing
- Inferential Analyses (Z- and T-Tests, ANOVAs)
- Inferential Analyses (Correlation and Regression)

Part III: Advanced Data Management

Just because your data are in SPSS format does not mean that they are in a format that is ready for data analysis or synthesis. Typically, data collected in the Social Sciences and entered into SPSS (called raw data) need to undergo transformations and/or manipulations before they are analyzed. Sometimes the information you want does not even exist in your raw data. In these circumstances, you need to *create* new variables that are summaries of your raw data (typically, these are called scale scores). Other times you will need to combine information from different datafiles (for instance, to get IV and DV information in the same file) or you will need to indicate that only some of your data (i.e. subgroups) is of direct interest to you. Early chapters in Part III focus on these issues of "getting your data in a format that conforms to desired analyses". Three chapters focus primarily on very common data manipulations:

- Manipulating Your Data
- Collapsing and Merging Data Files
- Differential Treatment of Data

Although information in Chapters 1 through 15 are likely sufficient for most beginner-level situations (changing variable values, merging datafiles, creating scale scores, running descriptive and inferential analyses), SPSS also has powerful capabilities that extend beyond these common functions. The final two chapters of Part III introduce you to just a few of these capabilities that we have found particularly helpful in our own problem-solving applications (for example, how to construct conditional if-then statements). The information in these final two chapters will primarily help you to work more *efficiently* with SPSS. In addition to efficient syntax commands, the use of notepad and the identification and eradication of errors are covered. Chapters include:

- Using Your Output
- Other Tricks of the Trade

Acknowledgments

We would like to thank three people who helped bring this book to life but who aren't officially recognized on the spine of the book – Emma Matheson, Jace Dallman, and Laura Olean. Emma, Jace, and Laura were all graduate student instructors of laboratory sections of undergraduate statistics that paralleled traditional instructional sections. These three really set the groundwork for this second edition to be a more useful reference for undergraduate students, and we are extremely grateful for their contributions.

Author Biography

John Kulas received his PhD in Industrial and Organizational Psychology from Northern Illinois University. He currently serves as Professor of Industrial and Organizational Psychology at Montclair State University. His research has tended to focus on issues of measurement in Psychological assessment. In his spare time, he likes to hunt (and eat!) wild mushrooms.

Renata Garcia Prieto Palacios Roji is completing her PhD in Industrial and Organizational Psychology from Montclair State University. She currently works as a Talent and Culture Analyst for Lockton Companies, and as Dr. Kulas' Graduate Research Assistant conducting research on work–life balance and telework among other topics. She is a llama lover and in her spare time, she likes to bake, read, and watch scary movies.

Adam Smith completed his PhD in Industrial and Organizational Psychology at Auburn University. He is an associate consultant at Kincentric, specializing in leadership assessment and development. Adam also serves as an adjunct faculty member at Wentworth Institute of Technology and an instructor at Harvard University, teaching courses on statistics and I/O psychology. On the weekends, he enjoys playing violin and taking trips up the New England coast.

Part I

Introduction

1

What is SPSS?

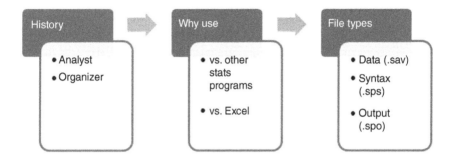

Chapter Learning Objectives

1. History of SPSS
2. SPSS uses and capabilities
3. Additional statistical programs
4. Importance of syntax

Welcome to the first stage of your adventure learning how to use SPSS®, one of the more commonly used statistical software programs. The name **SPSS** is an

IBM SPSS Essentials: Managing and Analyzing Social Sciences Data, Second Edition.
John Kulas, Renata Garcia Prieto Palacios Roji, and Adam Smith.
© 2021 John Wiley & Sons, Inc. Published 2021 by John Wiley & Sons, Inc.

acronym for Statistical Package for the Social Sciences, and is owned and sold by IBM®. As a valuable tool for running statistical analyses, SPSS is currently used by individuals across a variety of fields and disciplines, expanding past its original market solely within the "social sciences".

SPSS has two primary functions: (1) as a data organizer/manager and (2) as a data analyst. Both parts will be covered in detail throughout this book, and by the end you should be able to not only create and organize **data** efficiently, but also run statistical analyses based on a variety of data structures. It's important to keep in mind how crucial the process of data organization is, since analyses run on faulty data can lead to incorrect conclusions and some very confusing output from SPSS. Luckily, we are here to steer you in the right direction.

Like most software programs, SPSS is continually being updated, just like your constant Android or iOS mobile updates. SPSS updates are intended to improve the user experience as well as add additional functionality to help you better analyze and visualize your data. In the beginning versions of SPSS, users were required to use mainframe and DOS-based programs, which required users to *program* (enter computer code language) in order to organize and run analyses. Fortunately, the current version of SPSS (25 as this book is being written) includes a comprehensive set of click and dropdown menus in order to help you perform these functions.

In addition to perpetual software updates, the field of statistics changes over time (improvements and slight alterations are generally made) and new statistics are constantly being "discovered". To stay current with statistical advancements and platform limitations and changes (such as changes in Microsoft Windows), the SPSS program is frequently updated. Whether you are using the most recent or an older version of SPSS, the information in this book will still serve you the same. All figures and examples will be shown from a PC perspective, but the information is also applicable to a Mac audience.

What Is SPSS Used For

SPSS has the capability to perform a wide variety of statistical analyses, both *descriptive* and *inferential* (these terms will be covered later in Chapters 7 and 8). It is used by researchers (biologists, psychologists, sociologists, and economists) and public and private sector workers (accountants, human resources professionals, and actuaries). These individuals use SPSS to test hypotheses in experimental and field settings, summarize information, and create graphs and figures.

The primary power of SPSS lies in its wide variety of statistical options and its ability to perform these analyses quickly. There are other software programs available that do a nice job of, for example, creating customizable graphs and figures, but SPSS creates these *in addition* to its primary purpose of processing data using appropriate statically formulae.

The Power of SPSS

Given the vast array of options SPSS offers, running large numbers of analyses can become confusing, especially when trying to repeat something you did previously. For example, you could spend an hour running analyses in SPSS by clicking drop-down menus, and afterward you realized you made a mistake 30 minutes prior. How would you know where you made your mistake? How would you go about trying to fix the issue? Unfortunately, this happens on a frequent basis, even for well-seasoned SPSS veterans. But don't lose hope, because SPSS allows you to keep track of all the work you've previously done, and gives you a physical trail of everything you've done. It does this through what refer to as a **syntax diary**.

We previously mentioned how older versions of SPSS required users to write their own code to run functions. While this is still possible, SPSS also anticipated the needs and common mistakes made by modern users and currently has the capability to *generate code for you*. It then places this code in a file that serves as a record of what you've done (and, if you're a good diary writer, why you've done it). Later chapters will cover how this is done, but take our advice, this function will be your greatest ally in mastering SPSS and impressing your professor, boss, colleagues, or friends of your statistical genius.

SPSS Compared to Other Programs

SPSS was designed specifically for the purpose of performing statistical analyses. There are other software programs that perform statistics as their primary purpose (such as SAS, Minitab, and nQuery). In addition to these, open-source programs are becoming widely popular for performing statistical analyses, with R currently being the most popular. In general, individuals tend to pick one program and rely heavily on learning and using it exclusively, but there is much to be gained from being able to capitalize on a diverse set of tools. That being said, learning to use multiple software programs is no small feat and in terms of learning curves, SPSS is one of the easiest to navigate.

SPSS is also in competition with spreadsheet programs that have statistical potential. These programs (such as **Microsoft Excel**) are generally fine for organization and **descriptive statistical analyses** (statistics that *describe* a given set of numbers: means, standard deviations, and correlations), but they are usually less useful if your goal is to perform **inferential statistics** that make an *inference* about a larger group of numbers (these are the activities that will be further discussed in Chapters 7 and 8). If you are doing inferential hypothesis-testing, SPSS is the way to go.

Over the years, the SPSS data sheet has actually come to look quite similar in appearance to **Excel**. For the current version of SPSS, you can think of the program as a combination of Word and Excel (to cite the most commonly used word processor and spreadsheet applications). SPSS is conceptually a combination of the two, as data are stored in SPSS's Excel-like spreadsheet component and analyses are performed by writing commands (with text) in SPSS's Word-like processing component.

Summary

SPSS is used not only to perform data analyses, but also used to organize and manipulate data. SPSS is considered superior to data spreadsheet programs (such as Excel) because with SPSS you can *keep a record* of what you have done. This is done through keeping a *syntax diary*.

Key Terms

Data – Anything informative that can be entered into SPSS.
Descriptive statistics – Information summarizing a set of numbers.
Excel – Computer spreadsheet program.
Inferential statistics – Probability-based information relating sample to population characteristics (more to come on this topic later).
SPSS – Computer program used to do data manipulations and analyses.
Syntax diary – Record of "what you've done" to your data.

Discussion Questions

1 Why is SPSS superior to Excel?

2 What are some advantages and disadvantages associated with SPSS's evolution toward an Excel–Word hybrid?

2

Navigating SPSS

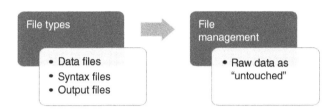

CHAPTER MENU

Chapter Learning Objectives

1. Opening and using SPSS
2. Understand the three important file types
3. Managing your SPSS life
4. Importance of raw data files

How the Program Works

When you access the program (selecting the SPSS icon from your desktop or start menu) for the first time, a couple of different things can happen. First, a "Welcome

IBM SPSS Essentials: Managing and Analyzing Social Sciences Data, Second Edition.
John Kulas, Renata Garcia Prieto Palacios Roji, and Adam Smith.
© 2021 John Wiley & Sons, Inc. Published 2021 by John Wiley & Sons, Inc.

to IBM SPSS Statistics" box might appear that basically asks "what would you like to do?" There is an option at the very bottom of this box that says "Don't show this dialog in the future" – go ahead and select that box (you don't actually want to see this box every time you open SPSS). The second thing that can happen (and in fact will happen when you close the "Welcome" window) is that an empty data file will open – this is the **data file**, one of three very important file types in SPSS.

Important File Types

There are three very important types of files used by SPSS. There is the aforementioned data file type (identified by a .sav file extension), a syntax file type (identified by a .sps file extension), and an output file type (identified by a .spv file extension).

Data Files

Data (.sav) files are where you store your numbers/data. Typically, you have one *original* data file for each major project that you are working on. Figure 2.1 shows what an empty .sav file looks like.

Notice that the empty data file looks similar to a spreadsheet, with a tool bar at the top filled with icons (including the typical "file", "edit", and "view" commands but also the nontypical "transform", "analyze", and "graphs" commands – the icons you see in Figure 2.1 may look a little different from SPSS version to a

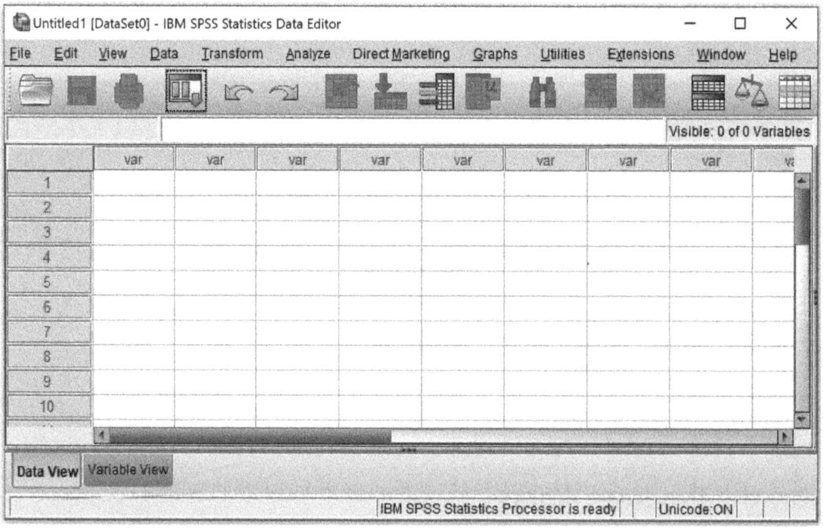

Figure 2.1 Empty .sav file.

different SPSS version or from one computer to another). The bottom of the file has two spreadsheet tabs labeled "data view" (the tab currently shown in the screen shot above) and "variable view". We will explain the variable view tab later in this book, but for now you should recognize that the Data View tab visually reveals the data.

Similar to Excel, data in this tab will be organized in rows and columns. Note that the columns (the top cells running from left to right) currently have the word "var" written in them. When you have data to enter in the .sav file, these top cells can be used to identify what the column data represent. As you record multiple observations (also called cases) of this variable, you will populate rows (identified by the numbers along the left side of the spread sheet above). When there is more than one case (rows) for each variable (columns), you will have a **data matrix**.

The matrix in Figure 2.2 contains four variables (Var1 to Var4) defining each column. For each variable, there are five rows, representing the five observations (aka *cases*) for each variable.

The .sav file technically contains everything a novice SPSS user needs to run analyses. 99% of the time, any command or manipulation you want to do can be completed using the dropdown options located in the commands at the top ribbon.

Although the .sav file can manage most of your statistical needs on its own, there is another important file that is crucial to maintaining and organizing your statistical work: the **syntax file**

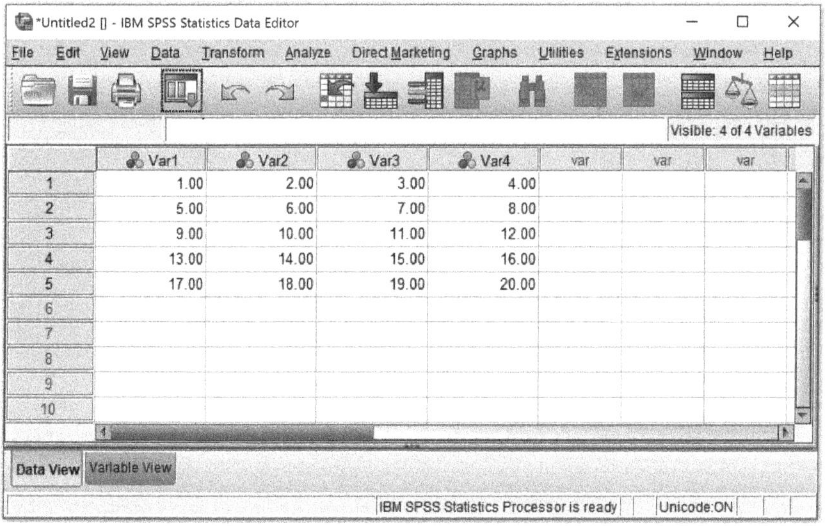

Figure 2.2 Matrix with four variables.

Syntax Files

Syntax (.sps) files are where you write your statistical diary (where your data came from, what analyses you'd like to do, the date or any other notes you would like to leave for yourself later on). An empty (no diary entries/statistical commands) syntax file is presented in Figure 2.3.

Just as you put your numbers in your data file, you identify what you would like SPSS to do with the data via the Syntax file (.sps). Notice that: (1) the commands along the ribbon of the page are similar to the options in the .sav file and (2) there is a lot of blank white space instead of grids (you can actually write in this file like you would in a word processor). These two file types (data [.sav] and syntax [.sps]) are the two files that you, the SPSS user, works with. You have to enter information into both the .sav file and the .sps file for each project that you do.

Output Files

Output (.spv) files are different from data and syntax files. *You* do not create output file – output files are created by the SPSS program. If you have a syntax file that is full (writing in it instead of a big blank space like Figure 2.3) and you have a data file that has numbers in it (e.g. Figure 2.2, instead of the blank white cells as in Figure 2.1), the result of the interaction of your syntax commands and your data will produce an output (.spv) file. As with the data and syntax examples, a blank output file is presented in Figure 2.4.

You will almost never see empty output files like Figure 2.4. The reason for this is because output files are "born", they're not typically conjured up as this one has

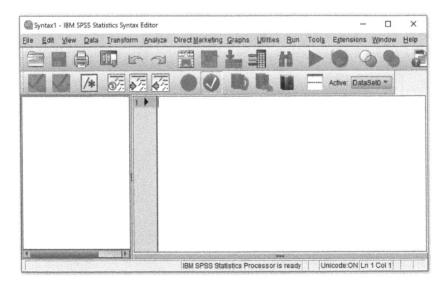

Figure 2.3 Syntax (.sps) file.

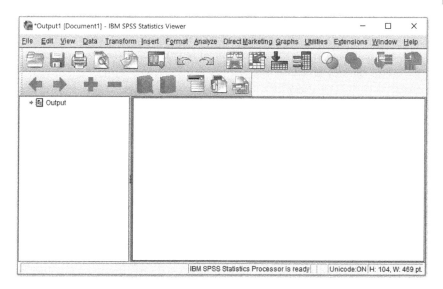

Figure 2.4 Empty output file.

been. When you perform an analysis or a data manipulation – boom – an output file appears. An output file will be created the first time you "do something" to your data. As more "things" are done to the data, the result will be added to this output file. Output files are therefore like SPSS messengers – anytime something noteworthy is done to your data, the output file will pop up and report the event.

The Output file has two "panels" (left and right). The right-hand panel presents all of the detailed output you request from your selected analyses. The left panel is merely an outline of the detailed information provided in the right-hand panel (this outline is sometimes useful to help you navigate through the detailed output on the right if you have a lot of analyses that have been performed).

The "Others"

There are other SPSS file types you will eventually encounter, but the big three that you should know are the data, syntax, and output files. You can pursue learning about SPSS's other capabilities after reading this book (if you decide that you like SPSS enough [or are going to use it enough] to learn more).

Managing Your SPSS Life

We've just presented the notion that SPSS has three important file types that you will be working with. If you're nervous about using new software (like many of us are), this fact can make learning this system feel even more daunting. Luckily, there are ways to manage how and where you save these files that will hopefully simplify the process (and declutter your desktop).

Before you start using SPSS, you will need to create a system for storing your syntax and data. You should start by choosing a location within your computer's file space that you can easily find. This **file space** may be somewhere in your personal file folder or on a designated external flash drive. It is also best to get in the habit of creating subfolders for each project or assignment. This will ensure that you can easily find the syntax file you need, open it up, and pick up right where you left off (even if it's been weeks or months since you last worked on the project). Figure 2.5 shows a flowchart of a system that works well if you are using this book to supplement a statistics course.

In the example above, the files are organized by class assignment folders. You can also organize them by topic or research area. Notice that within each HW folder, there is a separate space for the data and syntax files. If you've been paying attention, you might ask why there is not a place for the output file?

We have already mentioned that the syntax file is for writing and recording the manipulations and analysis that you will perform on your data file. The output file will pop up whenever you do something of note to the data. Because the output file is created by the interaction of the data file and the syntax file, there is not typically a need to save this file. Whenever you want the information again, you can simply rerun the syntax script on the original data file.

The Importance of Maintaining the Raw Data as an "Untouched" File

Maintaining the unadulterated status of your original (also called "raw") data file is key to using SPSS correctly, since this is what will enable you to redo and undo any errors that you make. In fact, early in your SPSS exploration, it is highly recommended that the raw data file be the only data file that you maintain for a given project.

Even the savviest of SPSS users are still human and make mistakes and errors that can compromise the data they are working with. Simple things such as filtering data on the wrong variable, accidently overwriting a number in a cell, or deleting a variable that seemed unneeded at some point in time can cause massive

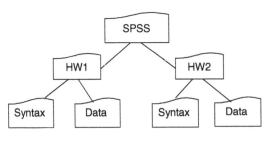

Figure 2.5 Flowchart to supplement statistics course.

problems down the road. These simple, common, and seemingly small mistakes can lead to misinformed conclusions (or at least a less-than-deserved grade on statistics homework) when they are not caught. When accidents like this are discovered, a raw data file and a properly recorded syntax file are like a magic do-over button that allow you to correct a mistake quickly and move on rather than spend hours trying to backtrack.

Summary

SPSS works through the interaction of a datafile (.sav) and a syntax file (.sps). When the numbers (data) and instructions (syntax) interact, the result is an output file (.spv). It's important to have an organizational system in place within your computer for saving these files.

Key Terms

Data file – Computer repository for information (aka "data")
Data matrix – Synonym for data file, but implying that the file holds actual values
Data (.sav) files – Where data are stored within SPSS
File space – System of drives and folders located on your computer (or on a server/cloud)
Syntax file – Script that documents requested computer actions
Syntax (.sps) files – Where operations are specified within SPSS
Output (.spv) files – Where results are reported within SPSS

Discussion Questions

1 In the text it is mentioned that _____ files look similar to a spreadsheet such as the ones you would find in Excel. On the other hand, there are _____ files which look similar to a Word Document, and are to be used as diaries to keep track of where your data came from, what analysis you have done, etc.

2 Why is it important to maintain your raw data "untouched"?

3

Introduction to Data

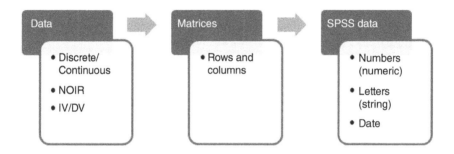

CHAPTER MENU

Chapter Learning Objectives

1. Understanding your data types
   a. Independent and Dependent variables
   b. Nominal, Ordinal, Interval, and Ratio
   c. Continuous versus Discrete
   d. Numeric and String data
2. Structure of SPSS data organization
   a. People organized as rows
   b. Variables organized as columns

IBM SPSS Essentials: Managing and Analyzing Social Sciences Data, Second Edition.
John Kulas, Renata Garcia Prieto Palacios Roji, and Adam Smith.

This book is intended to prepare you for your first experience working within SPSS. However, before you use the program, it is essential that you understand your data (outside of SPSS). If you understand your data independent of SPSS, it'll make the process of learning how it integrates with SPSS a lot easier. This chapter, therefore, first ensures that we're all in agreement on "what data is" before we delve into inputting that data into SPSS.

Understanding Your Data

Data is quite a broad term that can include any informative piece of information. For statistical analyses, data are most often organized into **variables**, which refer to anything that can take on more than one value. For example, pets can be a variable since it can take on the value of dog, cat, or any other (typically) domesticated animal.

Independent Versus Dependent Variables

Considering methodological/experimental concepts as we discuss variables, data can also be thought of as representing either an **independent variable (IV)** or a **dependent variable (DV)**. An IV refers to the predictor or manipulated variable in a study, whereas a DV identifies the outcome of some experiment or the criterion variable of interest. In a study that aims to study the effect of water intake on weight loss, amount of water drank would be the IV, whereas weight would serve as the DV/outcome.

There are of course other variable types relevant for data management and analysis. Two that you may encounter other than IV/DV are: (1) a covariate or (2) purely descriptive. A **covariate** is a variable that is measured or recorded but is not of *primary* interest to your research question. Usually these are considered *secondary* IVs. Demographic variables such as age, gender, or race are common covariates used in the social sciences. Purely descriptive variables are variables that simply organize your information (these could be, for example, participant ID or name).

Scales of Measurement

Outside of SPSS, the social and behavioral sciences commonly utilize the Stevens (1946) taxonomy of *nominal, ordinal, interval,* and *ratio scales of measurement* to govern the assignment of numbers to variable values. A variable measured at the nominal level represents the crudest form of measurement, and includes assigning numbers to things like sport jerseys (these numbers do not then convey any information other than identification). Measurement at the ordinal level is often described as rank placement, such as first, second, or third place. Here the numbers merely reflect an underlying sequence or ordering. Interval-level measurement maintains consistent spacings between each jump in variable value, and includes such commonly encountered scales as temperature as measured by either the Fahrenheit or Celsius scale. Ratio is similar to interval, except that the assignment of the number zero ("0") is held in extremely high regard – zero can only be used to reflect the complete absence of whatever is being measured. This type of measurement is more commonly encountered in the hard-physical sciences and includes concepts such as height and weight.

Within SPSS, the distinction between each of Stevens' four categories becomes a bit less important. Rather than these four levels, there are really only two categories of relative importance, and although these two categories are more closely aligned with levels of measurement, they are terms that are commonly applied to variables: these are *discrete* and *continuous* variables. For simplicity, think of nominal- and ordinal-level data as being associated with **discrete variables**, while interval- and ratio-level measurement occurs with **continuous variables**. These labels will sometimes be important when attempting to perform statistical analyses.

All of the information presented above is applicable regardless of whether you want to work with data within SPSS or any other statistical platform. Below, however, you will find information that is specific to how SPSS conceptualizes data.

The SPSS Data Perspective

We've discussed kinds of data from a measurement perspective (nominal, ordinal, interval, and ratio), from a methodological perspective (independent, dependent, and covariate), and from a hybrid of measurement and methods perspective (discrete, continuous), but we need to dig a bit deeper to get into the SPSS perspective. SPSS allows a great deal of flexibility in what you consider to be data. Essentially, you can store any little nugget of information you want in SPSS, but for 99% of your purposes, there is only one important SPSS distinction to make: is your data best represented by a number or a word?

Data Represented by Numbers (Numeric)

If your data is an IV, DV, or covariate, it should always be stored as a number. SPSS refers to all numbers (regardless of whether they represent a nominal, ordinal, interval, or ratio level of measurement or classified as discrete or continuous) as **numeric** variables. It is often difficult to think of values of nominal variables as being represented by a number, but entities that can be sorted into categories – such as (1) male or female, (2) dog, cat, or bird, or (3) army or navy – can just as easily have category labels such as: (1) 1 or 2, (2) 0, 1, or 3, or (3) 100 or 10,000. The numbers are meaningless in terms of quantity or order of importance, since they are meant only to identify a category. The numbers' primary function is to identify *which group* an individual belongs to. *If* you are eventually going to use group membership as a variable within a statistical analysis, it is important (within SPSS) that category membership is indicated with numbers, not words.

Data Represented by Words (String)

In addition to primary variables of interest, it is often convenient to record supplementary information about the elements of your data sample (most commonly, these elements are "people"). You may, for example, decide that it would be a good idea to record the names of individuals who are associated with particular records (rows) in your file. Although these names are not necessary for statistical analysis, they may prove useful if an individual record is lost, needs updating, or otherwise needs to be identified. SPSS by default, however, expects any data that you enter to be in numerical format – you therefore need to go through some prep-work prior to storing data as words (variables with word values within SPSS are referred to as **"string"** variables). We will cover how to do this prep-work in the next chapter. For now, just keep in mind that string variables cannot function as an IV, DV, or covariate, since inferential analyses in current versions of SPSS require data to be numerical.

The Other Variable Types

In addition to string and numeric variables, there are several others that can be stored within SPSS. For example, you may eventually want to store **date** information, perhaps as a reminder of when data were collected. SPSS, however, views dates a little differently than people typically do, tracking time by a smaller than commonly encountered metric: seconds. Therefore, if you were to ask SPSS to compute the difference between 8/10/2017 and 8/9/2017, instead of reporting a difference of "1" (one day), SPSS would give you a value of 86 400 (the number of seconds in a day). This is no big deal, however, as we can easily transform this information and have SPSS report values for any time period we are interested in (e.g. minutes, hours, days, weeks), and we will in fact cover these types of transformations later in the book.

Your Data in SPSS – Think Matrices

The way in which data is organized can look quite different on a classroom chalkboard than how it needs to look in SPSS. Data are typically entered and stored within SPSS as a **matrix** of information. A matrix consists of horizontal rows and vertical columns. Figure 3.1 illustrates a matrix in SPSS.

By convention, variables are identified with column headings, and people populate rows (not every project will collect data from "people" of course – rows may also therefore represent individual rats, pigeons, llamas, or any other members of a research sample).

SPSS is primarily concerned with variables (columns) and the entities (rows) that provide values for those variables. In a typical application, one "entity" – for instance, a person – will provide values to many variables (there is only one person per row, but many columns contain different pieces of information from that person). For instance, John is a male, he does not smoke, and on a scale of 1–10, he likes SPSS 10 (i.e. a lot). This information would be entered into one row within an SPSS data file. When more individuals provide more information, more rows are added. When more than one individual provides information on more than one variable, you end up with a matrix of information.

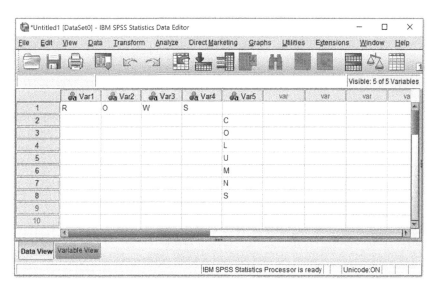

Figure 3.1 Rows and columns in an SPSS matrix.

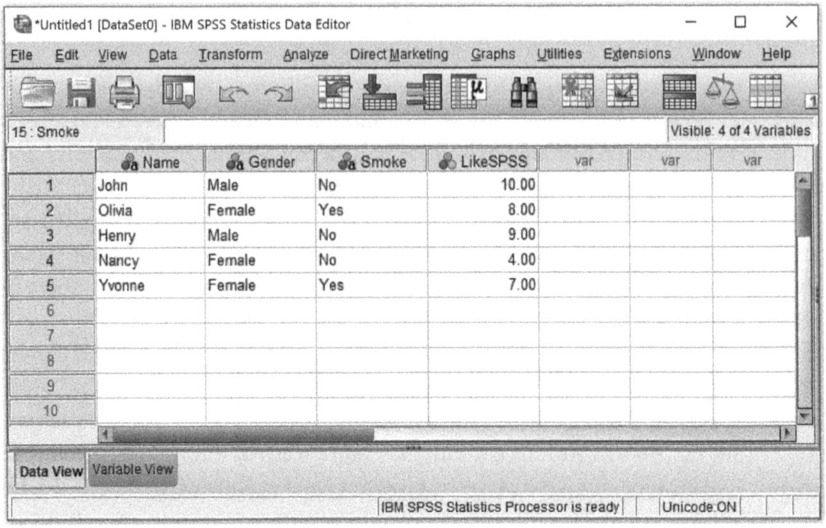

Figure 3.2 5 × 4 SPSS matrix.

Let's say we collected information from John, Olivia, Henry, Nancy, and Yvonne regarding their gender, smoking preferences, and how much they like SPSS, we would end up with a 5 × 4 matrix of information (shown in Figure 3.2). Matrix dimensions are always specified as (the number of rows with meaningful information) × (the number of columns with meaningful information). In SPSS, it is most likely that you will have more rows than columns. This is because it is most common to have more people than variables within a given project.

This is also a very important and extremely important consideration in the organization of your data: *the number of people you have in your experiment or project equals the number of rows you will have in your SPSS data file.* This little tidbit of information will help you immensely as you try to figure out how to organize your data to fit your analyses (if your unit of analyses is multiple people – that is, groups or teams – then you will have the same number of rows as groups).

Summary

Data can be represented in a variety of ways. As far as SPSS is concerned, data are most importantly either a number (numeric) or a word (string). If at all possible, numeric data are preferred to string data (e.g. you should try to store as much information as numbers as possible). Always remember that the number of people or objects you are dealing with defines the number of rows in your dataset, with the number of variables defining the number of columns.

Key Terms

Continuous variables – Variables that can assume a large number of possible values.
Covariate – Variable not of primary interest, but thought to be related to a DV.
Date – SPSS specification of a calendar date.
Dependent variable (DV) – Outcome or criterion variable.
Discrete variables – Variables that have only a limited number of possible values.
Independent variables – Predictor or manipulated variable.
Matrix – A grid formation of two or more rows and columns.
Numeric – SPSS specification of a number.
String – SPSS specification of a word.
Variable – Anything that can possess different values or quantities.

Discussion Questions

1 What numbers can be used to code the following values?
   a. Gender
   b. Military rank
   c. Height

2 Why would anyone include covariates in a data file?

3 Data represented by numbers are known as _____ variables, while data represented by words are known as _____ variables.

4

Getting Your Data into SPSS

CHAPTER MENU

Chapter Learning Objectives

1. Creating data files by hand and through syntax
2. Specifying types of variables
   a. Numbers versus Words (String)

Welcome to the part of the book where you will actually enter your own personal data into SPSS. By now you should know what an empty SPSS data file looks like

IBM SPSS Essentials: Managing and Analyzing Social Sciences Data, Second Edition.
John Kulas, Renata Garcia Prieto Palacios Roji, and Adam Smith.
© 2021 John Wiley & Sons, Inc. Published 2021 by John Wiley & Sons, Inc.

(see Figure 2.1) and what a data-filled file looks like (see Figure 2.2), but how did we actually get the Figure 2.2 numbers to appear in the grid cells? Good question! This chapter will help you accomplish this goal (populating an empty data shell with actual information).

When a researcher collects data, they have traditionally been stored on **hardcopies** (typically physical paper). Increasingly, however, data are being kept in some type of digital storage file (for example, if a survey was completed via online or phone response). This chapter will focus on **hardcopy** data that requires hand-entry into SPSS, as this is still quite common in a variety of research settings. The following chapter presents *how to access* datafiles that contain important information, whereas this chapter focuses only on *how to create* those datafiles that contain important information.

Before SPSS

Regardless of which statistical software program you are using, it's very important to understand your data before you imagine how the data may fit within the constraints of the software. Therefore, before we start to work within the software program (SPSS), please take a look at Appendix A, which presents an example of a survey questionnaire that is to be filled out "on paper". This is a personality assessment developed from the international personality item pool (IPIP; Goldberg, 1999; Johnson, 2005). It has a number in the upper right-hand corner indicating the participant's ID, asks for the respondent's gender, and presents 100 personality-related questions. Traditionally, researchers would gather many of these completed questionnaires and then transfer the information from each individual survey into an SPSS data file. For example, if 1000 people responded to all 102 items, the data file would be a 1000 × 102 matrix, reflecting the number of respondents × number of variables. When working with data "by hand" such as this, it is a very good idea to create a **code sheet** that helps you organize data that you eventually plan to somehow represent electronically. Here are a few simple steps to help you create a code sheet:

1. Find a blank questionnaire (no participant data has been recorded).
2. Determine what information should be recorded as numbers and what should be recorded as words.
3. For information that will be recorded as numbers, write those numbers on the code sheet (see Appendix B).
4. Give a short name (eight characters or shorter) to each of the variables in the questionnaire. While SPSS can handle variable names greater than eight characters, your life will be much simpler the shorter your variables names are. We will discuss this further along in the book (in a later chapter).

For this particular questionnaire, all information can be stored as numbers (numeric variables) rather than words (string variables), with 102 variables to create. The first variable (what we are calling the **case number** – you should always have this variable in your projects) identifies the respondent, the second identifies the respondent's gender, and the remaining 100 variables identify responses to 100 items on the personality questionnaire. The code sheet represents a linkage between your hard copies (e.g. the data itself) and your SPSS data file (e.g. a software repository where we hope to eventually perform statistical analyses on our data). We are going to use the code sheet first to help us create a file that can electronically store our 1000 responses – throughout the book, we refer to this type of empty but "data ready" file as a **data shell**.

Specifying Operations Through SPSS

Previously, we talked about syntax and how it provides a method to manually control operations in SPSS through typing words, otherwise known as **SPSS code**. However, there are two different categories of words that need to be elaborated on: (1) **commands** and (2) **objects** (e.g. your variable names). Commands tell SPSS *what* actions you want to perform; your objects (aka variables) tell SPSS *where* the actions should be performed (i.e. what variables to focus on). SPSS comes with built-in commands that are available for you to use, but you will need to decide appropriate variable names "on your own" (e.g. SPSS doesn't know or care what your variable names are). This feature of SPSS (and all other data processing applications) is why a code sheet is such an important resource. Additionally, before we begin writing syntax, keep in mind that SPSS reads syntax *sequentially, from "top" to "bottom"*. This becomes very important as our syntax documents (also called "scripts") become more elaborate – SPSS will always perform operations starting from the top of your script and proceed to **execute** commands line-by-line until the bottom of your script is reached. The "execute" command in our syntax tells the SPSS processor to start working, you could think of it as a "go" command – you'll notice it within our screenshots, as we use it to confirm that components of our scripting are indeed complete.

Creating a Data Shell

There are two primary ways to get from a completely empty and undefined new SPSS data file to one that is still empty, but contains information relevant to your project (what we call a *data shell*). The non-scripting way to create an empty (but variable-defined) data file will be covered first. Recall those two tabs at the bottom of an SPSS data file? They are circled in Figure 4.1.

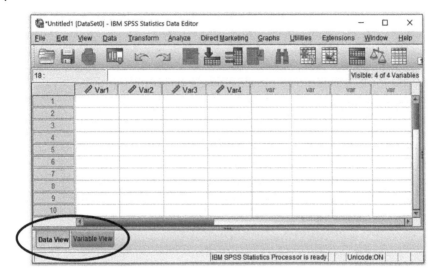

Figure 4.1 SPSS data file tabs.

These tabs in empty SPSS data files are there to facilitate your data file creation and data entry – you can *define* your variables by working in the **Variable View** tab, and you can *enter* your data by working within the **Data View** tab. Unfortunately, going from one tab to the other transposes your matrix; meaning that it turns columns into rows (see Figures 4.1 versus 4.2), which can be confusing to the unsuspecting user.

When the Variable View tab is activated, you can enter your **variable names** (which then will automatically "appear" in your Data View as column headers, if you happen to take a look [toggling between tabs]). While in the Variable View window, you will notice a variety of options allowing you to specify a variety of definitional elements of each variable (these options are circled toward the top of Figure 4.2). Don't worry about these options right now – although we will revisit them in a later chapter, default specifications will suffice for most variables that you create.

At this point, there are a few important rules about variable names that you should keep in mind. First, variable names should only contain letters, numbers, or the underscore symbol "_" (which can neither begin nor end a variable name). Capitalization is allowed, but SPSS is not case-sensitive (so an "S" is interpreted internally the same as an "s"). Lastly, no spaces are allowed in variable names, including at the end of a variable name (the underscore symbol is often in fact used by SPSS users as a placeholder for the "space" character).

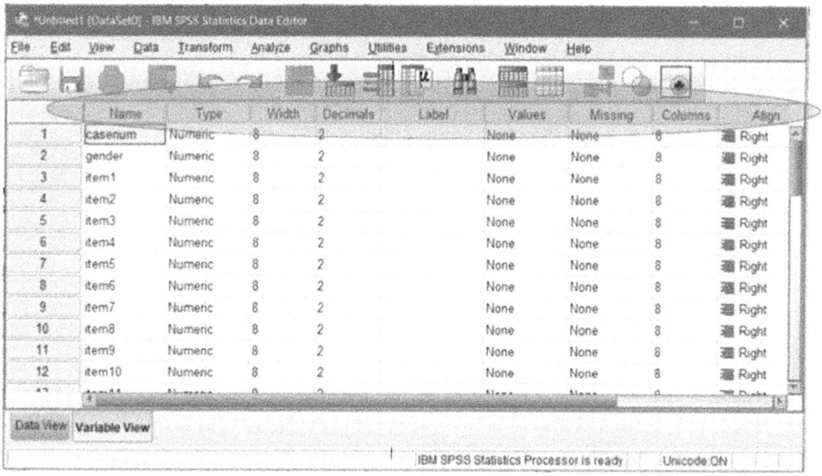

Figure 4.2   SPSS data file variable view.

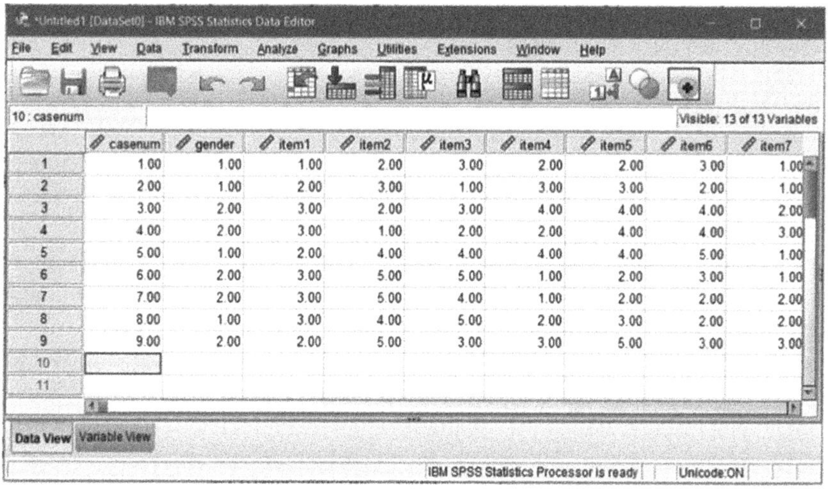

Figure 4.3   SPSS data file data view.

Once you have decided on your variable names (e.g. if we were creating a data shell for the Appendix B code sheet, we would specify 102 different variable names within the Variable View tab), you can then toggle over to your Data View and hand-enter your data into the individual cells. Figures 4.2 and 4.3 demonstrate this toggling of tabs for a small number (9) of responses to our Appendix A questionnaire.

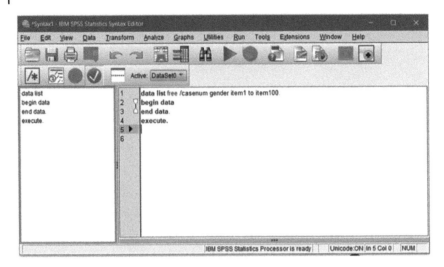

Figure 4.4 Commands to create empty data shell.

Creating Data Files Via Syntax

The second common option for creating empty data shells is to define your variables via syntax script. Especially when your data contain somewhat redundant information (e.g. "item1", "item2", "item3", etc. – such as what we have in Appendices A and B), you probably want to specify your data shell via syntax (because you can do so with just four simple commands).

Figure 4.4 shows how we would create an empty data shell for the code sheet in Appendix B. In this particular example, **"data list free /"**, **"begin data"**, **"end data."**, and "execute." are all examples of syntax commands, whereas "casenum", "gender", "item1", and "item100." are examples of your chosen variable names. The variable names will differ for different data shell creations, but the four "commands" will usually be retained.[1] If any aspects of the commands (including periods ".") are missing, your file may not be properly defined. Periods are especially crucial since they instruct SPSS that you are done with a major portion of your command.

To initiate the action you've requested in your syntax file, you need to highlight the commands you wish to run. You can do this a few different ways, however, the two most useful are:

---

[1] If your desired data shell contains a mixture of variable types (e.g. storing numbers *and* words), then these four commands will have to be tweaked a little – this situation is presented further along in the chapter.

1. Press **Ctrl+A**; this will select everything in your syntax file.
2. Select targeted actions by dragging the cursor to highlight the commands of interest.

It is good to get into the habit of using the Ctrl+A method, since once you become an SPSS expert, you will craft syntax files and then run them completely (from top to bottom) regardless of whether the information requested is redundant with previous requests or not. After you have highlighted your syntax, you click on the **"Play" button** on the Syntax Editor toolbar (the large green "right-pointing" arrow located to the right of the "Find" icon – the binoculars), and SPSS will act upon your requested commands. After running your syntax, you should go take a look at your data file. It should now be empty but will have variables defined and is therefore ready to receive data (e.g. it should resemble Figure 4.5 if you have the Data View tab activated).

Numeric Versus String Variables

If you want to have words in your data file in addition to values stored as numbers, you will need to (1) use a slightly different file creation command and (2) know the SPSS specification for words and numbers. SPSS refers to words as **string** variables, and the SPSS specification for a string variable is the letter **a**. SPSS refers to numbers as **numeric** variables, and the SPSS specification for these is the letter

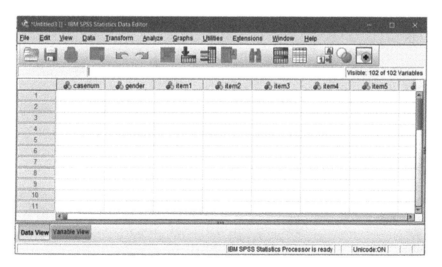

Figure 4.5   Empty data file with defined variables (aka data shell).

f. After either of these letters ("a" or "f"), you will also need to specify a number. This number will place boundaries on the number of letter or numbers that are presented to the SPSS viewer. The default specification for any variable is **f8.2** (an eight-character number with two decimals places [i.e. the *hundredths* spot]), so if all variables are numeric, you will not need to specify **f** or **a**. If you want to include string variables, however, you will need to know these specifiers, as well as a different syntax command term: **list** instead of free.

To demonstrate a scenario in which we may want to store information as words in addition to the more typical numerical variables, consider the data in Table 4.1. Here, we have three people who told us what type of car they drive as well as how many miles per gallon their car gets on any average week. To keep the data tidy, we'll also include each respondent's first name in our data file.

To see how a data file can be created that is capable of retaining both numbers and words as variable values (such as the data as is represented in Table 4.1), take a look at Figure 4.6. The only tweaking we needed of the previous script was

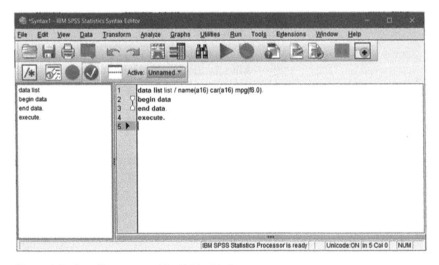

Figure 4.6   Data list command for Table 4.1 data.

Table 4.1   A mix of string and numeric data.

First name	Type of car	Average MPG
John-o	Mini	41
Adam	Maserati	12
Renata	Ferrari	15

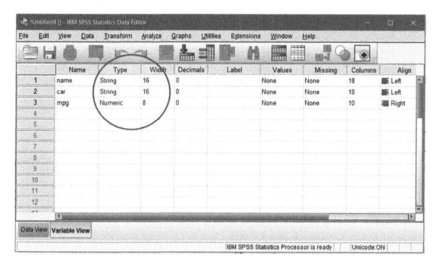

Figure 4.7   Resulting string and numeric variables in data file.

replacing a **command option** (command options are slight adjustments that can be applied to the more general request). In this circumstance, we merely replaced the word, "free" from Figure 4.4 with the word "list" (see Figure 4.6). These slight modifications of the "data list" command permit more or less flexibility with the types of variables we want to "list". In this example, our syntax commands request a data shell with two string variables (sixteen characters each) and one numeric variable (with no decimal places), and looking at the resulting datafile (Figure 4.7) we can get some feedback that our request was indeed fulfilled.

Data Entry Within the Syntax File

There are actually two options to *populate* our empty data shell with information. As mentioned previously, it is permissible to hand-enter data directly into the "Data View" editor. Alternatively, and especially preferable with small datasets, the empty data shells can not only be defined within the syntax editor, but data values themselves can also be specified within the script, and this has been requested in Figure 4.8.

By selecting Ctrl+A, this entire request will be processed, specifying both the data shell (consisting of string variables for "name" and "car" and a numeric variable for "mpg") as well as the data itself (values for three people along each of our three variables). Note here that "space" characters merely identify when one variable's information is complete and the next variable's information is incoming (this

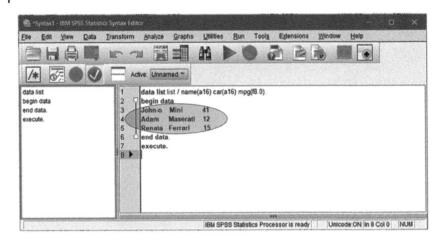

Figure 4.8 Populating data values via script.

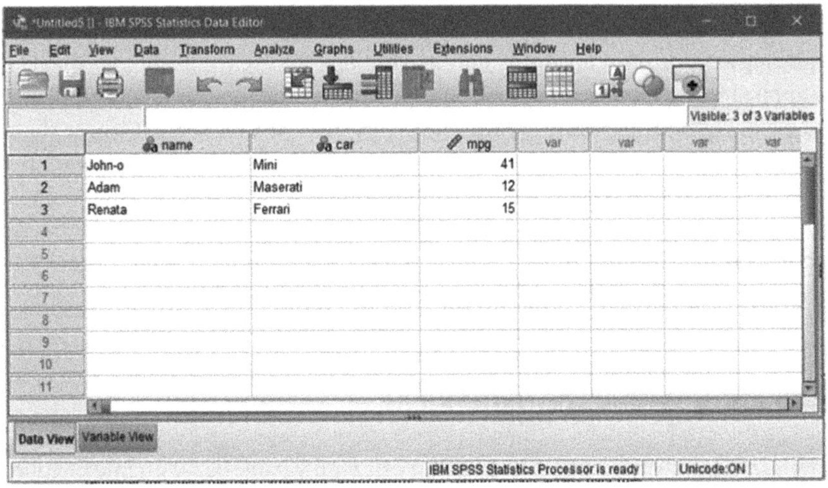

Figure 4.9 Data file result of specifying data values in script.

is one reason why space characters are forbidden in variable names). Figure 4.8 has used extra spacing characters in order to present the data in a more visually appealing manner, but it is not necessary to specify multiple spaces between variable values when entering data in this syntax manner. Figure 4.9 shows the result of requesting the entire Figure 4.8 script.

"Saving" Populated Datafiles

Once you are done inputting data in your syntax file (regardless of how it is entered – via syntax or "by hand"), you are going to then need to *save* your now information-filled data file. There are two methods that can be applied to save your data file. One is to click the ubiquitous "save file" icon that is available at the top-left hand corner of most windows-based programs. As the next chapter highlights, we recommend that you DO NOT get into the habit of saving your data files in this common manner. Rather, there is a syntax command that also performs this action for you: "**save outfile**". In addition to the "save outfile" command, you will also need both a file name and file location to fully enact the command. Figure 4.10 incorporates all of our current chapter lessons to: (1) create an empty data shell, (2) enter the data, and (3) save the now-populated data file as "rawdata.sav" within the "HW1" folder on the local computer's "C:" drive.

We now have a "saved" data file that can be retrieved for later use if we wish to access it (this "accessing a populated data file" is actually the focus of the following chapter). The data are hidden safely away in our system of folders, but it is wise practice to also get into the habit of saving your scripts! Look back to Chapter 2 and please note that there are two folders within each project directory – a "data" folder and a "syntax" folder. We placed our data within the data folder, but we will locate our data-generating script within the syntax folder.

Figure 4.10 Incorporating chapter lessons.

Figure 4.11 Saving your syntax.

Although we recommend avoiding the "save" shortcut icon for *data files*, it is perfectly acceptable to use this icon for the *syntax files*. Note that if you DO NOT save your script, the window heading will have placeholder names of "Syntax1", "Syntax2", "Syntax3", etc. (numbers indicate how many unsaved Syntax files you have open in your current SPSS session). It is good practice, however, to actually give these files a descriptive name – we have the habit of calling these initial data-shell creating files "data file creation" as seen at the very top of Figure 4.11. In the future, if we want to revisit how we created the data or explore whether or not there are any errors, we can simply access this syntax file and inspect it for information.

Having SPSS Auto-Generate Your Syntax

The premise of this book is that syntax is uber-important when using SPSS (or, really, any statistical software platform). Keeping a record of "what you've done" is crucial for competent data management. The primary obstacle to keeping syntax diaries for most SPSS newbies seems to be the daunting learning curve associated with "knowing what to write". This book has many screen-captures that are intended to serve as templates, so you do not need to "know what to write" – you can simply alter our syntax commands to fit your purpose.

In addition to these screen-capture resources, however, SPSS also has a built-in system to facilitate syntax generation. For almost all purposes (excluding data file creation, as is the focus of the preceding paragraphs), SPSS will generate syntax for you via the **"paste"** function within pull-down windows. Figure 4.12 highlights

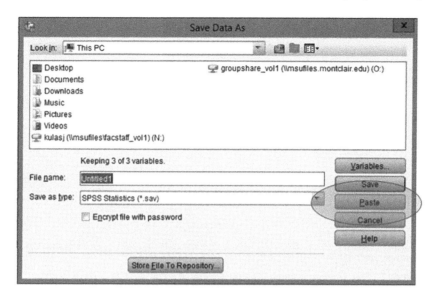

Figure 4.12 SPSS "auto-generating" syntax.

this option – when you select "paste", syntax will be generated for you and placed at the bottom of a syntax file. Throughout the book, you may notice script that we have generated via this method because when SPSS auto-generates script, the letters are typically CAPITALIZED. When we write script "by hand", we typically do not capitalize.

Controlling Your "Open" Datafiles

There are two housekeeping considerations that are important to note here at the end of this "create and save your datafiles via syntax" chapter.

One consideration is SPSS's addition of notation to our syntax file that we didn't write. In recent versions of the program, SPSS generates the comment: "**Encoding: UTF-8**", and places this as an asterisked (*) note at the top of your active syntax file (see, for example, Figure 4.11). Asterisks serve as an indicator that information after the asterisk is an internal comment, meaning that SPSS won't read or run this information (this will be further discussed in Chapter 6). SPSS does this annotating by default any time you "run" or save a syntax file – we have been deleting this comment in previous screen-captures but left it untouched in Figure 4.11. This "Encoding: UTF-8" is computer-speak for character encoding – it is differentiating our English alphabet characters from other possible computer languages – you can override this annotation, but it is generally harmless so we just wanted to point out that you may see this comment

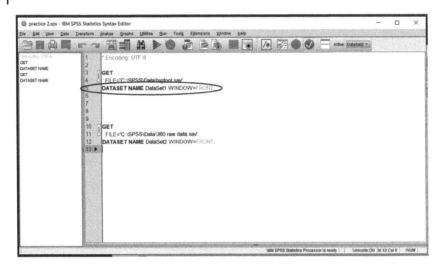

Figure 4.12   Dataset open commands auto-generated by SPSS.

pop up in your syntax files even though you did not request it. This is normal (and harmless) behavior characteristic of current versions of SPSS.

The second housekeeping consideration is a bit more important (because it's potentially impactful regarding the ultimate integrity of your data) and concerns your ability to manage "one open datafile at a time". If you "open" a new data file via pull-down menus (but properly choose to paste the command into your syntax), SPSS by default not only generates the appropriate script to access your data, but also generates a "nickname" for the new data file. As shown in Figure 4.12, the nickname generated is *DataSet1*.

If we have SPSS auto-generate another "get file" command for us (this time accessing a file named "360 raw data"), it will, by default, give this datafile a different nickname ("*DataSet2*" in Figure 4.12). Nicknames are useful for managing multiple datafiles – however, when using SPSS, we recommend that yhou only keep one datafile "open" at any given time. This means that nicknames are useless (as is the second command shown in Figure 4.12 – "**WINDOW=FRONT**"). WINDOW=FRONT is SPSS-speak for "this dataset is more important than are the other open datasets". Neither of these commands should ever be used. They are, by default, qualifying statements to your auto-generated "get file" command, but they should ALWAYS be deleted!

Running the entire syntax (Ctrl+A) as shown in Figure 4.12 will cause SPSS to pull up both datafiles (bigfoot.sav and 360 raw data.sav), which is NOT good.

The capability to open multiple datafiles simultaneously is a feature that is intended to increase the convenience of SPSS, but it is actually terribly

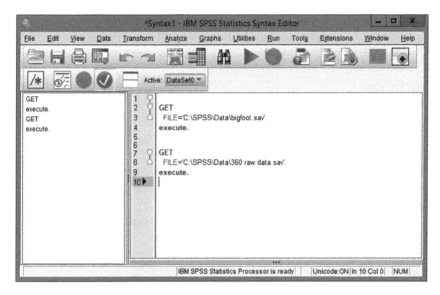

Figure 4.13 Script without SPSS dataset name.

inconvenient, since it introduces the possibility that you manipulate or change information in the wrong datafile without realizing it. In order to prevent this from happening, you can very simply delete the second line auto-generated by SPSS from both "**Get file**" commands (see Figure 4.13). This will allow us to run the entire script and only open the final datafile named in the script. In the case of Figure 4.13, running the entire syntax will open the "bigfoot" datafile, but then also close this file when opening the new "360 raw data" file. This sounds silly (because there are no manipulations done to the bigfoot data – we simply open, then ignore the data). However, the simple act of accessing different datafiles properly and sequentially is a very important behavior to learn and master. Having a single datafile open at a time is a very important habit to develop. It helps you to better manage your data and minimizes the likelihood that you will make errors.

Summary

There are syntax shortcuts to creating data files – you will find it helpful to use them especially if you have redundancy in variable names (such as, for example, a large questionnaire or survey). Every project should have a "data file creation" syntax file, whether the SPSS file was created from scratch or, as covered in the following chapter, imported from a different software program. Your data creation file should be annotated with comments and act as a reminder for where the data came from, and always be saved using the "save outfile" command.

Key Terms

* – Indicator that information after the asterisk is an internal comment "for your eyes only"; SPSS won't read or run this information.

"Begin data" – SPSS subcommand used with the "data list free" command.

Case number – Confidential person or case identifier. Nominal data form.

Code sheet – Hardcopy that specifies SPSS variable names and value codes.

Command – Wording that tells SPSS what to do.

Command option – Command options are slight adjustments that can be applied to the more general request.

Ctrl+A – Keystroke combination to "select all".

"Data list free" – SPSS command used to create a new data file.

Data "shell" – Empty data file, in which variables have been defined but numbers have not been entered.

Data view – Traditional view in data (.sav) files – data are stored here.

Encoding: UTF-8 – Auto-generated SPSS comment commonly placed at the top of active syntax files.

"End data" – SPSS subcommand to be used with the "data list free" file creation command, along with "begin data".

"Execute" – SPSS command that tells SPSS processor to start working.

f8.2 – The default format of SPSS variables.

"Get file" – SPSS command used to retrieve a specified data file.

Hardcopy – Paper version of data, measurement, etc.

Numeric – SPSS definition of a variable with *number* values.

Objects – Otherwise known as your variables, tell SPSS where the actions should be performed.

Paste – Command option within pull-down menus that auto-generates syntax for you.

Play button – SPSS button, located in syntax files, that activates selected syntax.

Save outfile – Syntax command to save your data file.

SPSS code – Language used by SPSS.

String – SPSS definition of a variable with *letter* values.

Variable names – Names, of eight characters or fewer, used in the SPSS data file.

Variable View – Capability that allows you to define variables from within the data (.sav) file.

WINDOW=FRONT – SPSS command that enables multiple datafiles to be open simultaneously.

Discussion Questions

1 What is the importance of the case number?

2 Why are the "get file" and "save outfile" commands so important

References

Goldberg, L.R. (1999). A broad-bandwidth, public domain, personality inventory measuring the lower-level facets of several five-factor models. In: *Personality Psychology in Europe*, vol. 7 (eds. I. Mervielde, I. Deary, F. De Fruyt and F. Ostendorf), 7–28. Tilburg, The Netherlands: Tilburg University Press.

Johnson, J.A. (2005). Ascertaining the validity of individual protocols from web-based personality inventories. *Journal of research in personality* 39 (1): 103–129.

5

Accessing Your Data

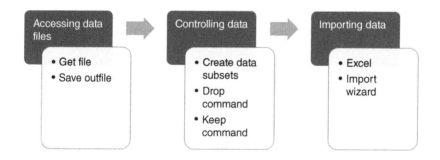

CHAPTER MENU

Chapter Learning Objectives

1. Accessing data files through syntax
   a) Controlling content in data files
2. Importing data from Excel

IBM SPSS Essentials: Managing and Analyzing Social Sciences Data, Second Edition.
John Kulas, Renata Garcia Prieto Palacios Roji, and Adam Smith.
© 2021 John Wiley & Sons, Inc. Published 2021 by John Wiley & Sons, Inc.

Accessing Your Data Files

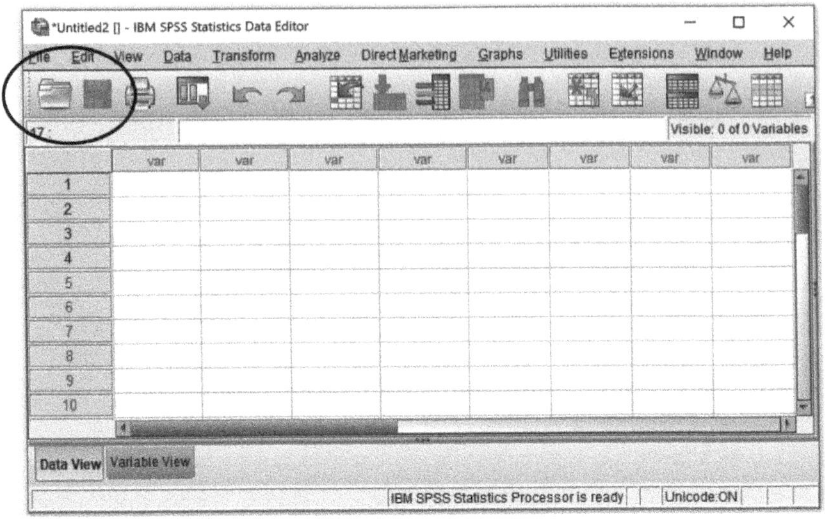

Figure 5.1 Open and save icons.

In Windows-based programs, the Open (file) and Save (file) icons are generally located adjacent to each other in the top left-hand corner of a window (see Figure 5.1 for the SPSS example of this). Have you ever mistakenly clicked on the "Save" button instead of "Open", accidently saving changes you did not intend to? This "unintentional saving" can actually have massive real-world implications when it happens to *data* files, because with any data analysis it is always imperative to maintain the integrity of original data (e.g. ensure that you can always revisit the raw, unaltered data at some later point in time).

The only instances in which you would want to intentionally "save" **raw data files** are when you are (1) entering additional data or (2) making corrections to typos (e.g. data that were initially entered incorrectly). Other than these two circumstances, you should *never* "save over" your original raw data file – which is why the "open"/"save" icon locations represent a design flaw (at least in data management software programs such as SPSS). Even if you make changes to your raw data that are intentional (such as the above two circumstances), be sure to make note of it in your syntax file via comments. This helps keep a record of what has changed in case of inquiries from an instructor or journal editor (or, most likely, yourself when you later revisit the project).

Because of this design flaw (really, these two options should not be located *anywhere* near each other), the way you interact with your data is going to be syntax-reliant. For whatever reason, this seems to be a difficult lesson to learn, but it's one that we do implore you to adhere to. *The only time it is permissible to access a data file directly (open a data file directly from the Data Editor) is if you are hand-entering data into the file.* If your intention is to manipulate or perform analyses, you should never open a data file directly from the data editor. In addition to this warning, you should also remember from the previous chapter that you should never open more than one data file at a time. The current versions of SPSS allow for multiple data files to be open concurrently, but this is more likely to result in unintended errors than not. By judiciously operating through the syntax commands of "get file" and "**save outfile**" (presented previously but further elaborated on below), you will achieve a high level of control over your data, and you will minimize the likelihood of common errors.

Get File and Save Outfile

In order to control data files via syntax, you will be primarily relying on two important commands: "*get file*" and "*save outfile*". "Get file" tells SPSS which data file (.sav) you would like to open, while "save outfile", as previously discussed, will save whatever changes you make to your data. The habitual use of these two very important commands bypasses the "accidental overwrite" scenario that we want you to avoid. When you use "save outfile", you should *almost always* change the name of your outfile (from the original raw datafile name) so you don't accidentally overwrite your raw data. Figure 5.2 shows a syntax file that utilizes these commands by grabbing the previous chapter's "rawdata" file, creating a duplicate mpg variable (don't worry about this now, we will cover data manipulations such

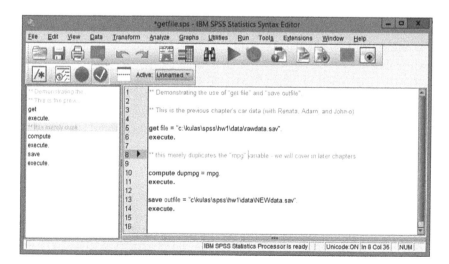

Figure 5.2   Syntax showing "get file" and "save outfile" commands.

as this in later chapters), and then saving this *new and slightly altered* datafile as "NEWdata".

Any time you make changes to your data file that you deem important enough to be stored separately from the original datafile, be sure to save your outfile with a new name!! Keep in mind that if you heed this advice, you will likely have several data files associated with any individual project (even if you have only one syntax file). Don't worry about cluttering your folders with data files – if you annotate your syntax files appropriately, you will have a great record of what information each data file contains. Your annotated syntax file (e.g. with comments) is therefore a crucial reference to help you keep track of "where you have been" and what you have done to your data.

Creating Subsets of Data

Using these advocated commands (especially "save outfile"), it is possible to select only targeted variables in a dataset and save them in a separate datafile. This is quite useful for larger datasets when you'd like to whittle your data file down to a more manageable size. The syntax for these commands can be seen in Figure 5.3, where only two variables (car and mpg) are retained from the slightly larger original file (name, car, and mpg). We can achieve this smaller datafile in two separate ways, by either keeping what we *do* want or omitting what we *don't* want.

To drop a particular variable or group of variables from a dataset, we will simply add a *subcommand* to our "save outfile" command. Syntactically, this is done by dropping down to the next line below "save outfile", inserting a slash character "/", typing the command "**drop=**", and then indicating the variables you want to drop (see Figure 5.3). Notice that the period "." is now located after the subcommand line instead of after the file name (this is different from, for example, Figure 5.2). This migration of the command terminator period will occur anytime we specify a subcommand within a broader syntax command. Be sure to keep track of where your period goes, since improper placement will result in error messages (these messages are generally quite helpful and will be elaborated upon in Chapter 16).

For an alternative to the "**drop**" command, you can instead specify the "**keep**" command which serves the same purpose, but instead indicates the variables that you would like to keep in your new file (also see Figure 5.3).

Importing Data from Excel

Increasingly, data are collected from (or at least stored in) formats other than hard paper copies or SPSS data files. Quite often, you will encounter data that are in the form of a datasheet (such as an Excel file), or one that can easily be transformed

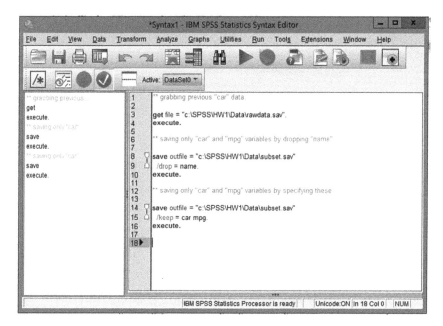

Figure 5.3 Syntax showing "drop" and "keep" commands.

into that format. For this reason, we will show you how to import data stored as Excel files into SPSS. Figure 5.4 presents a typical Excel file – note that this resembles an SPSS data file quite a bit – variables in columns and individual respondents occupying rows. The basic syntax commands for importing data from Excel can be found in Figure 5.5.

One advantage of using syntax to control "getting" and "saving" our data is that we can easily convert this Excel data into SPSS format, with the help of the "save outfile" command we just learned. Notice that we included this command in Figure 5.5, keeping a record of where the data came from and what it was saved as via asterisked comments. As always, this practice helps to avoid confusion and having to answer questions like "where the heck did this data come from?" If you highlight all of this syntax and run it, your new SPSS data file will appear in the designated folder.

Using the Import Data Wizard

If you are not comfortable tweaking existing scripts (altering minor elements to fit your unique situation), such as the syntax provided in Figure 5.5, you can have SPSS generate such commands for you via the **Import Data** wizard (see Figure 5.6). Indeed, we used the wizard to generate our 5.5 script, although

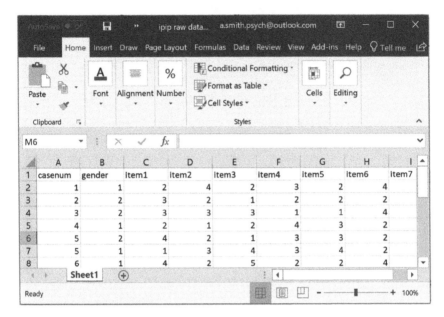

Figure 5.4   Data in Excel file.

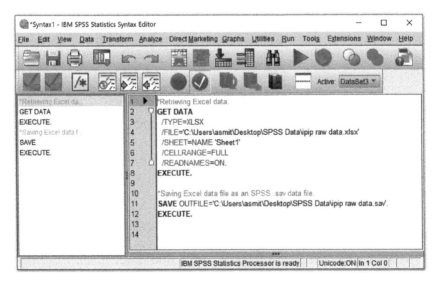

Figure 5.5   Syntax commands to import data from Excel.

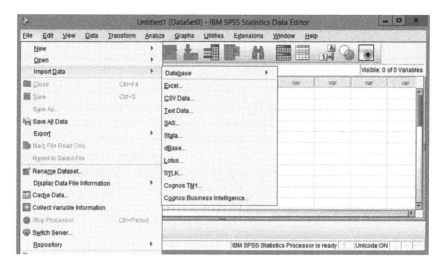

Figure 5.6 SPSS import wizard.

once we have this template, we would likely copy, paste, and tweak this syntax to meet future Excel to SPSS data imports (with different datasets). Even though you are not *directly scripting commands* within your syntax environment if you use the wizard, it is still important to make note of every step in the process, so in addition to our reliance on the "paste" function, we will also carefully annotate our syntax file.

The Copy–Paste "Option" (aka This Is a Terrible Idea)

There is one final data capturing method that we will *acknowledge*, but we hope that none of you actually ever utilizes (because it violates our "keep a record of what you've done" principle). Here, you simply copy the data in your Excel file (without copying the variable names) and paste it into the first cell within SPSS's data view tab. Now that you have your data in SPSS, you will need to add variable names by transitioning to the variable view tab. Then you can define the vari-able names and specify the variable characteristics (e.g. letter, number). Although this is an enticing method for data transfer, especially to SPSS newcomers, we hope that none of you reading this book falls into the habit of transferring data in this "copy–paste" manner – it is a method fraught with pitfalls and data dan-ger. Your syntax files should be thought of as diaries that record what you've done and why you've done it. "Copying and pasting" data is a procedure that bypasses record-keeping – BAD!

Summary

Always access data files through the "get file" command within your syntax editor (rather than the point-and-click data editor icons/options) – this allows you to control which data file is active and to avoid catastrophic mistakes. The "get file" and "save outfile" commands are probably the two most important syntax commands for you to master. If you access data from a different program, it is ok to have SPSS help you generate the syntax, just make sure to "paste" the commands into a syntax diary. The next time you access the data, you can do so straight from your syntax file (because the commands to access the other-formatted data have already been generated for you).

Key Terms

"Drop" – Subcommand used with "save outfile", specifying which variables are to be executed in the newly saved data file.
"Keep" – Subcommand used with "save outfile", specifying which variables are to be kept in the newly save data file.
Raw data file – Electronic storage of variable and person information (a data shell with information in it).
"Save outfile" – SPSS command used to save the currently open data file.

Discussion Questions

1 Why is it important to save a new data file every time you make changes to the data?

2 When would you want to create a subset of data, what command should you use?

6

Defining Your Data

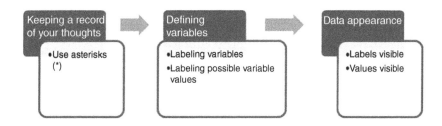

CHAPTER MENU

Chapter Learning Objectives

1. Annotating your syntax files (*)
2. Defining your variables
   a. Variable labels
   b. Value labels
3. How to view your data labels

You should now be familiar with the use of syntax files for the: (1) creation of variable-defined data shells, (2) control over saving data files, and (3) access of data from other sources (for example, Excel). You'll now typically want to take your

IBM SPSS Essentials: Managing and Analyzing Social Sciences Data, Second Edition.
John Kulas, Renata Garcia Prieto Palacios Roji, and Adam Smith.
© 2021 John Wiley & Sons, Inc. Published 2021 by John Wiley & Sons, Inc.

new data file and provide some additional information – primarily more specific definition to your variables.

Annotation

Remember that you will be working exclusively in the syntax environment: this keeps a diary of your steps in case you need to retrace what you did with your data. When you access SPSS, always open up a syntax file rather than a data file. The "get file" command will open up the data file for you – don't go messing around with opening data directly. Before you get too far with this method, however, you'll want to also get into the very important habit of annotating your diary. Figure 6.1 shows a note to ourselves (on line 1) that the syntax will create a new (empty) data file and that we were working on this project on December 3.

The important elements of a note are at least one asterisk (*) at the beginning and a period (.) indicating the end. We typically use two asterisks out of habit, just as a personal style choice, but this is not necessary.

Any asterisk tells SPSS to NOT interpret the ensuing information as a command or request, and the period indicates your note is finished. We also recommend recording the dates you were working within your syntax files – this serves as a

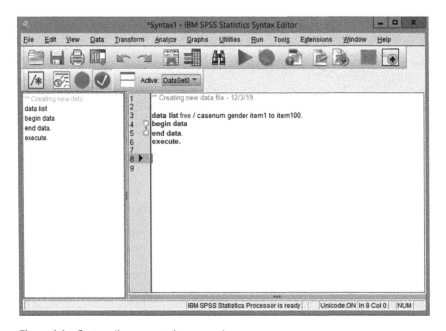

Figure 6.1 Syntax diary annotation example.

memory cue when you later revisit the project. You'll likely notice some old dates on screenshots throughout this book – they are legacies from the first edition of this book, but we kept them to: (1) remind the first author of how old he is and (2) stress the truism that SPSS commands are backward compatible (e.g. syntax that worked 15 years ago will also work with current versions of SPSS).

Defining Your Dataset

There are two important definitional commands that you will frequently use to help further describe your data. One provides more descriptive labels to your variables (remember, we use short – eight characters or fewer – variable names in our data files). The other command provides descriptors for possible *responses* to the variables (aka values).

Adding Variable Labels

To provide a bit more descriptive information to your data file's variables, the command is simply "**var labels**". You must use this command individually for every variable in your data file.

Figure 6.2 shows an example of giving labels to the variables from the questionnaire in Appendix A. This is a very useful data management tactic, because if you provide this level of specificity, SPSS output by default (when you eventually request it) will report these labels instead of variable names. Typically this is desired, although you can also "turn off" this option if you'd like.

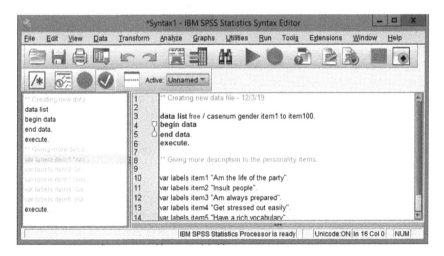

Figure 6.2 Labeling variables.

You may use single or double quotes when defining your variables, but it's important that you pay attention to which you are using, because if your longer description has a contraction in it (such as item 12 in the Appendix A – *Am not interested in other people's problems*), you need to either exclude the apostrophe from your variable label or make sure that you wrap the text with double quotes (such as those used in Figure 6.2). If you include a contraction within single quotes, you'll get an error message. Additionally, there are shortcuts to physically typing all of your item labels into your syntax file (see Chapter 17), and one of the main reasons to use these shortcuts is to get rid of pesky apostrophes or replace single quotes with double quotes (or vice versa).

Adding Value Labels

If you take a look at the example coding sheet in Appendix B, you'll notice that we're indicating a response of "male" as a "1" and "female" as a "2". Also, responses to the personality items are recorded as numbers, with numbers one through five corresponding to responses of "strongly disagree" to "strongly agree". It is useful to have SPSS know this information, and probably more important that you record these relationships in your diary so you can later remind yourself what the numbers "mean". After giving all of your variables labels, you should therefore identify responses to the variables as well.

Also note in Figure 6.3 that we've mixed the double and single quotes – you would not typically mix their usage like this, we just wanted to communicate here that, with either var labels or **add value labels**, it is permissible to specify either single or double quotes.

This process (adding *value labels*) is actually quite a bit less time-intensive than specifying variable labels, because you will typically have many variables with the same value labels (as with responses to our Appendix B personality items). You can specify ranges of variables instead of listing them all separately.

We like to indent with a few tabs when adding value labels, although this is not necessary. This practice seems to keep our diaries a bit more tidy-looking and facilitates error resolution when mistakes are made. You don't need to do this, but we do recommend that you get into this habit also. Notice that you don't use a period (.) until you have exhausted all possible responses.

If you run this syntax and decide to take a look at your data file, you'll now have the option of two views – one that displays the numbers you entered and one that displays the labels that you've defined. You can toggle back and forth between these two views by clicking the **Value Labels button** in the SPSS Data Editor – just remember to be careful about altering any of the data in your data file. Additionally, your more descriptive variable labels will be displayed if you hover your cursor over your data variables (see Figure 6.4).

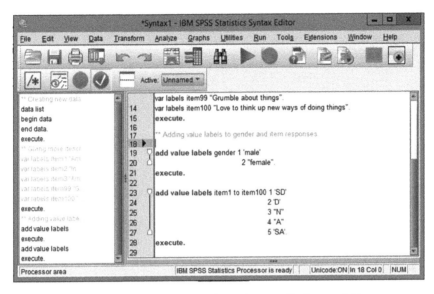

Figure 6.3 Labeling responses to the gender and personality item variables.

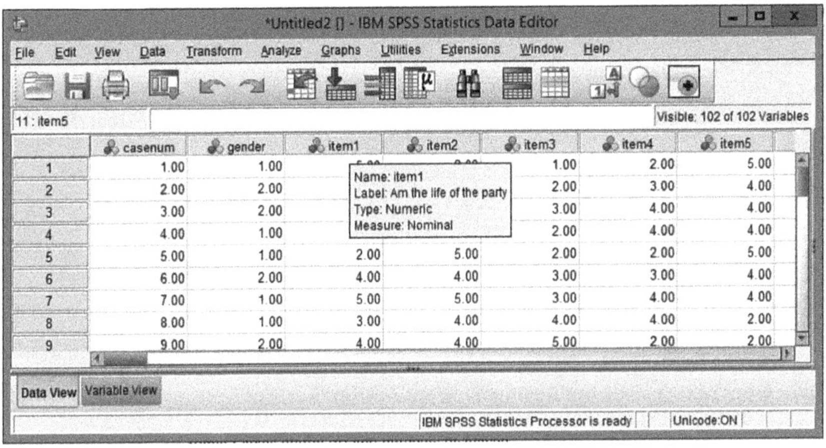

Figure 6.4 Variable label displayed when "hovering" cursor over variable name.

Figure 6.5 shows the Value Labels button off and numbers displayed, whereas Figure 6.6 shows the Value Labels button "on" and labels displayed.

Appendix C presents a step-by-step process for creating an empty data file and defining your variables (giving them descriptive labels). After your data file creation syntax looks like the syntax in Figure 6.3, you can save the data shell (the empty but variable-defined data file) and start entering data (if it's in hardcopy format).

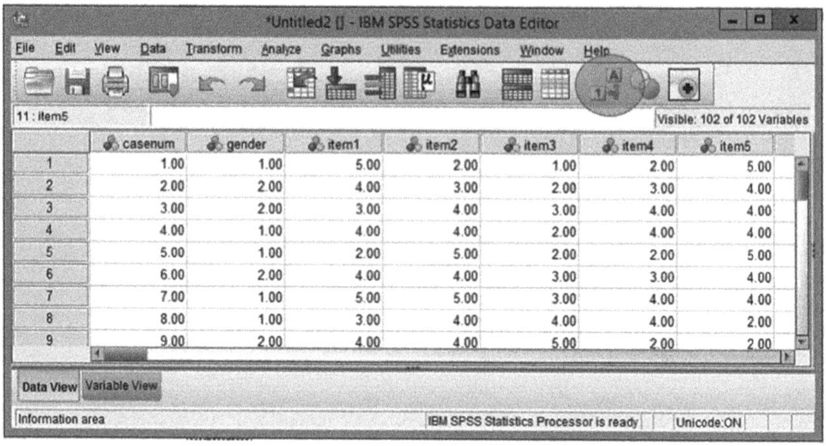

Figure 6.5   Value Labels button off and numbers displayed.

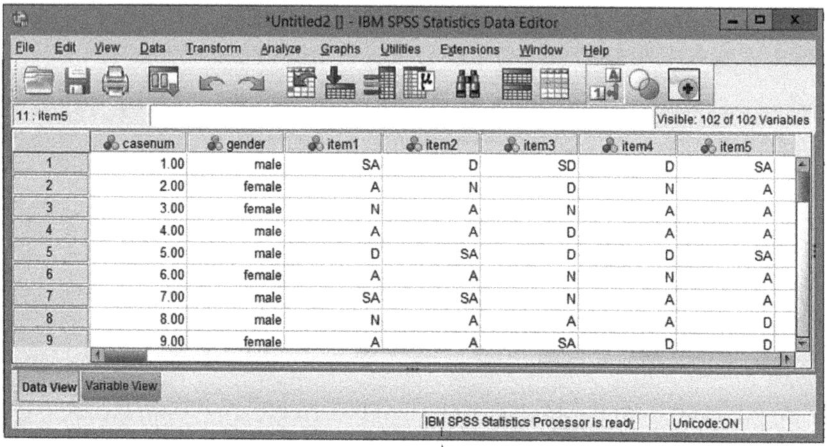

Figure 6.6   Value Labels button on and labels displayed.

Summary

All variables within your data files should be labeled as comprehensively as possible. Although SPSS variable names are kept short, you can be more descriptive by using the "var labels" command. When we have categorical (or ordinal) data that are represented within our data file by numbers (which is common), it is also considered good data management practice to specify labels for the numbers. If you want to view the labels, you can click the Value Labels button within the data file (although we don't want to spend too much time in the data or .sav file environment).

Key Terms

* – Symbol used to designate the *beginning* of a comment line within SPSS syntax.
"Add value labels" – SPSS command that describes your coding scheme for possible values on categorical variables (for example, does "1" represent male and "2" represent female or vice versa?).
. – Symbol used to designate the *ending* of a comment line within SPSS syntax.
Value Labels button – SPSS function allowing you to view category labels within the data file itself.
"Var labels" – SPSS command used to give your variables more descriptive definitions (more descriptive than the eight-character variable name).

Discussion Questions

1 If my variable names are self-explanatory, do I still need to give them labels?

2 Does the coding scheme make a difference if I add value labels?

Part II

Statistics

7

Descriptive Statistics

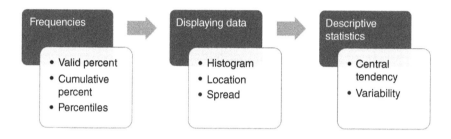

CHAPTER MENU

Chapter Learning Objectives

1. Requesting frequency distributions
2. Requesting descriptive statistics
3. Using frequency information to create new variables
4. Visual displays of data

IBM SPSS Essentials: Managing and Analyzing Social Sciences Data, Second Edition.
John Kulas, Renata Garcia Prieto Palacios Roji, and Adam Smith.
© 2021 John Wiley & Sons, Inc. Published 2021 by John Wiley & Sons, Inc.

In this chapter, we will be covering ways to request meaningful descriptive output (information) about our data. This is where we will actually begin to *request* output from SPSS (as opposed to the previous actions such as creating and saving data files where output files appeared but were *not directly requested*).

There are two basic but very useful commands that allow you to "get a good sense" of your data: **"descriptives"** and **"frequencies"**. These are the two most basic and common descriptive commands you will use (e.g. the SPSS commands that request descriptive information about your data). In this chapter, we will practice both using these commands as well as interpreting the output.

Frequencies

If you want a broad visual representation of what your data looks like, you can (and should) request a **frequency distribution**. This chapter demonstrates how to request this information in both table (using the "frequencies" command) and visual forms (e.g. requesting a histogram). The data we will be using throughout the chapter are presented in Table 7.1, and represents eight peoples' self-reported estimates of how many tacos they eat per week (both barbacoa and al pastor tacos).

To enter the data into SPSS, we will follow the recommendations of Chapter 4 to create variable names, enter data, and save the file as a raw data file (named "tacos" – see Figure 7.1).

To obtain a snapshot of the data, we can utilize a fresh syntax file (because we're no longer *creating* data, we are now doing manipulations or requesting transformations of the data). Figure 7.2 accesses our newly created "tacos" file, and requests a tabular frequency distribution for barbacoa tacos using the simple command, "frequencies".

Table 7.1 Frequency distribution for number and type of tacos consumed.

Name	Barbacoa	Al Pastor
Rachel	2	4
Monica	3	6
Phoebe	3	7
Joey	3	7
Chandler	2	5
Ross	1	2
Gunther	5	7
Tag	3	1

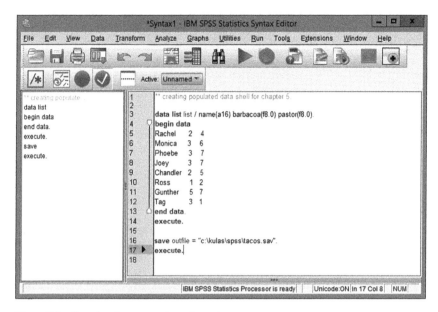

Figure 7.1 Entering frequency data through syntax.

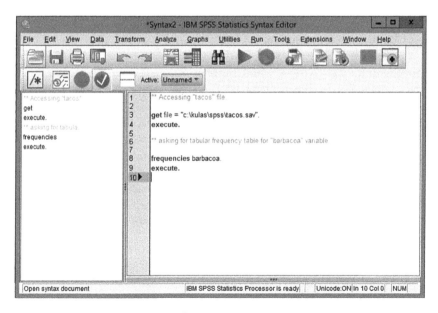

Figure 7.2 Accessing new data file "tacos" and requesting a frequency table.

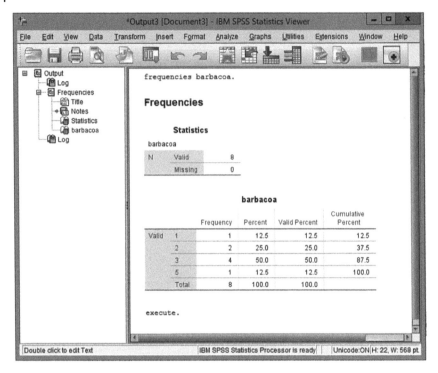

Figure 7.3 Frequencies output file.

Highlighting (e.g. "Ctrl+A") and running the Figure 7.2 syntax results in a meaningful output file popping up (one that contains directly requested information), and this output file is shown in Figure 7.3.

Looking at our distribution of responses to the barbacoa variable, we can see that all eight people (as seen in the Frequency column of Figure 7.3) provided a response of either 1, 2, 3, or 5 (furthest-left shaded column in the table). Furthermore, the most common response was "3 barbacoa tacos". Four people (50% of our respondents) indicated that they eat, on average, three barbacoa tacos in a typical week. Note the **"cumulative percent"** column presented in the frequency table. Although not of central focus here, this column becomes important later in the book when we discuss the concept of **percentiles.**

Displaying Data Graphically

In addition to reviewing the frequencies of values given to our variable, it is also useful to create visual representations of these values. SPSS can create a wide variety of graphs and charts that simplify the task of interpreting information such as this.

For example, instead of (or in addition to) looking at a frequency table, we can create a **histogram** that visualizes how many individuals selected a particular score for a variable of interest. This type of graph can be requested with the syntax shown in Figure 7.4, where the responses to our barbacoa variable are presented as a frequency distribution (see Figure 7.5).

In this chart, we can see that the most frequent response option selected was three. This finding can be confirmed by looking back at our frequency distribution table in Figure 7.3.

Location and Spread

The frequency distribution actually conveys two very important pieces of information regarding a set of numbers: (1) the **location** of the set of numbers (at what location along the x-axis do numbers tend to be found) and (2) the **spread** of the set of numbers (e.g. how similar or different responses are). This information is easiest to visualize with larger datasets, so Figure 7.6 presents two different frequency distributions that exhibit differences in both location and spread. Here, the distribution of values for men is *located* to the left of the distribution of values for women. This means that women tend to love tacos more so than do men (if

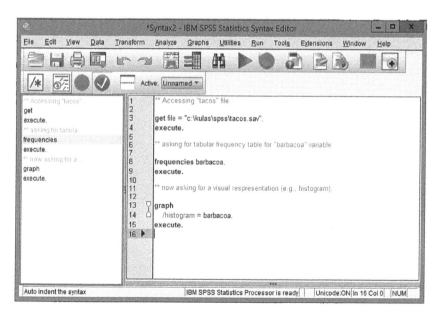

Figure 7.4   Requesting a histogram though syntax.

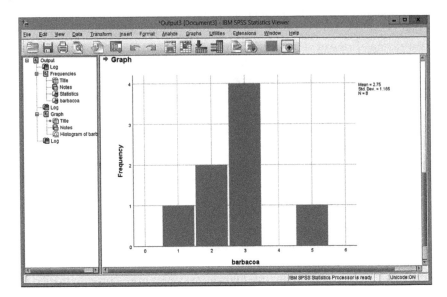

Figure 7.5   Histogram with frequency distribution.

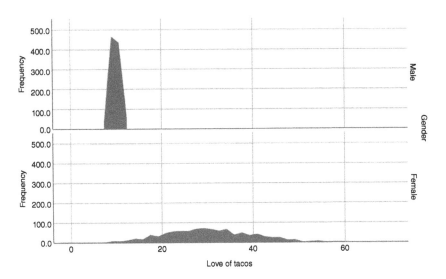

Figure 7.6   Frequency distributions differing in location and spread.

higher numbers indicate "more love" of tacos). Additionally, the spread of these two distributions is quite different. Men have more *similar opinions* about tacos, whereas women have less agreement regarding their love of tacos (e.g. greater distributional *spread*).

Descriptive Statistics

Similar to visual and tabular representations of frequencies, **descriptive statistics** convey information about the location and spread of a set of numbers, but they do so via *numerical* as opposed to tabular or graphical means.

Measures of Central Tendency and Variability

In addition to tables and figures, you'll commonly need some communicable *numbers* that describe the spread and location of a set of values. These are usually discussed as indices of variability or central tendency, which simply refer to where numbers tend to be grouped in a distribution (central tendency aka location) or how similar the numbers tend to be to each other (variability aka spread).

If we want to know this information for any variable within our dataset, the command is simply "**descriptives**" (see Figure 7.7). This command is requesting summary information in the form of descriptive statistics. Therefore, similar to the frequencies command above, we expect information to be reported in an output file.

Note that in Figure 7.7 we merely added a request to our previous "frequencies and histogram" script. If we highlight and run the syntax shown in Figure 7.7, we'll get a brief summary of the barbacoa variable in an *output* window as shown in Figure 7.8 – note that nothing in our data file has been altered by this analytical request, so there is no need to "save outfile" as a new dataset.

This table gives us some very important (and basic) information. First, we can see that there were eight "valid" barbacoa taco ratings (this "valid" term refers to the number of cases who provided a *non-missing* value). If we also know that our data file contains responses from eight people, this means that no one *did not* provide a response to this item. Next, looking at the **minimum** and **maximum scores**, it seems that these values are reasonable (within the range of likely scores – for example, no one claimed to eat 800 tacos per week). Scores outside of the plausible range of scores can help you identify data entry or other errors that may exist in your data file.

Because the mean and standard deviation are the most commonly requested and reported measures of central tendency and variability, respectively, these are the default statistics presented by the descriptives command. The minimum

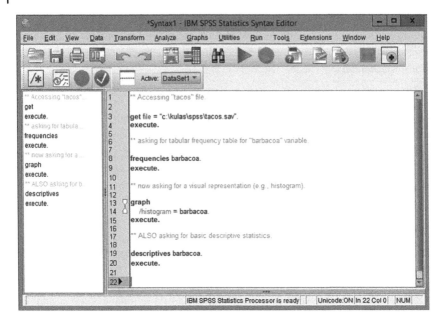

Figure 7.7 Requesting descriptive statistics through syntax.

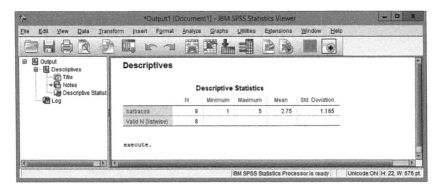

Figure 7.8 Descriptive statistics output.

and maximum values can be used to compute a range (an alternative measure of variability). If you want to know the values of the other common measures of central tendency and variability, you will need to do a little extra work. The variance is simply the squared value of the reported standard deviation (in our case, $1.165 \times 1.165 = 1.36$), whereas the mode and median are best sought-for in our histogram and frequency table, respectively. The histogram's "high point" is the mode (referring to Figure 7.5, the distribution peaks at an x-axis value of "3", therefore the mode is "3"). The median can be trickier to find, but it is the value associated with the number "50" in our frequency table's "Cumulative Percent" column. Referencing Figure 7.3 reveals that our "50" is actually hidden by the value of 87.5. Our "50" is here, but it is not explicitly reported. We need to infer its existence by recognizing that it resides between the two reported values of 37.5 and 87.5. The median value here is therefore "3", because this is the barbacoa rating associated with a cumulative percent of 50.

There are additional statistics that can be generated with the "descriptives" command, but range, mean, and standard deviation should be sufficient for most of your applications.

A General Note on Analyses

It was stated earlier that you do not need to know SPSS syntax code to use the syntax file organizing system, yet we have given examples of simple code commands that are useful for your SPSS life (such as "get file", "save outfile", "descriptives", and "frequencies"). These commands are so common that they are useful for you to remember, but it is not *necessary* that you remember them. Remember that SPSS will find the command language for you and write your syntax files for you via the Paste function. Although you will soon become familiar with basic syntax *manipulation* commands, it's less likely that you will become as proficient at remembering *analysis* commands. Therefore, it's expected that you will use the drop-down menus for analyses; just make sure that you only use these menus to generate commands that you then paste into your syntax diary.

When you use the drop-down menus to find and run analyses, it's also useful to know that SPSS organizes the available menu options from simple to more complex. Analytical options toward the top of the menu are more common and simple. Analytical options toward the bottom of the menu are more complex and generally less common. If you aren't sure which analysis you should be running, choose the "higher" (simpler) alternative – it's most likely to be correct for your purpose (especially if you are taking an undergraduate statistics course).

ALSO, if you *do* use pull-down menus to generate syntax, make sure to also cut and paste the generated command to the appropriate location in your syntax diary. This is an important consideration when relying on SPSS to generate your syntax for you, because SPSS will always paste the menu-generated command *at the bottom* of your syntax file. Usually that's not where you want the command to be located (remember, syntax runs sequentially from top to bottom).

A General Note About Output Files

This chapter dealt with commands that result in meaningful output files. We very rarely save output files. If you save your syntax files, you will receive output whenever you activate your syntax. There's typically therefore no need to directly save output. Treat it like a newspaper – read it over, take note of the important information, then use it to line the bottom of a birdcage or to wrap a nice cut of halibut – just like a newspaper, you can get a new one tomorrow.

Summary

You will eventually want to directly request output when working with SPSS – almost every project will require you to look at either descriptive information or frequency distributions (or both). The descriptive and frequency information that you request can be used for other data manipulative purposes, such as categorizing people or determining percentile ranking – and these advanced applications will be addressed in a later chapter. When you receive an output file, take note of the important information, but do not save the output file itself.

Key Terms

Cumulative percent – Frequencies output column presenting percentile information (cumulative **valid percent**).
Descriptives – SPSS command requesting (by default) the mean, standard deviation, minimum, and maximum values of a variable.
Frequencies – SPSS command requesting the number and percent of cases within each observed variable value.
Frequency distribution – Visual representation of what your data looks like regarding to the frequency of scores.
Histogram – Visual representation of data that utilize bars to represent frequencies.
Location – Location along the x-axis do the numbers tend to be found.
Maximum score – Largest data value within a column or variable.
Minimum score – Smallest data value within a column or variable.
Percent – Frequencies output column summarizing the number of cases for a given value divided by the total number of data file cases.
Percentile – Percentage of individuals at or below a given value or score.

Spread – How similar or different a set of responses is, represented through the span it covers within a distribution.

Valid percent – Frequencies output column summarizing the number of cases for a given value divided by the total number of responses to the variable of interest.

Discussion Questions

1   What are some applications of the "descriptives" information?

2   What are some applications of the "frequencies" information?

8

Hypothesis Testing

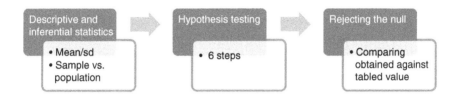

Chapter Learning Objectives

1. Descriptive versus inferential statistics
2. Six-step hypothesis testing
3. SPSS's focus on Step 5

This book is primarily intended for a very specific audience: students who are learning statistics in a classroom format while also learning how to perform statistical analyses in a separate lab course. This book is not intended to teach you statistical analyses. Rather, it assumes that you already know about analyses (from your statistics instructor) and have a need or desire to *compute* statistical indices via SPSS. This book, then, is a guide to help you learn SPSS, not statistics. This

IBM SPSS Essentials: Managing and Analyzing Social Sciences Data, Second Edition.
John Kulas, Renata Garcia Prieto Palacios Roji, and Adam Smith.
© 2021 John Wiley & Sons, Inc. Published 2021 by John Wiley & Sons, Inc.

chapter, however, does provide a brief overview of how we believe you should think about statistics and where SPSS fits within that thinking.

Descriptive Versus Inferential Statistics

One of the most important distinctions you make as a statistician is between **descriptive** and **inferential statistics**. This is because there are two primary purposes for statistics: the simple description of data or the desire to say something about a larger group of individuals based on information taken from a subset. Although it is important for you to be able to distinguish between these two categories of statistical indices, you must also be prepared for others to not be explicit in this distinction. That is, individuals will use the term "statistics" in a very broad sense and will very rarely explicitly specify whether they are referring to descriptive or inferential statistics. The previous chapter was focused on **descriptive statistics**. If you are at a cocktail party surrounded by baseball fans, and you overhear someone mention the word "statistics", you can be fairly confident that they are discussing *descriptive statistics* (many of these statistics are some version of a mean [for example, batting average or earned run average in the parlance of seamheads]).

Moving forward (in this textbook), however, we are entering the realm of *inferential statistics*. This is the category of statistics that would be implicated if you overheard the term "statistics" at a political candidate's headquarters on the night of an election. Here, individuals would likely be focused on polling numbers, and whether the polling numbers are truly predictive of what voters will do (or not). Specifically, inferential statistics are a category of procedures that facilitate inferences about a **population** based on information that are obtained from a **sample**. Descriptive statistics typically require only simple computations and the results of these computations are easily communicated to others. The computation and communication of inferential statistics, on the other hand, are greatly facilitated by adherence to a rigid procedure commonly referred to as **hypothesis testing**.

Hypothesis Testing (A *Process* for Interpreting Inferential Statistics)

Inferential statistics are not stand-alone indices as are descriptive statistics. They require context. Inferential statistics are therefore necessarily embedded within a framework of considerations (in the framework we provide below, the inferential statistic is not even considered until the fifth of six important steps). You must not think of an inferential statistic as a mere index – instead, you need to understand that the inferential statistic is only one component of this six-component *process* (the process is generally referred to as "hypothesis testing"). SPSS is good at one thing: computing a statistical index. You must be good at six things, because it is really not the inferential statistic that you are ultimately interested in, it is the inference that the inferential statistic permits.

Six Steps of Hypothesis Testing

Your goal in computing an inferential statistic is *not* to simply obtain a number. Your goal is quite different (and actually quite distinct from anything having to do with numbers) – your goal is to make a decision regarding the viability of something called the **null hypothesis**. You make this decision by systematically advancing through the ensuing six-step process.[1]

Step 1 – Set Alpha. **Alpha** can refer to many different things without proper context. It may represent the first letter in the Greek alphabet, or reliability within measurement contexts, or, most germane to the current presentation, it may communicate your **Type I** error rate in hypothesis testing. Your Type I error rate is your willingness to **reject the null hypothesis** when in fact you "shouldn't do so" (e.g. in the vast truthfulness of the Universe, your null is in fact correct). By convention, alpha is commonly set to 5% (0.05). This means that you will make an error of commission (say an effect is present when in reality it is absent) 1 out of 20 times. This is typically an acceptable level of error across disciplines; however, if the consequences of making a Type I error are considered substantial, then you may choose to select a different value. Commonly encountered values for alpha include 0.05, 0.01, and 0.001, although it is fully permissible for you to choose whatever alpha you desire. It is an important first step, because this is the point at which you determine how bold or cautious your prediction (aka hypothesis) is.

Step 2 – State your Hypotheses. That's correct, "hypotheses" (plural). There are always at least two mutually exclusive conditions that you will proclaim. One is called the null hypothesis (for the purposes of this book, the null hypothesis will be annotated as H_0). This literally means "I expect nothing of interest to occur". The other hypothesis is the one that is reflective of your prediction. This is the "interesting" hypothesis, even though it is referred to as the **alternative hypothesis** (we will annotate the alternative hypothesis as H_1). The naming convention for these two competing predictions stems from the backward logic

---

1 Some instructors may deviate slightly from this and favor a five- or seven-step process (by expanding or collapsing one of these six steps). Regardless of number of steps, the general process is always consistent across hypothesis testing applications (e.g. the performing of inferential statistics).

that hypothesis testing utilizes – statisticians set up likely scenarios (through the specification of sampling distributions) and then look for unlikely events. If an event is likely, then the null hypothesis is perfectly viable. If an event is deemed *unlikely*, however, then we look upon the null hypothesis with greater apprehension – perhaps even rejecting it outright. If we are able to reject the null hypothesis, then that means that the mutually exclusive yet complementary alternative hypothesis must be viable.

Step 3 – Collect Data. Hypothesis testing is an **empirical** venture. This means that numerical data must be collected. This may be done through a traditional experiment, administration of a survey, or even coding of qualitative data. The manner in which you collect data is governed by your experimental methodology, and some are better methodologists than others.

Step 4 – Find your Critical Value. Your **critical value** is the point in your appropriate sampling distribution that is identified by your alpha (declared in Step 1), your alternative hypothesis (stated in Step 2), and, very often, the size of your sample (calculated from Step 3). The metric of your critical value depends on the analysis that you are performing. If you are probing the association between two variables, your critical value will be an r_{cv}. If you are interested in whether two groups differ along some dependent variable of interest, your critical value will be a t_{cv}. With more than two groups, it's an F_{cv}. Critical values are usually found in appendices at the end of statistics textbooks. SPSS does not use critical values (because, remember, your critical value is partially a function of decisions that *you* make at Steps 1 and 2). SPSS cannot know what is going on inside your head regarding these decisions, so it never bothers with critical values – we will come back to this point in Chapter 9 once we begin to look at the output from inferential analyses.

Step 5 – Obtain your Observed Value. Finally, this is the point at which SPSS becomes useful. You will typically receive a lot of superfluous information with the output of an analysis in SPSS, but you should only be looking for one thing – your **obtained value**. The obtained value is the computed statistic based on your collected data. This is the value that is compared against your critical value.

Step 6 – Make your Statistical Decision. Your final step is to either **reject** or **fail to reject** your null hypothesis. Remember, the logic of hypothesis testing is a bit backward – your goal is to reject the null hypothesis (recall the null hypothesis is the "uninteresting" one that says, "nothing really interesting is happening here"). If you reject the uninteresting, then you can accept the alternative as viable. The terminology used at this stage is unfortunately confusing, but, happily, your route to making a decision is quite clear and obvious: if your obtained value (what SPSS gives you in Step 5) is bigger than your critical value (what you look up in the back of your statistics text), then you reject the null hypothesis.

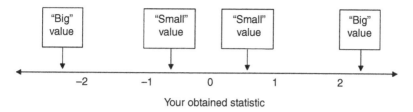

Figure 8.1 The concepts of "bigger" and "smaller" as germane to hypothesis testing.

If your obtained value is smaller than your critical value (see Figure 8.1), then you **fail to reject the null** hypothesis.[2]

Summary

If you aim to make inferences about broader groups of individuals (aka a population) from the collection of individuals you currently have access to (aka your sample), you likely want to consider applying inferential statistics. The traditional *process* of inferential analysis employs a procedure called "hypothesis testing". We recommend following six steps when you apply inferential statistics through hypothesis testing. SPSS tries to facilitate your hypothesis testing via the computation of significance estimates, but we recommend relying on tabled critical values as opposed to software estimates of significance.

Key Terms

Alpha – Percent of occasions you're willing to erroneously reject the null hypothesis.
Alternative hypothesis – The hypothesis that is reflective of your prediction, and is mutually exclusive and exhaustive of the null hypothesis.
Critical value – Statistical value corresponding to your alternative hypothesis, alpha, and (usually) sample size.
Descriptive statistics – Information summarizing a set of numbers.
Empirical – Data-based.

---

2 One note on "big" versus "small" in the realm of inferential statistics: This distinction is all about the "distance from zero". Therefore, a statistic of value −3 is "bigger" than a statistic of value −2. "How big" is interpreted relative to a starting point of zero (see Figure 8.1). The boundary between what can be labeled "big" and what should be labeled "small" is determined by your critical value.

Fail to reject the null – Statistical absence of an effect. You're either correct or making a **Type II error**.

Hypothesis testing – The process of claiming the presence or absence of an effect (typically a difference or association).

Inferential statistics – Probability-based information relating sample to population characteristics.

Null hypothesis – The hypothesis that contradicts your prediction, and is mutually exclusive and exhaustive of the alternative hypothesis.

Obtained value – Value computed via application of the statistical formula (this is typically the focus of software packages).

Population – Larger group of interest you wish to make a claim about (an effect is present or absent).

Reject the null – Statistical presence of an effect. You're either correct or making a Type I error.

Sample – Smaller subset you have access to, ideally randomly sampled from the broader population.

Type I error – When you reject the null hypothesis, when in fact the null hypothesis is true.

Type II error – When you fail to reject the null hypothesis, when the null hypothesis is false.

Discussion Questions

1   What is the goal when computing an inferential statistic?

2   Explain the differences between Type I and Type II errors.

3   What would you conclude (Step 6) if your obtained value is equal to 0.027, while your critical value is equal to 0.05?

9

Z- and T-Tests

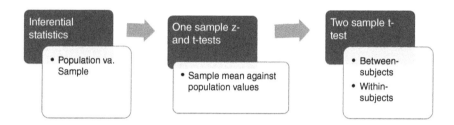

Chapter Learning Objectives

1. Select the appropriate analysis for your data
   a. One sample z-test
   b. One sample t-test
   c. Two independent samples t-test
   d. Two correlated samples t-test

IBM SPSS Essentials: Managing and Analyzing Social Sciences Data, Second Edition.
John Kulas, Renata Garcia Prieto Palacios Roji, and Adam Smith.
© 2021 John Wiley & Sons, Inc. Published 2021 by John Wiley & Sons, Inc.

2. Identify important and unimportant output
   a. Mean difference
   b. Standard error
   c. "t"
   d. "p"

Welcome to the wonderful world of inferential analyses. These chapters are *not* "best practice" recommendations on performing statistics – you need to get that information from your statistics instructor (alphas and hypotheses and similar stuff summarized in Chapter 8). Here, we're just trying to show you how to run some common analyses and navigate the output. All analyzed data are pictured in the screenshots, so you can enter data and follow along if you are so inclined.

The One Sample Z-Test

The most basic analytical procedure you'll want to perform involves a determination of whether or not two numbers differ from each other. Most often, the analysis you'll use in these situations is some type of **t-test**. Invariably, however, statistics texts first introduce you to the **one-sample z-test**. This is not a very practical analytical procedure, because it requires that you *know* two things about your population of interest (called parameters): the population mean (μ) and the population standard deviation (σ). Outside of a statistics classroom, you will never encounter either of these parameters (which is why the one-sample z-test is not a very *practical* analytical procedure). It is, however, a good stepping stone into the realm of **inferential statistics**.

SPSS example. Suppose you are a cookie manufacturer and you want to know if your cookies are better or worse than your competitors' cookies. *If* you were to know something about the average competitor rating (μ = 5.2, from perhaps the International Cookie Guild's yearly census of cookie-eaters' opinions), *and* you also, from this same census, knew what the variability in opinions was (e.g. σ = 1.3), then you could collect some ratings on your cookies and perform a one-sample z-test to determine whether your cookies are better or worse than your competitors'.

Proceeding through Chapter 8's six steps (we won't do this for all examples, but, as this is our first inferential analysis, we will do so here): (1) we'll use the conventional 0.05 alpha, (2) we're not very confident bakers, so we'll test whether our cookies are *either better or worse* than the average.

Step 1: $\qquad\qquad\qquad$ $\alpha = 0.05$

Step 2: $\qquad\qquad\qquad$ $H_0: \mu_{\text{my cookies}} = 5.2$

$\qquad\qquad\qquad\qquad\quad$ $H_1: \mu_{\text{my cookies}} \neq 5.2$

Table 9.1 7 random peoples' ratings.

Person	Rating
Bob	10
Persephone	9
Sally	8
Jane	9
Snoopy	9
Alexander	10
Yoseph	8

For our third step, you can ask seven random people to try your cookies and rate them along the same 1 → 10 scale that was used by the International Cookie Guild as seen on Table 9.1.

Your fourth step requires a statistical text – a **critical value** of z associated with an **alpha** of 0.05 (found in a *t-table*) and a nondirectional alternative hypothesis is:

Step 4: $$z_{cv} = \pm 1.96$$

Now, the fifth step is where SPSS usually steps in. Unfortunately, the one-sample z-test is *such* an impractical analytical procedure, that SPSS does not calculate this index directly. Instead, we'll have to alter a bit of syntax on a problem-by-problem basis, using the four values needed to calculate the obtained z: the sample mean (in our case, $\overline{X} = 9$), the population mean ($\mu = 5.2$), the population standard deviation ($\sigma = 1.3$), and the sample size ($n = 7$) as seen on Figure 9.1.

If those four values are placed into the above syntax and the entire script is highlighted and run, then the output window provides us with a value: 7.73. This is our "obtained" statistic.

Step 5: $$z_{obt} = 7.73$$

Step 6 is a simple comparison of our **obtained value** (7.73) and the value we took from the statistical table (± 1.96). Our obtained value is indeed "bigger", so…

Step 6: reject the null hypothesis

Indeed, our cookies are better than the average…

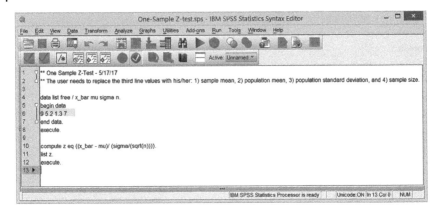

Figure 9.1 One sample z-test on SPSS.

The t-Test

The one-sample z-test is impractical because it requires information regarding your population of interest that is not typically available. More often, you will be missing information about the population. In these circumstances, the appropriate analysis is going to be some form of t-test. There are three different t-tests that we're going to learn. One is to be used when you want to compare your set of numbers against a known population value (again, μ), but this time you are not given σ – this is called the one sample t-test. This is still a bit impractical (because obtaining μ is a difficult venture indeed), but a bit more realistic than needing both μ and σ. The other two are very much practical and don't require any information about populations – these are called **two-sample t-tests**.

One-Sample T-Test

If you want to know if a mean calculated from your set of numbers is different from a **known mean**, you'll want to perform a **one-sample t-test**. You won't really encounter this situation very often outside of a statistics classroom (unless you're a sasquatch hunter). Imagine you are walking through the woods in the Pacific Northwest and you come across multiple sets of footprints. You record all of these sizes and then want to compare your estimate against the average human shoe size (which you look up on the Internet). We have the footprints we found in a SPSS file that we access through syntax as shown in Figure 9.2. After running the "get file" command, Figure 9.3 shows that data file that we've retrieved.

To see how likely it would be to find these 11 footprints from the normal **population** of people, we look up the average shoe size of people – 9.5. Next, we perform

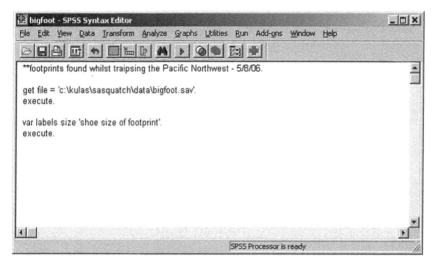

Figure 9.2 Accessing file with found footprints.

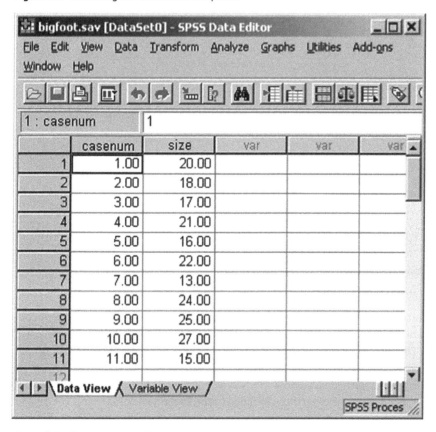

Figure 9.3 Footprints data file.

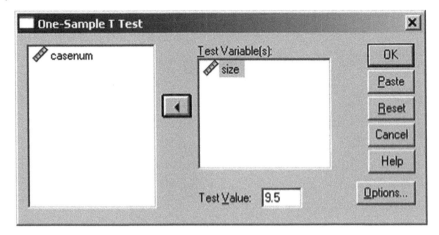

Figure 9.4 One sample t-test dialogue box.

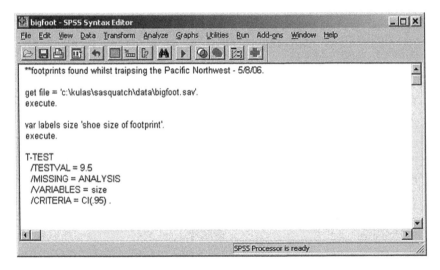

Figure 9.5 Pasting one sample t-test to syntax.

the one-sample t-test by selecting (from my syntax environment) analyze → compare means → one-sample t-test as shown in Figure 9.4.

The information we enter into this dialogue box is the dependent variable (also called test variable) and the number we're using as a comparison (in this case, the average person's shoe size). As shown in Figure 9.5, pasting this information to our syntax gives us everything we need to run this t-test.

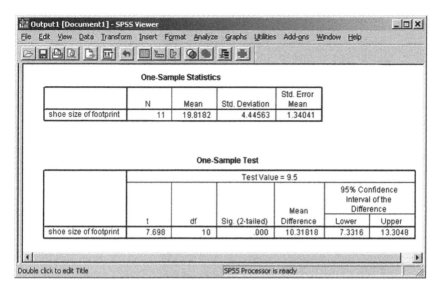

Figure 9.6 One sample t-test output.

Selecting all (Ctrl+A) and running results in the following output (we've mini-mized the outline to the left of the main output window for space-saving purposes; see Figure 9.6).

The first reported table contains descriptive information (the "**std. error** mean" is the standard deviation of your *sampling* distribution). The second table presents our t-test results. In order to make a determination regarding whether our mean (19.8) differs from the expected population mean (9.5), the **degrees of freedom** (10) can be used to select a critical t-value from a statistics book appendix and you can compare the tabled value against your obtained (7.698) value. Alternatively, a specific **significance estimate** is also provided. You "want" this significance estimate to be small (below your alpha), although you should note that the reported significance estimate is "conservative". If you had specified a directional (sometimes called one-tailed) hypothesis, the significance estimate would be even smaller (i.e. further to your alpha). In this case, it is quite obvious that there is a difference between our 11 Pacific Northwest footprints and the average shoe size – the implication is that these 11 footprints were not sampled from the human population. The formula used to calculate the obtained t-value is the mean difference (10.3) divided by the **standard error** (1.34), and this information is also provided in the tables (in your SPSS output). The 95% confidence interval is redundant with the significance information. If the significance estimate is less than 0.05 (as it is in this case), the 95% confidence interval will exclude 0; if the significance estimate is greater than 0.05, the confidence interval will include 0. You can change this

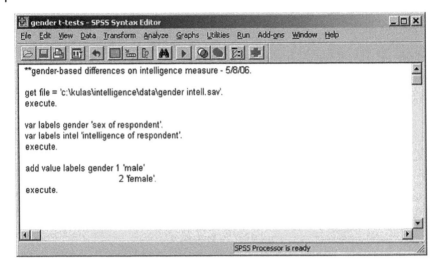

Figure 9.7 Running intelligence scores data through syntax.

confidence interval if you want to use a different alpha (look at the last line of our syntax specification on Figure 9.5).

Two Independent Samples T-Test

For our two **(independent) samples t-test** example, we're using information regarding intelligence scores from 25 men and 25 women. These 50 people have no relation to each other. If there's no reason to "link" people, we perform an independent-samples t-test. Loaded with the knowledge of the appropriate analytical procedure, we first access and run our existing syntax as shown in Figure 9.7.

The above syntax retrieves data and defines variables within the datafile seen on Figure 9.8.

To perform the t-test, we select from the analyze option within our syntax environment (analyze → compare means → independent samples t-test) and put our IV/Grouping Variable (gender) and DV/Test Variable (intel) in the appropriate SPSS windows as shown in Figure 9.9.

Because your grouping variable/IV may have more than two levels[1], you need to "define your **groups**", which is really SPSS's way of asking: What are the levels of your IV? The numeric codes for our gender levels are "1" and "2" as shown in Figure 9.10.

If we "continue" past this window, we can now paste the command into our syntax file as shown in Figure 9.11.

---

1 Well, it would be difficult (and painful) given the current example but generally its possible.

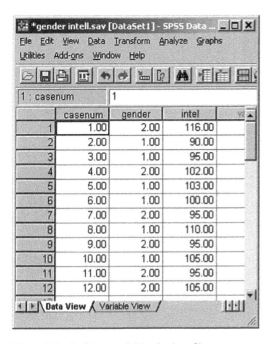

Figure 9.8 Defining variables in data file.

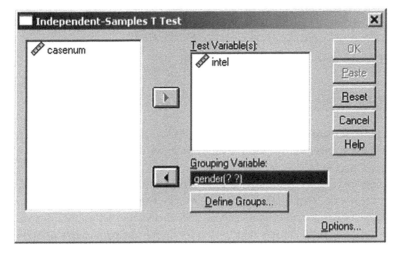

Figure 9.9 Specifying variables in independent samples t-test dialogue box.

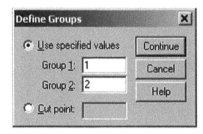

Figure 9.10 Defining groups dialogue box.

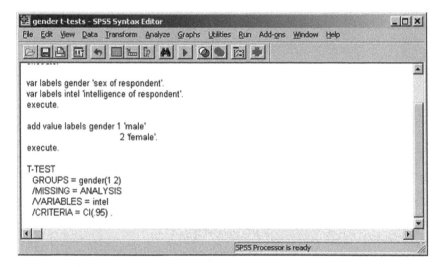

Figure 9.11 Paste defining groups command on syntax.

Running the entire syntax file at once (Ctrl+A) gives us the output file shown in Figure 9.12.

We can see that there is only a small mean difference in the samples – not likely to achieve significance, but we did the analysis so we should check our t value anyway (see Figure 9.13).

Good thing we looked – who's this Levene person and why has he hijacked our analysis? It turns out that one of the assumptions of the t-test is that your two samples have similar distributional shapes. SPSS checks this assumption for you through computing a **"Levene's test"**. It's a bit disconcerting because not only does SPSS run this check for you, but it gives you an alternative set of numbers to report if the Levene's test is significant (i.e. if you have a big **"F"**). This is why there are two rows of information reported in your t-table. Our "F" is small, so we don't have to worry about Levene and focus only on the top row of the table (see Figure 9.14).

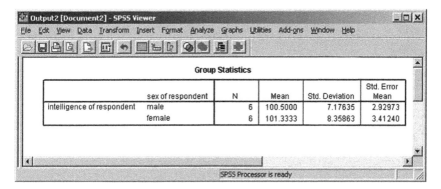

Figure 9.12   Output for groups statistics.

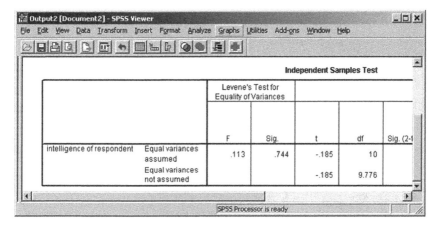

Figure 9.13   Output for independent samples t-test.

Our **obtained "t"** is −0.185. Because we specified "males" before "females" in our syntax, the female mean was subtracted from the male mean. If we change the order of our groups in our syntax, we'll change the valence of our obtained statistic, but nothing else (see Figure 9.15).

Running the above syntax (once again in its entirety – there's no waste associated with doing this) results in the t-test summary table found in Figure 9.16.

This table is identical to the previous summary except that the **valence** of your obtained statistic has flip-flopped. Regardless of whether the obtained t is positive or negative, it's small. Too small for us to say that there's a difference in intelligence between men and women. To conclude the analysis, we close out of the output (don't save), save the syntax, and call our grandma to let her know that she's been wrong about grandpa all these years.

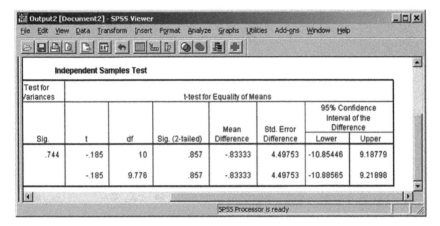

Figure 9.14 Independent samples t-test output information.

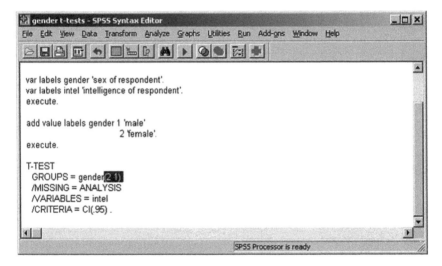

Figure 9.15 Changing valence of "t" statistic in syntax.

Two Correlated/Paired Samples T-Test[2]

Our **paired-samples** example concerns employees' productivity on the third shift versus the first shift. In this sample, all employees have tried working both shifts.

---

2 Social sciences terms of between-subjects and within-subjects (referring to treatments that are administered between or within participants) are sometimes referred to in statistics contexts as randomized groups and repeated measures. We know – multiple names for the same thing kinda sucks – get used to it. The difference between your two options for the two-sample t-test is most commonly decided by a consideration of design.

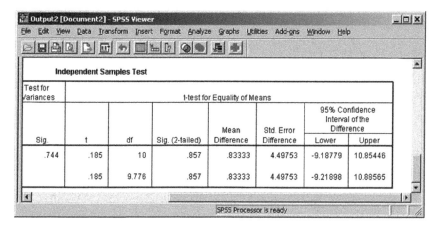

Figure 9.16   Independent samples t-test output after changing order of groups.

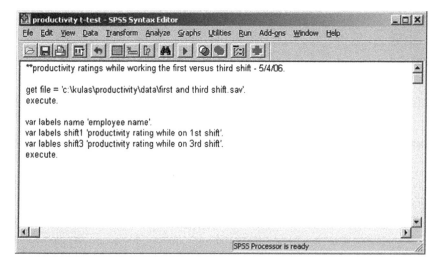

Figure 9.17   Preparing syntax for paired samples t-test.

The most appropriate analysis is therefore the **paired-samples t-test**. Remember from Chapter 3 that the number of people equals the number of rows in SPSS. This will help you determine both how to enter your data and also the most appropriate analysis. Calling up the syntax for this example can be found in Figure 9.17.

Running this syntax brings up the datafile shown in Figure 9.18 – note that although there is one IV (shift) and one DV (productivity), these variables are presented a little differently because all people experienced both first and third shifts.

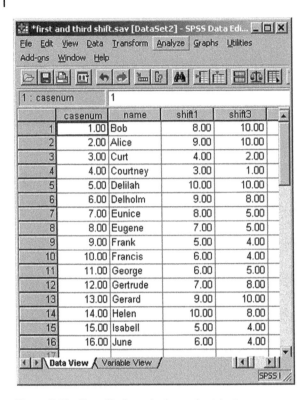

Figure 9.18 Data file for paired samples t-test.

Going through the same steps as the one-sample and independent sample t-tests, we select (from within our syntax environment) analyze→compare means→paired samples t-test as shown in Figure 9.19.

This window is a bit different from the others because you're not expected to have separate IV and DV columns. With a paired-samples situation, you have to store your data by "combining" your IV and DV information. If we paste the above, we get the syntax command shown in Figure 9.20.

Selecting Ctrl+A gives us the output shown in Figure 9.21.

This first table is the same as the first table in the independent samples t-test, the only difference being that the 16 first shift workers are the same people as the 16 third shift workers. Here, there is a larger mean difference – it will be interesting to see what our t-test will yield (see Figure 9.22).

Because the DV information is stored in separate columns, SPSS is able to calculate a correlation between first shift productivity and third shift productivity. Correlations will be covered in more detail in Chapter 11. From this correlation,

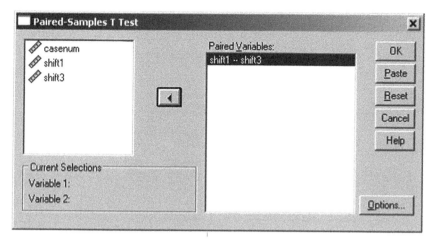

Figure 9.19 Paired-samples t-test dialogue box.

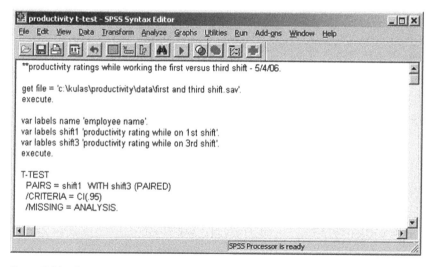

Figure 9.20 Syntax command for paired samples t-test.

you get a sense that people who were productive in the first shift were also generally productive in the third shift – it does not tell us anything about whether there are *mean* differences between shifts, however.

The third table (labeled "Paired Samples Test") is our requested output. Once again, the formula for the t-test (mean difference divided by standard error) is fully represented in the table. Workers were, on average, rated as being 0.875 more

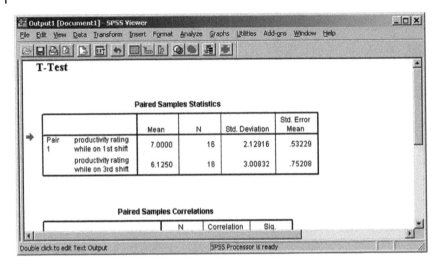

Figure 9.21 Paired samples statistics output.

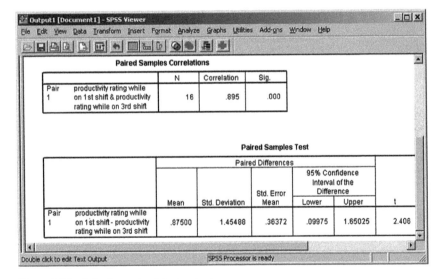

Figure 9.22 Paired samples t-test output.

productive when working the first as opposed to third shift. Dividing this average difference by the standard error gives us a t estimate of 2.406 as shown in Figure 9.23.

We can use the df information to look up a tabled critical value, or we can simply take the conservative significance estimate as evidence for the effect (if we had

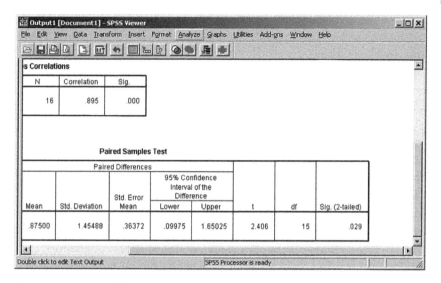

Figure 9.23 Value of "t" on paired samples t-test output.

thought that first shift workers would be more productive and specified a directional hypothesis, the reported significance estimate would be too high). Regardless of which approach we take to using this information, it is clear that workers are more productive on the first shift than the third (at an alpha of 0.05) – the boss had better invest in some 24-hour coffee makers.

Summary

T-tests are fairly simple inferential analyses. If you have information from only one group of individuals, you can only perform a one-sample t-test. To do this, you need to provide a comparison mean. If you have information from two groups, you can perform a two-sample t-test, but you need to determine whether those numbers come from the same people (paired samples) or different people (independent samples).

Key Terms

Alpha – Percentage of the time you're willing to incorrectly state an effect exists when in fact it does not. Set by the researcher, but the common social sciences convention is to set alpha at 5%.

Critical value – Tabled value of a test statistic (i.e. t, F, r) that is associated with a particular α and df. The threshold that the obtained statistic has to breach to be considered "significant".

Degrees of freedom (df) – A mutual consideration of the number of statistical parameters estimated and the number of numbers used to estimate the parameters.

F – Ratio of treatment to error variance.

Groups – SPSS label for "levels" of an IV within the t-test analysis.

Independent samples t-test – The two-sample t-test to be used with between-subjects situations.

Inferential statistics – Procedures estimating the probability that a given sample effect would occur if there was no effect present in the population.

Known mean – A value that is given instead of being computed.

Levene's test – Estimate of the t-test assumption of equal group variances.

Obtained value – The computed value of a test statistic (i.e. t, F, r). To be compared against a tabled/critical value.

One-sample t-test – Difference between a sample mean and a given mean.

Paired-samples t-test – Two two-sample t-test to be used with within-subjects situations.

Population – The larger group of interest from which the sample was drawn.

Significance estimate – Alternative to comparing obtained and tabled/critical test

Statistics – SPSS reports specific probabilities associated with each estimated obtained test statistic.

Standard error – Standard deviation of a sampling distribution. Commonly the denominator in inferential analyses.

T-test – Analysis used to determine if sample mean differences indicate population differences (or not).

Two-sample t-test – Difference between two estimated sample means.

Valence – "sign" (+/−)

Discussion Questions

1 What would happen to my obtained t if I ran a paired-samples t-test situation as an independent-samples t-test?

2 How practical is the one-sample t-test?

3 Your parents claim college students sleep too much. They claim the average amount of sleep "normal" people get is eight hours. You survey 7 of your classmates, who sleep 9, 11, 7, 8, 13, 12, and 10 hours per night. Do college students sleep more than what your parents claim is "average"?

4 You believe llamas from Peru are able to spit farther than llamas from Australia. You travel to Peru to measure the distance llamas are able to spit and obtain the following: 22, 26, 28, 19, 24 cm. You catch a flight to Auburn, Australia, and find a llama farm where you are able to measure the distance to which those llamas are able to spit: 20, 15, 40, 23, and 18 cm. Are llamas from Peru able to spit (on average) further than the llamas from Auburn, Australia?

5 You want to know the effect of caffeine on reaction time. You recruit your friends on two different occasions. Once you have them drink five cups of coffee before you throw foam-tipped darts at them; on the second occasion you have them drink five cups of water before trying to hit them with darts. You record the following number of hits (out of 20 throws):

	Caffeine	Water
Bob	5	10
Sally	15	16
Persephone	12	15
June	4	6
Eunice	8	12

Does caffeine affect reaction time?

10

Inferential Analyses (ANOVAs)

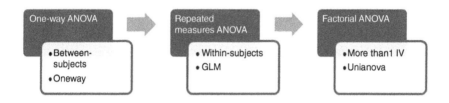

CHAPTER MENU

Chapter Learning Objectives

1. One-way Command
2. GLM Command
3. UNIANOVA Command

When you are still interested in mean differences but find yourself dealing with more than two means at a time, you need to perform an **analysis of variance (ANOVA)** instead of a t-test. There are three different ANOVAs that we're going to cover (although there are more types of ANOVA that could be specified).

IBM SPSS Essentials: Managing and Analyzing Social Sciences Data, Second Edition.
John Kulas, Renata Garcia Prieto Palacios Roji, and Adam Smith.
© 2021 John Wiley & Sons, Inc. Published 2021 by John Wiley & Sons, Inc.

You can think of ANOVAs as superordinate analyses to the two-sample t-tests. ANOVA *can* be applied to the two-sample t-test situation (except it reports an F instead of a t), but ANOVA has the flexibility to accommodate more than two means simultaneously. The one-way ANOVA is used in an independent-samples t-test situation, the repeated-measures ANOVA is used in a correlated samples t-test situation, and the third ANOVA (factorial) doesn't really have a straight t-test analogy – it is used when we have more than one predictor or independent variable (IV).

One-Way ANOVA (One-Way Command)

We'll use a prototypical drug and placebo example for the **one-way ANOVA**; Figure 10.1 shows our syntax.

Running this syntax calls up the data file shown in Figure 10.2.

For the actual ANOVA analysis, we have two options. We can run a straight-forward one-way ANOVA and receive a simple summary table, or we can run a **general linear model (GLM)** and get a bunch of supplementary information. We'll be forced to run the GLM with different ANOVA designs, so whenever possible, run the easier one-way ANOVA. As shown in Figure 10.3, the dialog box (Analyze > Compare Means > One-Way ANOVA) will give us our **"ONEWAY"** command. You can also see the command for the one-way ANOVA via syntax in

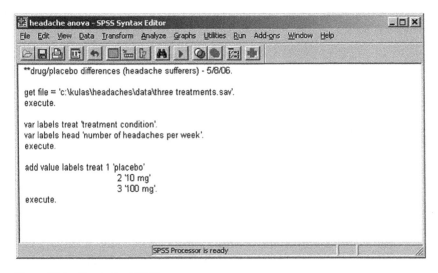

Figure 10.1 Headache ANOVA.

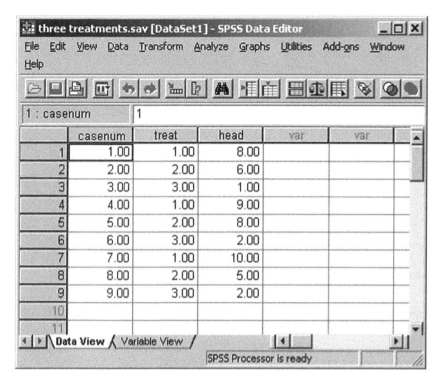

Figure 10.2   Drug and placebo data file.

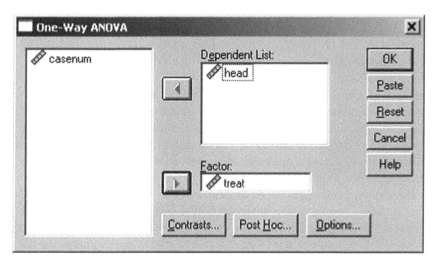

Figure 10.3   One-way ANOVA dialog box.

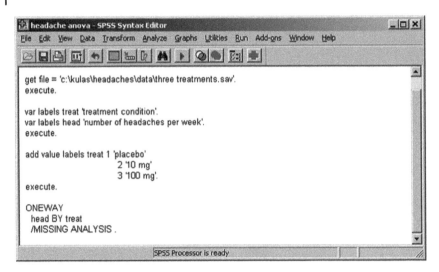

Figure 10.4 Headache ANOVA syntax.

Figure 10.4 in which the treatment condition variable is subdivided into three distinct categories.

This should look very similar to the Independent-Samples T-Test dialog box. The main difference here is that we don't have to specify our groups (in the **Factor** field) because the ANOVA can accommodate an infinite number of levels. Pasting this (and ignoring Contrasts, Post Hoc, and Options) will give us a simple ANOVA table, as shown in Figure 10.5.

The table in Figure 10.5 contains all the information you need to know for the **omnibus** (overall) **ANOVA,** and is one of the simplest pieces of output you will ever see from SPSS. Similar to the t-test, you could find a statistics table and look up the critical value of F at 2 and 6 degrees of freedom, then compare that tabled value against your obtained value of 33.82. Alternatively, you could simply use the specific significance information provided for your obtained F (that is, 0.001 is less than $\alpha = 0.05$). It all boils down to your level of comfort in using the test statistic to make a decision (the obtained F, as you are taught in statistics classes), or using the significance estimate (the Sig., as SPSS wants you to do). Both paths lead to the same conclusion (rejection of the null), but you may feel a little uncomfortable at first when you rely on the SPSS significance number. Note here that, unlike the t-test situation, all hypotheses with an ANOVA are, effectively, nondirectional (the F ratio is always only a positive value – it is impossible to obtain a "negative" F). This makes interpretation of the SPSS "Sig." value a bit more straightforward with the ANOVA (as contrasted with the t-test, where the "Sig." is dependent on your choice of alternative hypothesis directionality).

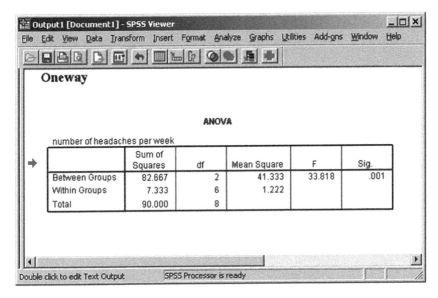

Figure 10.5 One-way ANOVA results.

Repeated-Measures ANOVA (GLM Command)

For the *repeated measures* (aka within-subjects' design) situation, we're going to use GPA information across years in college as the example. First, let's look at the syntax calling up the data file, as shown in Figure 10.6.

Running this syntax accesses the data file shown in Figure 10.7.

You'll note in Figure 10.7 that there is no IV identifying column – this is because we are in a repeated-measures, **within-subjects** situation. In these cases, you'll always have a different organization of your data (because the number of rows in SPSS has to equal the number of people). The variable headings therefore are not truly "variables" but rather the *levels* of the variable (e.g. the nominal values that the Independent Variable can take). To select the **repeated measures ANOVA**, we have to use the GLM option from the SPSS drop-down menu (Analyze > General Linear Model > Repeated Measures). Choosing this menu opens the dialog box shown in Figure 10.8.

Because you do not have an IV or predictor column for your within-subjects variable, you need to specify which of your columns contain IV level information in this window. For our analysis, there are four **IV levels** – freshman, sophomore, junior, and senior – so we name our IV, specify four levels, and add to the analysis, as shown in Figure 10.9.

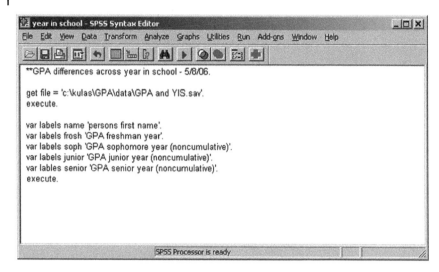

Figure 10.6 Year in school syntax.

	casenum	name	frosh	soph	junior	senior
1	1.00	Bobby	2.30	4.00	3.00	3.50
2	2.00	Jane	2.40	2.50	3.20	3.30
3	3.00	Sue	3.00	3.30	3.30	3.40
4	4.00	Martinique	3.90	3.80	3.90	4.00
5	5.00	Sally	1.50	1.60	2.80	4.00
6	6.00	Sobriquet	2.00	2.50	2.90	3.90
7	7.00	Persephone	2.30	2.20	2.80	3.10
8	8.00	Snoopy	2.00	1.50	3.00	3.20
9	9.00	Woodstock	1.90	1.50	2.50	3.10
10						
11						

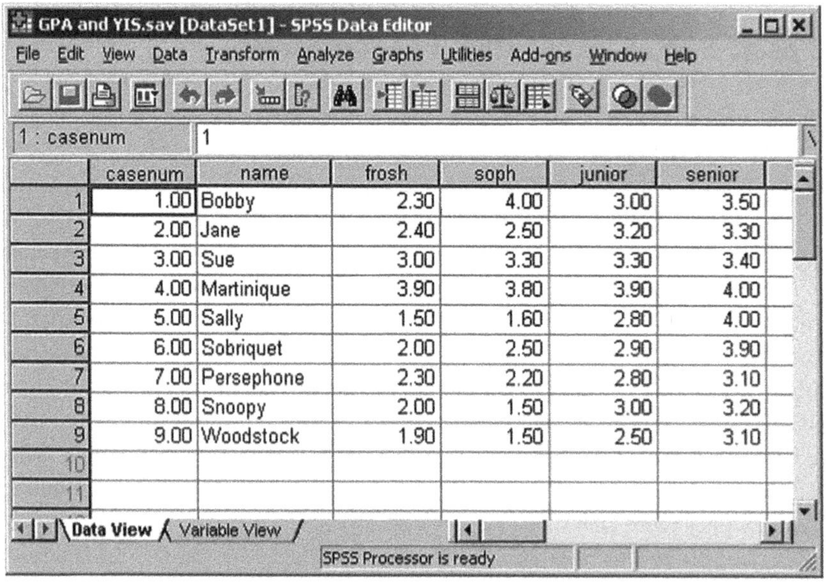

Figure 10.7 GPA and YIS data file.

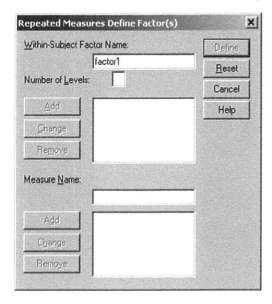

Figure 10.8 Repeated measures define factor(s) dialog box.

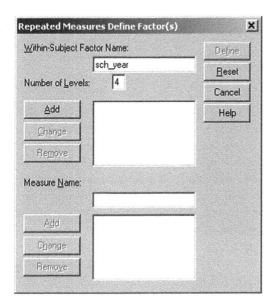

Figure 10.9 Repeated measures define factor(s) dialog box.

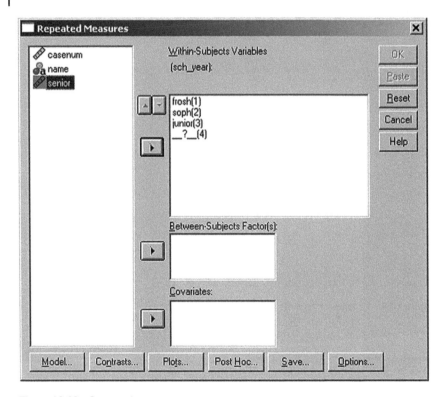

Figure 10.10 Repeated measures.

Choosing the Define option, we're able to specify which of our columns are associated with the different levels of our within-subjects IV, as shown in Figure 10.10.

The Between-Subjects and Covariates dialog boxes are letting you know that if you want to complicate your design beyond a simple repeated-measures ANOVA, SPSS is OK with that. We don't need to complicate things any further with the current example, so we'll paste the syntax shown in Figure 10.11 into our diary.

Running the full syntax file (Ctrl+A) gives us a complete mess of an output file (you can do basically anything with the GLM command – except simplify your output). We'll take the output one table at a time, starting with Figure 10.12.

Not much there: this first table, the GLM simply identifies our IV. On to the next table, shown in Figure 10.13.

This table is more interesting, but a little overwhelming. Because the GLM is a very flexible command, you're given all kinds of output. This table actually contains four different multivariate options that you may choose to report as your overall effect, but you don't have to. If you do report these, you report the values

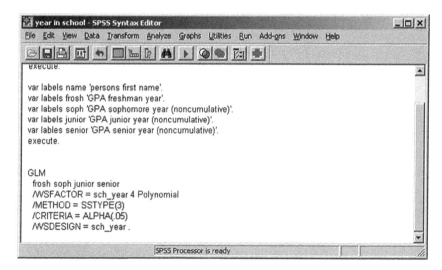

Figure 10.11   Year in school.

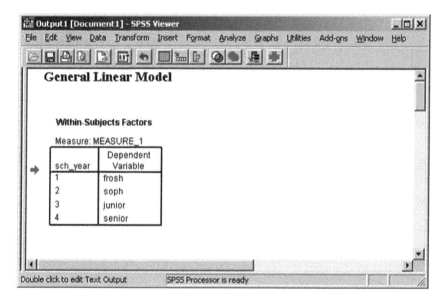

Figure 10.12   General linear model.

under the Value column, not the associated F. On to the next table, shown in Figure 10.14.

Sphericity is an overarching assumption of repeated-measures ANOVA (it essentially combines all of the repeated measures assumptions into one). If

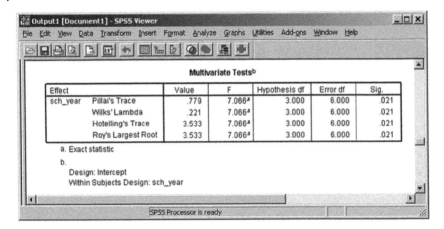

Figure 10.13 Multivariate tests.

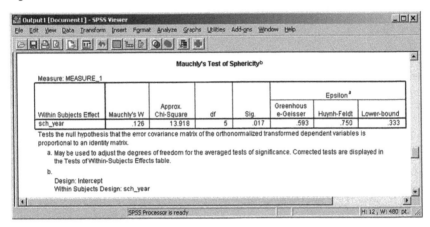

Figure 10.14 Mauchly's test of sphericity.

sphericity is *violated*, as it is here (significance is less than our $\alpha = 0.05$), it is recommended that you go back to the multivariate table and report **Wilks' Lambda**. If the significance estimate had been greater than $\alpha = 0.05$, you could go on to the tests of within-subjects effects, as shown in Figure 10.15.

The **Sphericity Assumed** row contains your traditional F – this is what you generally want to report from this analysis (for example, $F_{(3,24)} = 10.62$, $p < 0.05$). This is the F that you would obtain if you had done the analysis by hand, and is therefore the primary statistic you are looking for in this entire output. However, if sphericity is violated, you may want to ignore Sphericity Assumed and consider the **Huynh-Feldt** (which has a greater significance level reported due to the adjusted df results).

Tests of Within-Subjects Effects

Measure: MEASURE_1

Source		Type III Sum of Squares	df	Mean Square	F	Sig.
sch_year	Sphericity Assumed	7.079	3	2.360	10.617	.000
	Greenhouse-Geisser	7.079	1.778	3.981	10.617	.002
	Huynh-Feldt	7.079	2.250	3.145	10.617	.001
	Lower-bound	7.079	1.000	7.079	10.617	.012
Error(sch_year)	Sphericity Assumed	5.334	24	.222		
	Greenhouse-Geisser	5.334	14.224	.375		
	Huynh-Feldt	5.334	18.004	.296		
	Lower-bound	5.334	8.000	.667		

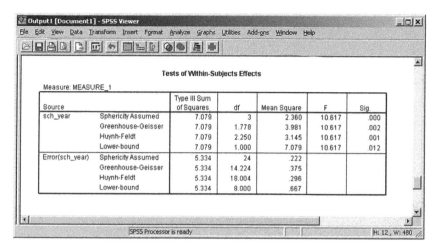

Figure 10.15 Tests of within-subjects effects.

Tests of Within-Subjects Contrasts

Measure: MEASURE_1

Source	sch_year	Type III Sum of Squares	df	Mean Square	F	Sig.
sch_year	Linear	6.845	1	6.845	21.020	.002
	Quadratic	.174	1	.174	1.412	.269
	Cubic	.061	1	.061	.277	.613
Error(sch_year)	Linear	2.605	8	.326		
	Quadratic	.984	8	.123		
	Cubic	1.745	8	.218		

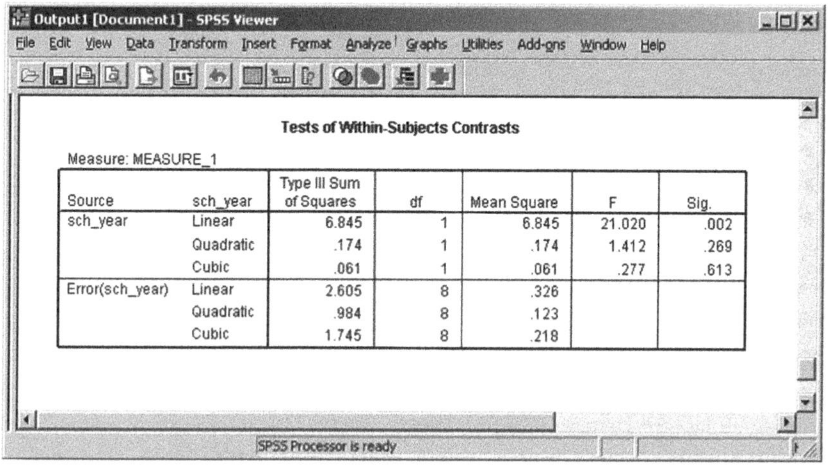

Figure 10.16 Tests of within-subjects contrasts.

The F column results in Figure 10.16 are useful if your *IV is* **quantitative** (that is, increasing drug dosages). Our situation with progressive years in school probably qualifies to make this table relevant, although more commonly it won't apply to your situation. Our linear trend is significant, meaning that GPA is linearly related to progressive year in school; that is, it tends to get better as you approach your senior year. We don't really care, as this isn't typically the focus of an ANOVA – let's move on to the final table, shown in Figure 10.17.

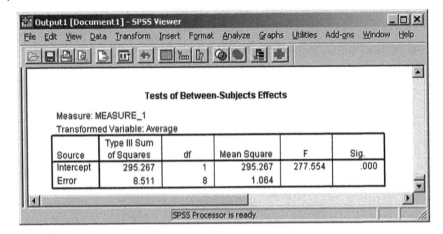

Figure 10.17 Tests of between-subjects effects.

GPA (DV)	SS	df	MS	F
Between Groups/Treatment	7.079	3	2.36	10.617
Subjects	8.511	8	1.064	
Within Groups/Error	5.334	24	0.222	
Total[a]	20.924	35		

[a]SPSS does not report tatals – you need to calculate these yourself if you want them

Figure 10.18 Summary ANOVA table for GPA (DVs).

The Error row actually contains your repeated measures' **subjects effect**. If the GLM command was capable of producing a nice and simple summary table as it did for the one-way ANOVA (instead of the reams of output that it provides), it would look like the table in Figure 10.18.

You should be able to construct one of these simple tables for every repeated-measures ANOVA that you conduct, if you follow the progression of tables that we have just visited. Out of all that output, we needed only these few pieces of information, but we had to pull them from different locations – quite confusing. Additionally, there was a lot of information in the output that we did not need – also confusing. Note that SPSS does not report total estimates for the repeated measures ANOVA – you'll have to compute those yourself by summing your three Sums of Squares estimates.

Factorial ANOVA (Unianova Command)

The **factorial ANOVA** is similar to the repeated-measures ANOVA in terms of SPSS specification (we have to do the GLM approach once again). However, because the example we're using has only *between-subjects* variables, our output is simplified. If one or both of our IVs were within-subjects, we would have to wade through the excessive output of the repeated measures analysis again. Instead, with between-subjects variables we get something that looks more similar to the simple one-way table. The syntax to define our data file is shown in Figure 10.19.

Running this syntax gives us the data file shown in Figure 10.20.

Choosing Analyze > General Linear Model > Univariate from within our syntax diary gives us the Univariate dialog box shown in Figure 10.21.

The IVs for this (and all) between-subjects situations can be specified as either **fixed** or **random IVs**. Generally, social sciences designs use fixed IVs – this means that the researcher or statistician intentionally *chooses* what levels are investigated; as shown in Figure 10.22, these are male, female, and placebo, 10 mg, and 100 mg. If the researcher does not specify what specific levels he or she is interested in and stumbles across them randomly, the random factor option should be used. Note that this is just SPSS trying to be as flexible as possible once again. It's not *trying*

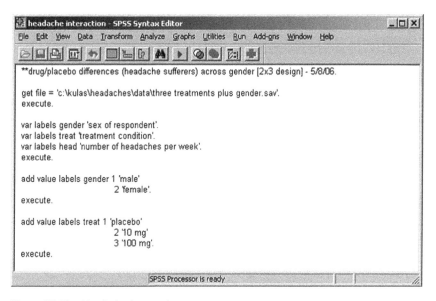

Figure 10.19   Headache interaction syntax.

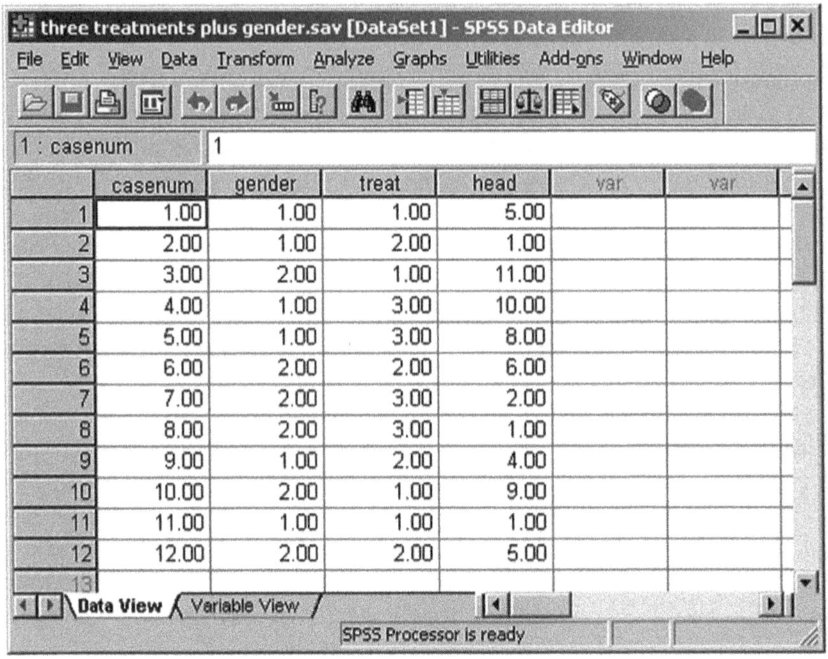

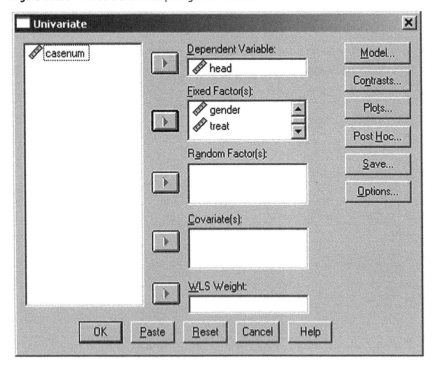

Figure 10.20 Three treatments plus gender results.

Figure 10.21 Univariate dialog box.

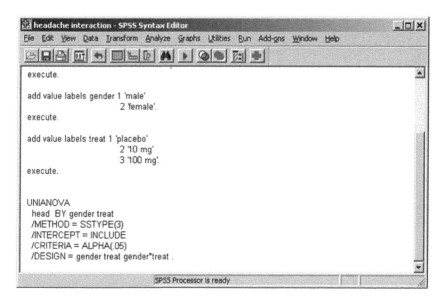

Figure 10.22   Headache interaction syntax file.

to confuse you, but just being accommodating to all possible researchers. Use the Fixed Factor(s) option when you're running an ANOVA; you can also run a simple one-way ANOVA with the same Analyze > General Linear Model > Univariate choice; this option gives the researcher more flexibility and options, whereas the "one-way" command is clean and simple. Figure 10.22 shows the command pasted into our syntax diary.

Selecting Ctrl+A and running our entire analyses gives us the output shown in Figure 10.23.

This first table just summarizes how many individuals we have in each condition. There are six males and six females, and there are four people who received the placebo, four who received 10 mg of the drug, and four who received 100 mg of the drug: a total of 12 people. The table shown in Figure 10.24 is the only other piece of output reported.

We have a significant interaction (drug effectiveness depends on gender; $F = 19.23$, $p < 0.05$) and no main effects. If we were to construct a simplified version of this table, it would be as shown in Figure 10.25.

Note that totals are reported in the SPSS table in Figure 10.24, but the row you actually want is labeled **Corrected Total**. The **Corrected Model** row presents the summated results of all three effects – it is used to estimate the R^2 at the bottom of the table, which is an estimate of the percent of total data variance that is associated with all of your IV effects. You do not typically report the Corrected Model F, although the R^2 may be of interest to you.

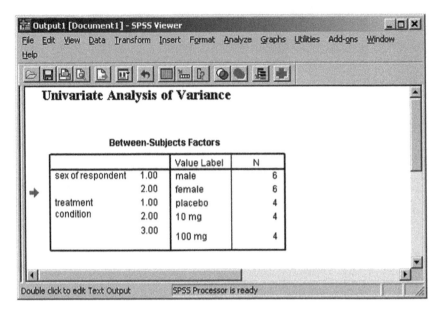

Figure 10.23 Univariate analysis of variance results.

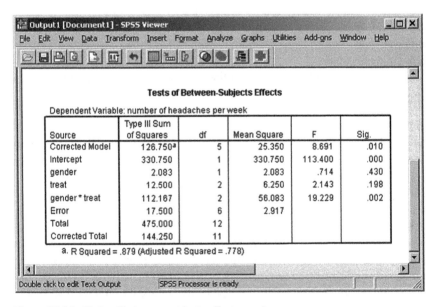

Figure 10.24 Tests of between-subjects effects results.

Headaches (DV)	SS	df	MS	F
Gender	2.08	1	2.083	0.71
Drug	12.5	2	6.25	2.14
Gender × drug	112.17	2	56.08	19.23
Error	17.5	6	2.92	
Total	144.25	11		

Figure 10.25 Summary ANOVA table for number of headaches (DVs).

Follow-Up Contrasts

We performed only **omnibus ANOVAs**, since it greatly simplifies the output. When people first interact with the drop-down menu capabilities of SPSS (especially with inferential analyses), they have a tendency to "check" everything – by that we mean they are so nervous about what they are doing that they request all of the available options. With most of these ANOVAs you can request assumption checks, **follow-up contrasts**, descriptive statistics, different alphas, and so on. This makes a complete mess out of your output file. With the ANOVA, we recommend requesting and reporting only the omnibus F. If you want to make another run at the analysis and check assumptions, that's fine, but the first run-through should be "bare bones" so you know what you're dealing with in the output. As far as follow-up contrasts go, we very generally recommend using t-tests. Although you can request these directly through the ANOVA menus, again, it's probably best to do these separately through t-test commands (it keeps your output clean, manageable, and interpretable).

The recommendations in this chapter for what output to report were mainly summarized from Tabachnick and Fidell (2007). If you need further guidance in conducting and reporting ANOVAs, this is the best ANOVA text we have encountered.

Summary

There are three different commands to be specified with the three different types of ANOVAs. The simple one-way (to be used with one between-subjects variable) uses a "one-way" command. The repeated measures (to be used with one within-subjects variable) uses a "GLM" command. The factorial ANOVA (to be used with multiple independent variables) uses a "**UNIANOVA**" command. The output is fairly straightforward with the one-way and factorial ANOVAs – but with the repeated measures ANOVA, the output is complex and tough to navigate. Follow-up contrasts can be performed by doing targeted t-tests.

Key Terms

ANOVA – General term used to classify a series of mean-difference testing procedures.

Corrected model – Combined impact of all estimated main and interaction effects.

Corrected total – SPSS label for the total sums of squares and df estimates in a factorial ANOVA summary table.

Factor – Term sometimes used for IVs, especially in ANOVA contexts.

Factorial ANOVA – ANOVA model to be used when there are two or more IVs of interest.

Fixed IVs – Researcher-determined levels.

Follow-up contrasts – Targeted analyses to determine where differences may exist, given the occurrence of a significant omnibus F (for example, what levels differ from each other).

General linear model – Encompassing theory from which most common analyses are derived.

"GLM" – SPSS command for the general linear model; many different analyses can be specified through the GLM command.

Huynh-Feldt – Recommended alternative to the "sphericity assumed" F if you have a violation of sphericity.

IV levels – Specific values of an IV/factor (for example, male and female are two levels of the gender IV).

Omnibus ANOVA – General, broad analysis assessing the ratio of column to row variance.

"ONEWAY" – SPSS command for a one-way ANOVA.

One-way ANOVA – ANOVA model to be used in a between-subjects situation.

Quantitative IV – Independent variable that differs in magnitude as well as category.

R^2 – Percent of DV variance associated with all estimated IV effects.

Random IVs – randomly determined levels.

Repeated measures ANOVA – ANOVA model to be used in a within-subjects situation.

Sphericity – Lack of association among tested variables.
Sphericity assumed – F ratio obtained on calculating a repeated-measures ANOVA by hand (type III SS).
Subjects effect – Estimate of the amount of variance in a matrix of numbers that is attributable to differences across people.
"UNIANOVA" – SPSS command for the factorial ANOVA (alternatively, "GLM" could also be specified).
Wilks' Lambda – Multivariate statistic ranging from possible values of 0 to 1.
Within-subjects IV – Independent variable, all levels of which are administered to all participating
individuals.

Discussion Questions

1 Why does SPSS use different terms than the terms that social science students learn?

2 Why is the repeated measures output so over-the-top?

3 Thirty chronic headache sufferers were assigned to one of three conditions: watch cartoons, go for a walk, or eat ice cubes. The researcher hopes that one of these treatments may help their suffering. Over the course of one month, the 30 people record the following number of reported headaches:

Cartoon watchers	Walkers	Ice-eaters
5	20	5
2	16	6
13	25	20
8	8	25
20	6	6
25	9	30
15	11	11
11	15	5
6	5	15
8	6	8

Are any of these treatments more or less effective than the others?

4 Maybe the effectiveness of these treatments depends on the gender of the headache sufferer. Organizing the data a little bit differently, we want to know if there is a difference in number of headaches across treatments for men and women.

	Cartoon watchers	Walkers	Ice-eaters
Men	5	20	5
	2	16	6
	13	25	20
	8	8	25
	20	6	6
Women	25	9	30
	15	11	11
	11	15	5
	6	5	15
	8	6	8

Is there a difference between the number of headaches according to gender?

5 Run the appropriate t-test as well as the appropriate ANOVA for the caffeine example from Chapter 9. What's the relationship between your obtained F and t?

Reference

Tabachnick, B.G. and Fidell, L.S. (2007). *Using Multivariate Statistics*, 5e. Allyn & Bacon/Pearson Education.

11

Inferential Analyses (Correlation or Regression)

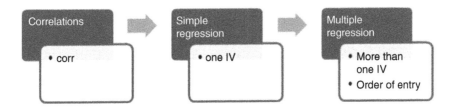

Chapter Learning Objectives

1. Select the appropriate analysis for your data
   a. Correlation
   b. Regression
2. Identify important and unimportant output
   a. r
   b. a
   c. b

IBM SPSS Essentials: Managing and Analyzing Social Sciences Data, Second Edition.
John Kulas, Renata Garcia Prieto Palacios Roji, and Adam Smith.
© 2021 John Wiley & Sons, Inc. Published 2021 by John Wiley & Sons, Inc.

   d. β

   e. p

Welcome to the penultimate chapter on data analyses. This chapter presents analyses that look a little different from ANOVAs and t-tests because the current analyses are used most commonly when you have **continuous IVs** (although they can also be used when you have categorical IVs). Just as ANOVAs are superordinate to t-tests, regression is superordinate to ANOVA (that is, anything you do with t-tests you can do with ANOVAs; anything you do with ANOVAs you can do with regression). Although you can apply regression to previous situations, we don't recommend doing that – instead, use the t-test and ANOVA when you have categorical IVs and use the regression or correlation when you have continuous IVs – it is possible (depending on your field of study) that future advisors will recommend a deeper understanding and application of regression, but for an introduction, it is generally preferred that you retain all three procedures (t-tests, ANOVAs, and regression).

Correlation

Much as the t-test is a simplified ANOVA, the **correlation** can be thought of as a simplified regression. Indeed, the correlation is so simple that we aren't going to use drop-down menus at all. We're not even going to look at them. First, we call up a data file with multiple continuous variables, as shown in Figure 11.1.

This syntax, when activated, brings up the data file shown in Figure 11.2.

If we want to know the correlation between height and shoe size, the command is a simple "**corr vars**" as shown in Figure 11.3.

Selecting all (Ctrl+A) and running gives us the small **correlation matrix** shown in Figure 11.4.

We generally recommend requesting one correlation at a time, although if you prefer, you can request a larger correlation matrix, as shown in Figure 11.5.

You do not need commas between your specified variables (we don't use commas with these correlation commands), but if you prefer to use commas, SPSS will still interpret and run the correlations. Correlations between these four variables are reported in Figure 11.6.

Among the four variables specified, there is only one significant relationship (at $\alpha = 0.05$). The number in the Pearson Correlation row is your **r** ($r = 0.88$ for the "significant" shoe size and height association). The number in the **Sig. (2-tailed)** row is your associated level of significance. Just like the t-test significance estimate, the significance level that is reported *by default* with the correlation should be considered conservative. If we had specified a directional hypothesis (as we

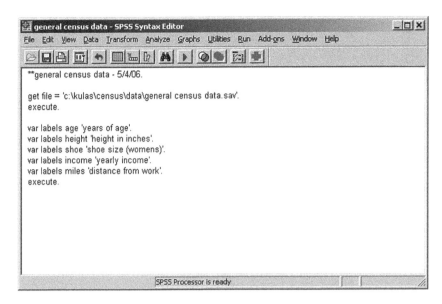

Figure 11.1   General census data syntax.

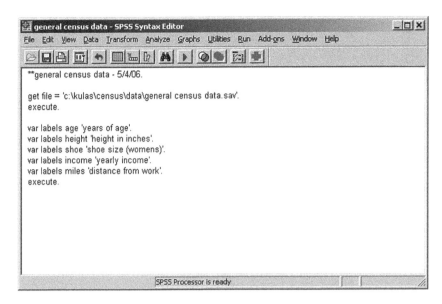

Figure 11.2   General census data file.

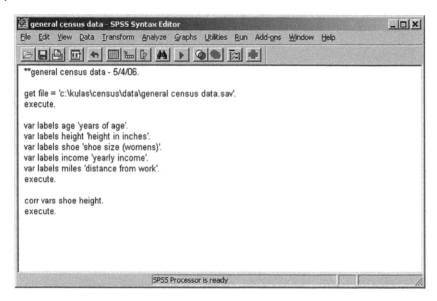

Figure 11.3   Request of correlation between shoe size and height.

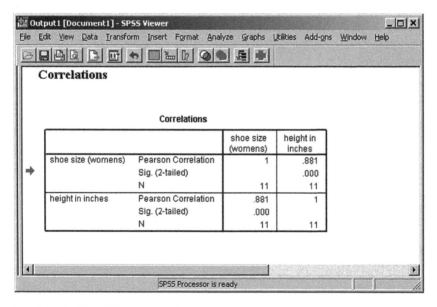

Figure 11.4   Correlation command output.

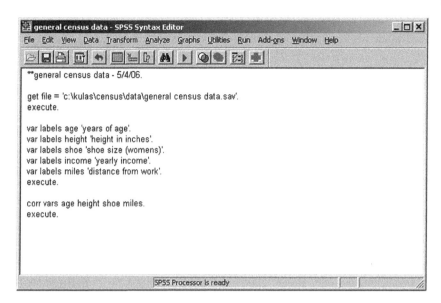

Figure 11.5 Request correlations between age, height, shoe size, and distance.

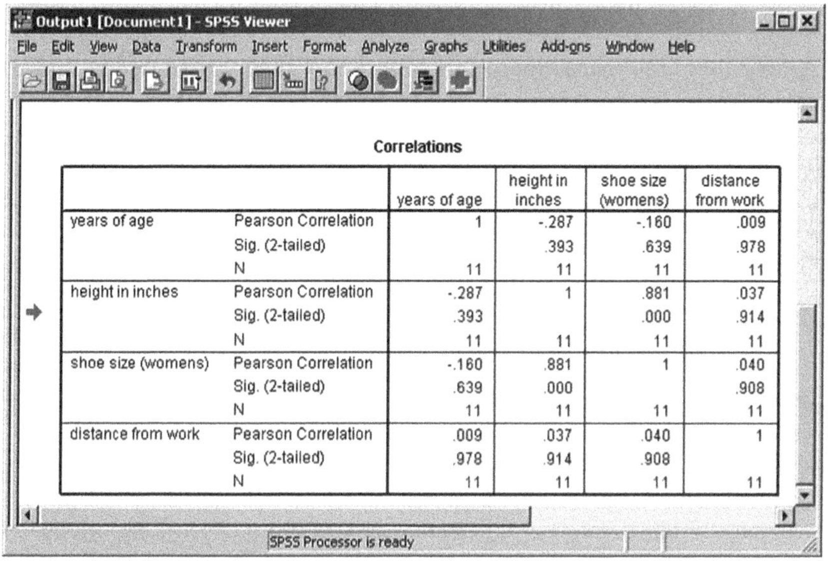

Correlations		years of age	height in inches	shoe size (womens)	distance from work
years of age	Pearson Correlation	1	-.287	-.160	.009
	Sig. (2-tailed)		.393	.639	.978
	N	11	11	11	11
height in inches	Pearson Correlation	-.287	1	.881	.037
	Sig. (2-tailed)	.393		.000	.914
	N	11	11	11	11
shoe size (womens)	Pearson Correlation	-.160	.881	1	.040
	Sig. (2-tailed)	.639	.000		.908
	N	11	11	11	11
distance from work	Pearson Correlation	.009	.037	.040	1
	Sig. (2-tailed)	.978	.914	.908	
	N	11	11	11	11

Figure 11.6 Correlation matrix (four variables) output.

likely would have with the shoe size–height relationship), the reported significance value would actually be smaller (closer to zero).

Simple Regression

Simple regression gives you some of the same information as correlation, but also a little additional. Using regression to replicate the relationship we estimated between shoe size and height, we now need to specify which variable should be an **X variable** and which should be a **Y variable**. This X/Y assignment is done implicitly when you compute a correlation – but with the correlation, the choice of assignment was fairly arbitrary (e.g. by variable sequencing [the first variable is assigned "X" and the second is assigned the "Y" designation]). With regression, the X and Y designations usually matter – the Y is the DV or criterion or outcome of interest, and the X is the IV or variable you hope will predict the DV. If you were a carnival barker interested in predicting a person's height once you find out his or her shoe size, you would want *height* to be the Y variable. If you were a shoe salesperson and wanted to predict shoe size once a customer told you his or her height, you would want *shoe size* as the Y. We'll take the carnival barker route to demonstrate simple regression. From within our syntax diary, choosing Analyze > Regression > Linear gives us the Linear Regression dialog box shown in Figure 11.7.

Pasting this information into our syntax diary gives us the syntax shown in Figure 11.8. Notice that we've placed asterisks in front of the correlation command from the previous run. Typically, we'll use asterisks instead of deleting commands that we don't want to run – you don't want to clutter up your output file when you select all (Ctrl+A), but similarly you don't want to forget what you've done. Using asterisks is therefore a good alternative.

Selecting the entire syntax file gives us the output shown (partially) in Figure 11.9.

The Variables Entered/Removed table is not relevant for your simple regression – if you do a multiple regression (as we do below) this table becomes more important. In the table shown in Figure 11.10, the R is "**multiple R**" using regression terminology – for the simple regression, it is also our Pearson's correlation. The **Adjusted R^2** here reflects **shrinkage**, which is also more useful in multiple regression; don't worry about it here.

The table in Figure 11.11 is an ANOVA table that has crashed our regression party. This table contains all of the "behind-the-scenes" numbers that were used to create the nice Model Summary table in Figure 11.10. The point is, the ANOVA table contains a lot of information, but all you *need* from it is the significance estimate. This tells us that the Multiple R/R^2 from the nice summary table is likely different from zero ($F = 31.24$, $p < 0.05$).

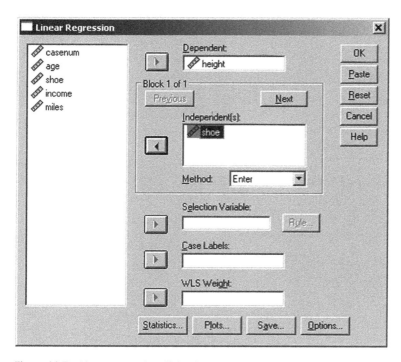

Figure 11.7   Linear regression dialog box.

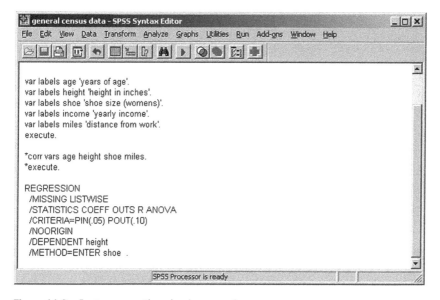

Figure 11.8   Syntax requesting simple regression.

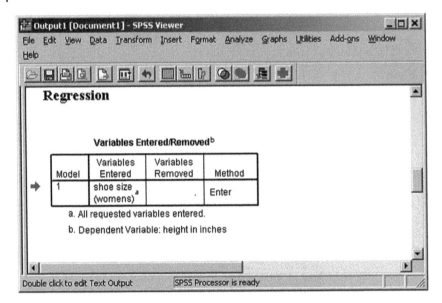

Figure 11.9 Simple regression output – variables entered/removed.

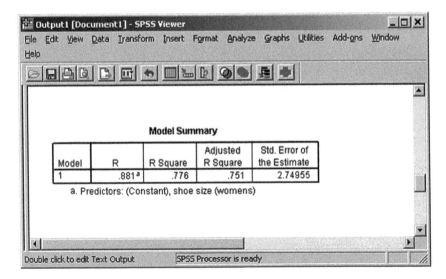

Figure 11.10 Simple regression output – model summary.

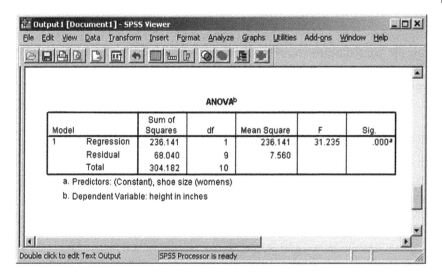

Figure 11.11 Simple regression output – ANOVA.

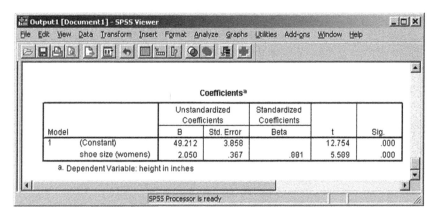

Figure 11.12 Simple regression output – coefficients.

The table in Figure 11.12 presents information needed to create a regression equation. This table also (once again) presents the Pearson's correlation in the form of a "Beta" coefficient. From this table, we can construct the following **regression equation**: predicted height = 49.212 + 2.05 × (shoe size). This is commonly written as $Y' = 49.212 + 2.05(X)$.

Multiple Regression

To SPSS, **multiple regression** follows the same procedural specification as simple regression – the only difference is we are now considering more than one X variable (e.g. IV), so we have the *opportunity* to make decisions regarding **IV priority** if we wish to do so. We are going to do two multiple regressions with the same dataset: one a bare-bones, no prioritization regression (straight regression), the other using variance partitioning or prioritization (**hierarchical regression**).

Straight Regression

One approach to multiple regression involves not placing priority on any of your IVs – we call this a **straight regression** to differentiate it from variance partitioning methods, although we are not sure if it has a specific name other than "multiple regression". Activating the syntax diary, as shown in Figure 11.13, we see we're dealing with a geography/geology/biology example.

Activating this Figure 11.13, syntax accesses the data file shown in Figure 11.14.

If we want to see if our geographic variables (soil, elevation, humidity, temperature) can predict plant coverage, we can access the same drop-down menu that we did with the simple regression (Analyze > Regression > Linear). The only difference between the new screenshot in Figure 11.15 and the simple regression example (Figure 11.7) is the inclusion of multiple IVs in the current example.

Pasting to our syntax gives us the syntax shown in Figure 11.16. Take note that the only difference is an expansion of the variables listed along the last line of script.

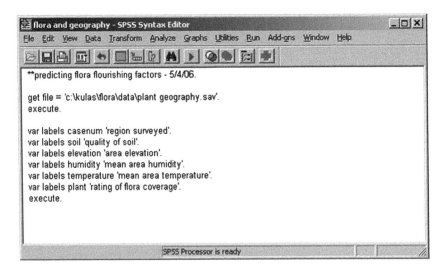

Figure 11.13 Flora and geography data.

	casenum	soil	elevation	humidity	temperature	plant
1	1.00	7.00	520.00	31.50	67.20	6.00
2	2.00	6.00	610.00	31.65	64.00	11.00
3	3.00	8.00	530.00	27.30	64.60	4.00
4	4.00	9.00	540.00	32.60	65.60	8.00
5	5.00	10.00	620.00	32.05	70.50	13.00
6	6.00	6.00	520.00	30.10	70.00	3.00
7	7.00	9.00	480.00	29.80	67.20	2.00
8	8.00	10.00	530.00	30.40	61.20	10.00
9	9.00	4.00	500.00	31.25	63.40	3.00
10	10.00	4.00	590.00	32.06	68.40	11.00
11	11.00	2.00	550.00	28.40	65.80	1.00
12						
13						

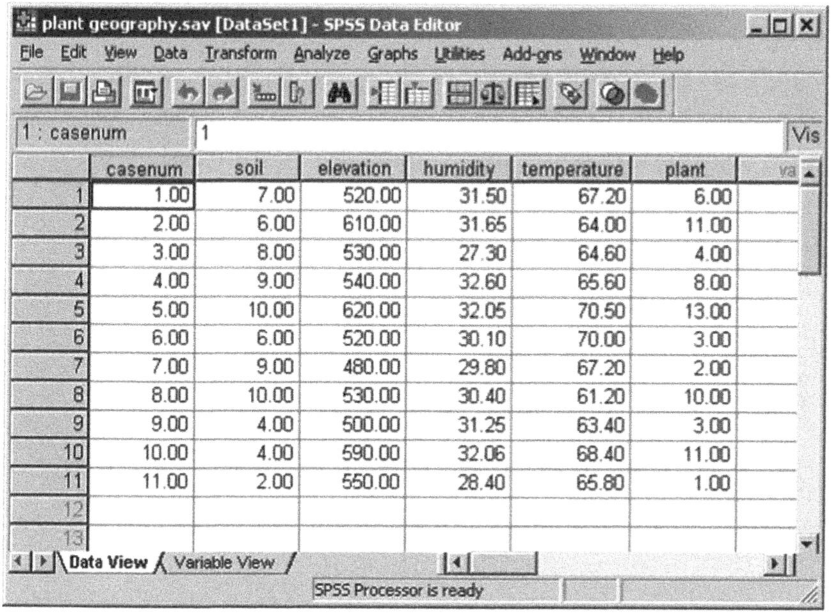

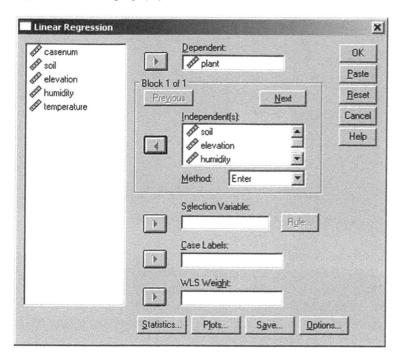

Figure 11.14 Plant geography data file.

Figure 11.15 Linear regression dialog box.

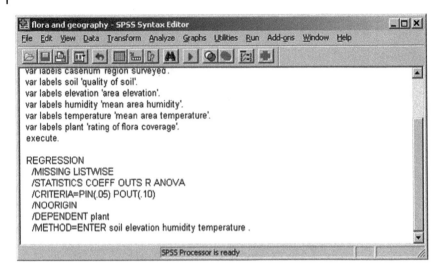

Figure 11.16 Syntax for pasted straight regression.

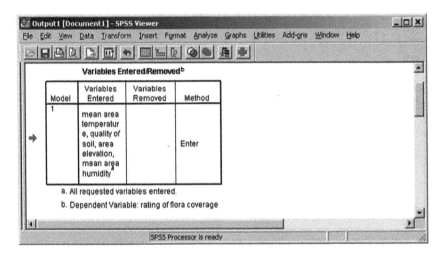

Figure 11.17 Multiple regression output – variables entered/removed.

Selecting all (Ctrl+A) and running this syntax brings up the output table shown in Figure 11.17. Like the simple regression, this table is not outrageously informative, although if you have extreme **multicollinearity** (excessive association) among your IVs, SPSS might "remove" one of them for you. Therefore, if you have any removed variables, you need to check your multicollinearity estimates. No problem identified here, however – all four IVs "made it".

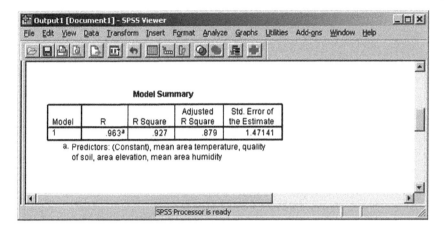

Figure 11.18 Multiple regression output – model summary.

In the results shown in Figure 11.18, as in the simple regression, these are omnibus statistics for your entire regression model (four IVs and one DV). We are explaining a lot of the variability in plant ratings (92.7%) by mutual consideration of our four predictors.

The table in Figure 11.19 tells us whether this 92.7% estimate can be considered to be significantly different from zero. Yes, the significance estimate is less than our α of 0.05, so we can consider the entire model to be useful.

The last table, shown in Figure 11.20, lets us know which of our predictors are contributing to this very high multiple R.

![Output1 [Document1] - SPSS Viewer]

ANOVA[b]

Model		Sum of Squares	df	Mean Square	F	Sig.
1	Regression	165.737	4	41.434	19.138	.001[a]
	Residual	12.990	6	2.165		
	Total	178.727	10			

a. Predictors: (Constant), mean area temperature, quality of soil, area elevation, mean area humidity

b. Dependent Variable: rating of flora coverage

Figure 11.19 Multiple regression output – ANOVA.

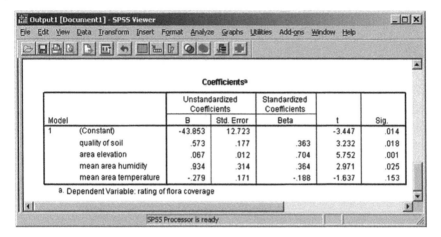

Figure 11.20 Multiple regression output – coefficients.

Here we have three significant predictors. Note that even though the temperature variable is not significant, if we remove it and rerun the analysis, our multiple R/R^2 estimate will change (so will the regression coefficients for the three retained predictors). The regression equation that results in a predicted/obtained DV correlation of 0.96 (Multiple R from Figure 11.18) is

Plant = −43.853 + 0.573(soil) + 0.067(elevation) + 0.934(humidity)

       − 0.279(temp)

Alternatively, this could be written as:

$Y' = -43.853 + 0.573(X1) + 0.067(X2) + 0.934(X3) - 0.279(X4).$

The correlation between this composite (predicted) score and our actual flora coverage DV is 0.96 within our plant geography.sav dataset.

Hierarchical Regression

An alternative approach to "throwing all IVs into the equation at once" is to successively enter IVs into the regression equation in different **stages**. There are two methods commonly used to do this: *hierarchical* and **stepwise**. With **stepwise regression**, the computer selects IV priorities based on correlations; with hierarchical, the researcher selects IV priorities based on theory, logic, or methodological considerations. As shown in Figure 11.21, we again call up the same syntax diary as in Figure 11.15, choosing Analyze > Regression > Linear again.

From the authors' limited knowledge of geography, geology, and biology, we have an idea that elevation tends to be the best predictor of plant coverage in a

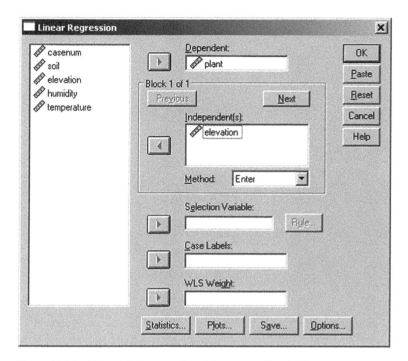

Figure 11.21   Hierarchical regression dialogue specification box.

region. So, in our regression model, we're really interested in whether our other three predictors give us *any additional information* after we've already considered elevation. To test this model, we first enter the elevation predictor into the equation, then click Next to enter the remaining three predictors, as shown in Figure 11.22.

With any regression that you conduct in stages, you need one option from the statistics window shown in Figure 11.23: **R² change** (the other two checked boxes are defaults).

Now we can paste into our syntax diary, as shown in Figure 11.24.

Notice that we've asterisked out the previous regression and made a note to ourselves. The output for this hierarchical regression is shown in Figure 11.25.

You'll notice that this first table looks a little different – elevation is entered in the first stage, and the remaining three predictors are entered in the second stage (labeled "Model" in Figure 11.25).

In the table shown in Figure 11.26, because we selected R^2 change from the drop-down menu, we receive information about whether our additional three predictors are adding valued information, located in the second row. According to this table, they do ($\Delta F_{(3,6)} = 8.49$, $p < 0.05$).

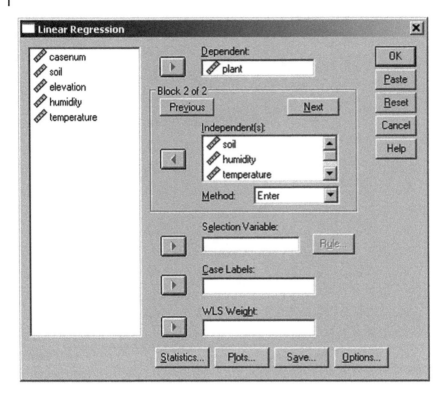

Figure 11.22   Hierarchical regression dialogue box – multiple predictors.

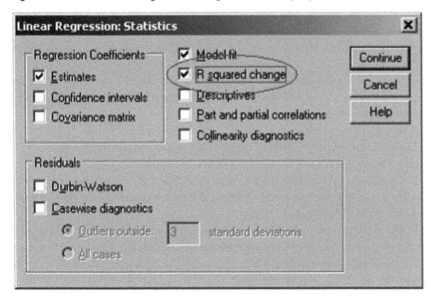

Figure 11.23   Linear regression: statistics.

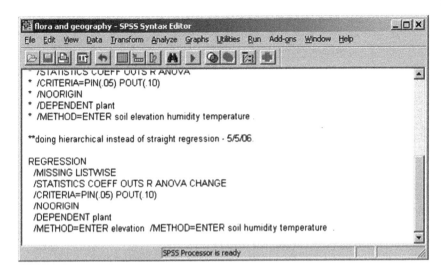

Figure 11.24 Hierarchical regression syntax.

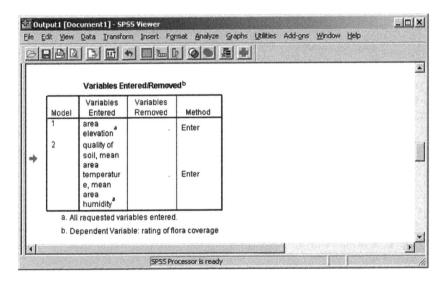

Figure 11.25 Hierarchical regression output – variables entered/removed.

If you don't select "R^2 change" when generating your syntax, the next table (shown in Figure 11.27) could lead to erroneous conclusions. This is because Model 1 presents the information needed to compute the first row statistics in the "Model Summary" Figure 11.26 table. The second model ANOVA statistics, however, are referring to all four IVs, not just the additional three that are included in the second step.

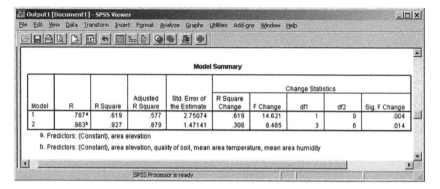

Figure 11.26 Hierarchical regression output – model summary.

Model Summary

Model	R	R Square	Adjusted R Square	Std. Error of the Estimate	R Square Change	F Change	df1	df2	Sig. F Change
1	.787[a]	.619	.577	2.75074	.619	14.621	1	9	.004
2	.963[b]	.927	.879	1.47141	.308	8.485	3	6	.014

Change Statistics

a. Predictors: (Constant), area elevation

b. Predictors: (Constant), area elevation, quality of soil, mean area temperature, mean area humidity

ANOVA[c]

Model		Sum of Squares	df	Mean Square	F	Sig.
1	Regression	110.628	1	110.628	14.621	.004[a]
	Residual	68.099	9	7.567		
	Total	178.727	10			
2	Regression	165.737	4	41.434	19.138	.001[b]
	Residual	12.990	6	2.165		
	Total	178.727	10			

a. Predictors: (Constant), area elevation

b. Predictors: (Constant), area elevation, quality of soil, mean area temperature, mean area humidity

c. Dependent Variable: rating of flora coverage

Figure 11.27 Hierarchical regression output – ANOVA.

In the Coefficients table for our hierarchical regression output (see Figure 11.28), you will find the same information you would have received if you had run a straight regression. The main thing you want to pay attention to in a hierarchical regression is that change in R^2 across stages, as you can see in Figure 11.26.

There is one additional table that you receive with a hierarchical (or stepwise) regression, shown in Figure 11.29. This table is simply an acknowledgment that, in the first stage, three IVs were not entered (we knew this because we in fact chose the ordering of IVs across the two stages).

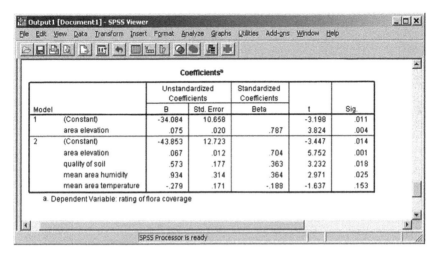

Figure 11.28   Hierarchical regression output – coefficients.

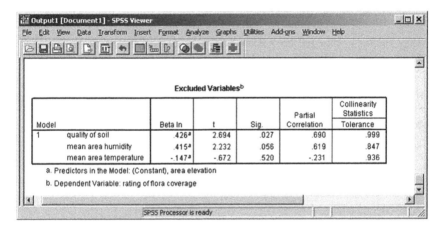

Figure 11.29   Hierarchical regression output – excluded variables.

Visualizing Your Relationship

Whether you do a regression or a correlation, visual representations of the relationship are typically informative. With a correlation, the relationship is pretty straightforward – it's the association between your two variables ("IV" and "DV"). With a regression, the relationship you'd like to visualize is likely a bit different because most regression applications specify more than one IV. For this reason, the visual representation you seek is commonly between the *actual* DV and the *predicted* DV. Both of these relationships can be visualized via a scatterplot – the only difference is what is being plotted (IV and DV or predicted and actual DV). This current chapter focuses only on the IV and DV scenario, as this is by far the more common scatterplot circumstance.

Figure 11.30 shows the command to request a simple scatterplot between two variables (here, height and shoe size). Note that the ordering of variables will transpose which variable goes on which axis (the first variable is always represented along the x-axis). Traditionally, this is your IV, and your DV is represented along the y-axis. With correlation, of course, this methodological distinction is arbitrary, so Figure 11.30 also requests a scatterplot with shoe size represented on the x-axis and height represented on the y-axis. Figure 11.31 presents the resulting scatterplot from the *second* requested scatterplot (with height on the y-axis).

The regression equation estimated between shoe size and height from earlier in the chapter is actually the "line of best fit" for this scatterplot. Commonly, you can eyeball this line with a scatterplot, but in doing so you must also be careful to pay attention to your axis values. It is not uncommon (and indeed represented in Figure 11.31) for computer packages such as SPSS to represent picture "close-ups" instead of maintaining axes' origins at values of "zero". This will throw off your

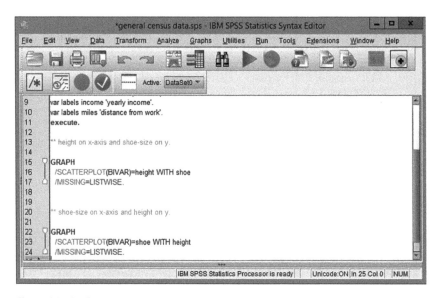

Figure 11.30 Requesting scatterplots - height and shoe size.

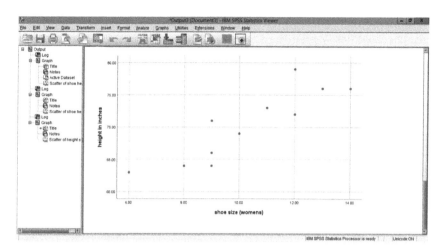

Figure 11.31   Scatterplot between shoe size and height (with height on the x-axis).

eyeball estimate of your intercept (where the line crosses the y-axis *at an x-axis value of zero*).

Summary

Correlation is a very simple analysis in SPSS. Regression analyses can take a number of different forms, including a standard, straight multiple regression (where all IVs are entered at one time) and hierarchical or stepwise regression (where IVs are assigned different priorities and entered in stages). If a stage-based regression is requested, it is important to ask SPSS to report the change in R^2.

Key Terms

Adjusted R^2 – Estimate of the population R^2, based on sample size and number of predictors.
Continuous IVs – Predictor variables that are measured along a continuum (instead of by categories).
"Corr vars" – SPSS command to request a bivariate (Pearson's) correlation.
Correlation – Index of association between two variables.
Correlation matrix – Square and symmetric matrix containing correlations from at least two variables.

Hierarchical regression – Variance partitioning procedure in which the researcher specifies IV priority.

IV priority – Relative importance of IVs, which can be specified through the use of variance partitioning regression models (such as stepwise or hierarchical).

Multicollinearity – Excessive association among IVs.

Multiple R – Correlation between your obtained and predicted DV scores.

Multiple regression – Regression analysis with one DV and two or more IVs.

r – Pearson's product moment correlation.

R^2 change – Percentage of incremental DV variance explained by the contribution of additional IVs.

Regression equation – Application of the regression analysis (an attempt to predict an unknown DV score based on known IV information).

Shrinkage – Acknowledgment that the obtained multiple R tends to overestimate the population multiple R: a regression equation generated in one sample will typically exhibit a smaller predicted or observed correlation (multiple R) if applied to a different sample.

Sig. (2-tailed) – Significance estimate based on a two-tailed hypothesis; this will always be more conservative than a significance estimate based on a one-tailed hypothesis.

Simple regression – Regression analysis with one IV and one DV.

Stages – Different blocks of IV specifications. The hierarchical and stepwise procedures are comprised of at least two stages.

Stepwise regression – Variance partitioning procedure in which the computer specifies IV priority.

Straight regression – Regression that does not assign IV priority.

X variable – Regression term for IV or predictor.

Y variable – Regression term for DV or outcome variable.

Discussion Questions

1   Why is there an ANOVA table in my regression output?

2   Why doesn't SPSS include R^2 change as a default reported statistic?

3   Based on the following data, is there a relationship between shoe size and height? Number of siblings and height? Shoe size and number of siblings?

	Shoe size	Height	Number of siblings
Hector	12	68	2
Sue	7	66	10
Sally	17	75	9
Eugene	14	70	8
Valencia	8	64	7
Penelope	9.5	60	3
Fernando	5	63	2
Norbert	15	74	10

4 If I wanted to predict how tall someone might be, given their shoe size and number of siblings, how would I go about doing that?

12

Nonparametric Analyses

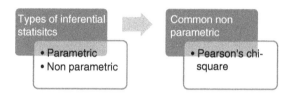

CHAPTER MENU
Chapter Learning Objectives, 141 Parametric Versus Nonparametric Analyses, 141 "The" (Pearson's) Chi-Square: χ^2, 143 Summary, 150

Chapter Learning Objectives

1. Parametric versus nonparametric analyses
2. Chi-square

Parametric Versus Nonparametric Analyses

All of the procedures covered in the previous three chapters are appropriately classified as inferential statistics, but the category of "inferential statistics" can

IBM SPSS Essentials: Managing and Analyzing Social Sciences Data, Second Edition.
John Kulas, Renata Garcia Prieto Palacios Roji, and Adam Smith.
© 2021 John Wiley & Sons, Inc. Published 2021 by John Wiley & Sons, Inc.

also be further divided. One common division is between **parametric** and **nonparametric inferential statistics**. All of the previous inferential analyses (z-test, t-tests, ANOVAs, regressions, correlations) are considered parametric procedures because they either: (1) estimate a population parameter (for example, using the sample statistic [s] as an approximation of the population parameter [σ] as is done with t-tests), or (2) are dependent on assumptions about an underlying population distribution (for example, that scores are distributed approximately normally).

Not every empirical situation is characterized by (at least) one of these above conditions, however. There are, therefore, statistical procedures that have been developed for situations where a population parameter is not estimated and no assumptions are made about underlying population distributions. This category of procedures is commonly given the label of nonparametric statistics. Sticklers to the importance of assumptions of parametric procedures (for example, **homogeneity of variance** within ANOVA applications) turn to nonparametric procedures when assumptions are violated. There are also non-sticklers, who tend to believe most parametric procedures are relatively **robust** to violations of assumptions, and are less likely to turn to nonparametric procedures.

For purposes of thoroughness, we will acknowledge the existence of some of these procedures, but will only focus on the most popular/commonly used nonparametric procedure. It should also be mentioned here that we identify and use two categories of nonparametric procedures: unique and parallel.[1] Many researchers turn to nonparametric procedures only when they "run into trouble" with their preferred parametric analysis. Nearly every parametric test has a nonparametric counterpart, and we therefore label one set of nonparametric procedures as "parallel" because these parallel a parametric test. Examples of these are the Kruskal–Wallis One-way ANOVA (which is used if data violate assumptions of the parametric ANOVA) and Wilcoxon's rank-sum test (which is used if data violate assumptions of the independent samples t-test). There are also "unique" nonparametric procedures, however, that have independent usefulness and answer questions that are different from the types of questions that are usually answered by parametric procedures. An example of a unique nonparametric procedure is the Chi-square test, which evaluates differences in category membership across (and within) groups.

---

1 These are not terms that you will find outside of this textbook. Other divisions such as inferential versus descriptive or parametric versus nonparametric are widely known and accepted – the only time you will see the unique versus parallel distinction is within the pages of this book.

"The" (Pearson's) Chi-Square: χ^2

"Chi-square" can refer to multiple things, and therefore requires some context. In its broadest use, a mention of "chi-square" most commonly refers to the nonparametric analysis developed by Karl Pearson (and this is also the chi-square we are focused on). This procedure is applied to **contingency tables** that reflect frequencies of category membership for either one or two variables.

For an example scenario, consider that you were interested in determining which is better: Coke or Pepsi. You could recruit 40 individuals, ask 20 to try Coke (and then rate how good it is on a scale of 1[bad] to 10[excellent]), and then ask the other 20 individuals to try Pepsi (also rating it on the same scale of 1 to 10). You could then probe for differences in average rating using the independent samples t-test as we did in Chapter 9. This would be a "parametric" approach to determining whether Coke or Pepsi is better.

Alternatively, we could just ask the 40 people to tell us which they prefer: Coke or Pepsi. What we end up with in this scenario is a contingency table (see Table 12.1) that reflects frequencies of category membership for two levels of one variable (soda pop).

Data collected and organized in this manner (e.g. do frequencies differ across categories?) can be analyzed using the chi-square test.

In SPSS, you can construct a very simple datafile with one variable, as can be seen in Figure 12.1, "Type" that has two potential values: 1 = "Coke" and 2 = "Pepsi" across the 40 individuals you sampled.

There are several ways to obtain a chi-square value, but we recommend using the "chi-square" command available from the "Analyze" > "Nonparametric Tests" > "Legacy Dialogs" option tree (see Figure 12.2).

Within the wizard, we'll be identifying our single variable of interest and moving it into the "Test Variable List" option box (see Figure 12.3).

And then pasting into our syntax file (see Figure 12.4).

Selecting all and running gives us the following output (see Figure 12.5) that tells us our observed statistic value ($\chi^2 = 2.5$), which does not exceed our tabled critical value for an alpha of 0.05 that we looked up ($\chi^2_{CV} = 3.84$). Therefore, we *fail* to reject the null hypothesis, meaning that there is no difference in preference between Coke and Pepsi within our sample:

Table 12.1 Category frequencies table.

Prefer Coke	Prefer Pepsi
25	15

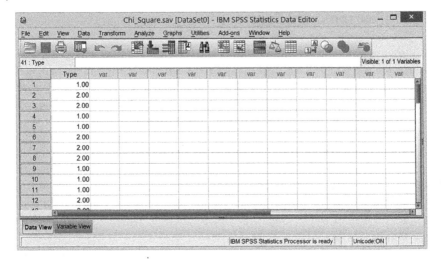

Figure 12.1   Soda preference data.

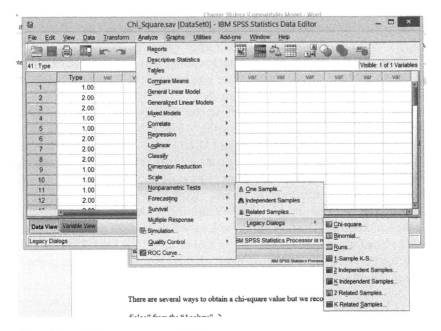

Figure 12.2   Chi-square command SPSS.

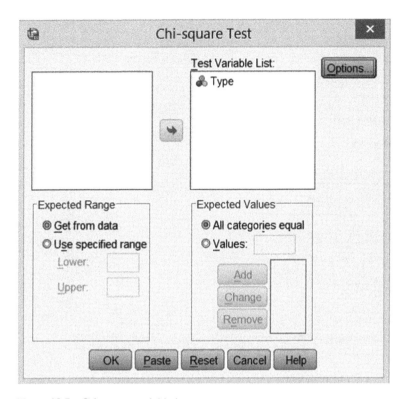

Figure 12.3 Chi-square variable box.

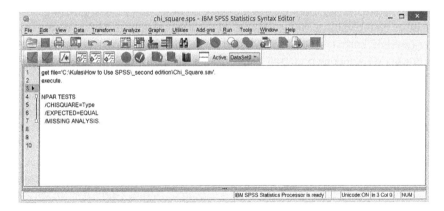

Figure 12.4 Chi-square syntax.

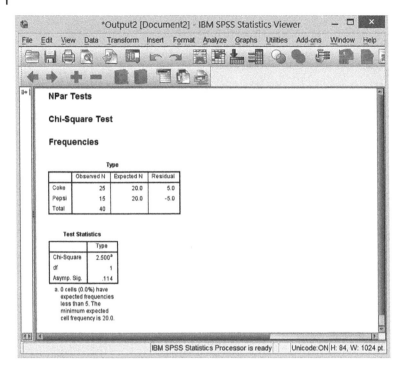

Figure 12.5 Chi-square output.

Two Variable Example

The chi-square test is more commonly used to probe for differences in frequency of category membership within **cells** created by joint consideration of two variables. For example, consider the possibility that we collected information regarding not only whether someone preferred Coke or Pepsi, but also which Hollywood movie star they most liked: Elvis Presley, James Dean, or Marilyn Monroe:

This is a true contingency table, containing information at both the cell and **marginal** levels. There are six cells (Elvis loving Coke drinkers, Elvis loving Pepsi drinkers, James Dean Coke drinkers, James Dean Pepsi drinkers, Marilyn fans who like Coke, and Marilyn fans who prefer Pepsi). Additionally, there is "marginal" information. This information is shaded in Table 12.2, and tells us how many individuals prefer Coke versus Pepsi (we already knew this from our previous analysis), but also how many prefer Elvis (n = 10) versus James Dean (n = 10) versus Marilyn Monroe (n = 20). This type of information can also be handled by the chi-square test (see Figure 12.6) if we incorporate favorite movie star or celebrity (coded as 1 = "Elvis", 2 = "James Dean", 3 = "Marilyn Monroe") into the datafile and label it "Celeb".

Table 12.2 Soda and movie star preference table.

	Prefer Coke	Prefer Pepsi	
Elvis Presley	5	5	10
James Dean	5	5	10
Marilyn Monroe	15	5	20
	25	15	

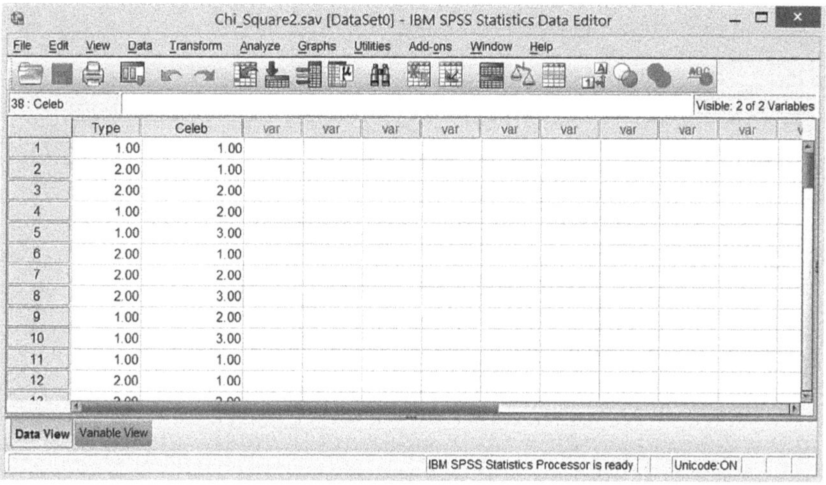

Figure 12.6 Data file with movie star variable.

As seen in Figure 12.7, the route to finding the syntax is a bit different when we're interested in two variables ("Analyze" > "Descriptive Statistics" > "Crosstabs").

From here you can assign your two variables to either a table row or column within the Crosstabs box.

Clicking on the "Statistics…" button (see Figure 12.8) brings up the critical piece – an option to perform a chi-square test on the contingency data (see Figure 12.9).

Pasting yields the syntax in Figure 12.10 – this syntax can obviously be modified for different applications and is likely a bit easier to work with than is the step-laden wizard.

Selecting all and running here gives us a larger tract of output (see Figure 12.11), the most important piece of which being, again, the observed value ($\chi^2 = 2.667$), which again does not exceed our tabled critical value for an alpha of 0.05 that

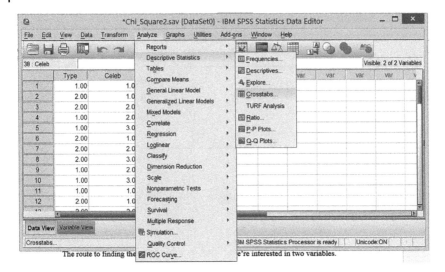

Figure 12.7 Command pathway to syntax for two variables.

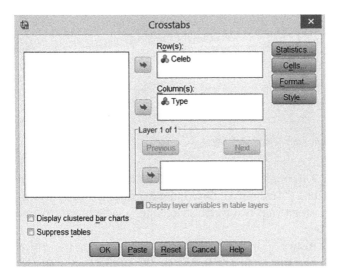

Figure 12.8 Crosstabs box.

we looked up ($\chi^2_{\text{CV}} = 5.99$). The interpretation this time is usually framed as *independence* of the two variables (type of soda preferred and favorite movie star). Meaning that the preference of soda type is independent from the preference of movie star.

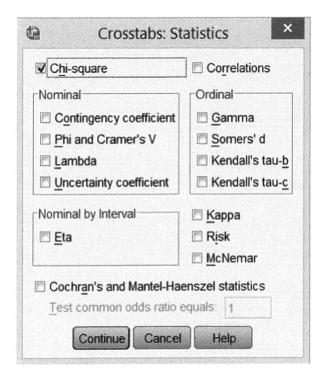

Figure 12.9 Statistics command box.

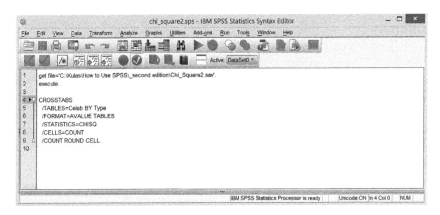

Figure 12.10 Crosstabs paste syntax.

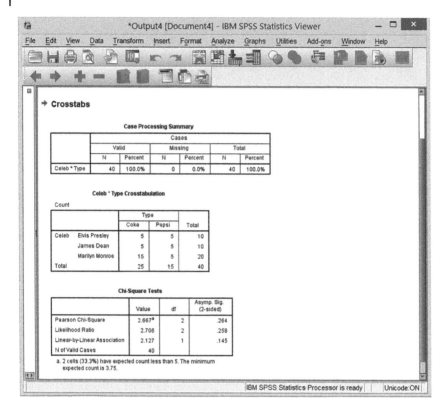

Figure 12.11 Crosstabs output.

Summary

A category of inferential statistics exists that is called "nonparametric". There are nonparametric procedures that parallel a parametric counterpart, but there are also unique nonparametric procedures that accommodate a different type of data (for example, frequency counts). The unique nonparametric that you will most commonly encounter is "Pearson's chi-square". This statistic can be applied to one variable (with several possible values) or two. A significant chi-square indicates a difference in frequencies across categories.

Key Terms

Cell – Joint contingency table location (*both* row and column).
Contingency tables – Tabular presentations of frequency estimates across *levels* of one or two variables.

Homogeneity of variance – Statistical assumption in ANOVA application whereby all treatments are expected to exhibit similar within-group variability.
Parametric inferential statistic – Characterized by parameter estimation and/or population assumptions.
Marginal level – Single-variable table location (*either* row or column).
Nonparametric inferential statistic – Neither estimates parameters nor makes assumptions about populations.
Robust – Statistical phenomenon whereby estimated coefficients are unaffected by assumption violations.

Discussion Questions

1   When a population parameter is estimated, or assumptions are made about the underlying population, you have a _____ analysis. On the other hand, when you conduct an analysis where there is no estimation of the parameter, and no assumptions are made, you have a _____ analysis.

2   An industrial psychologist is interested in determining whether there is a relationship between the education level of employees and the number of jobs they currently have. Accordingly, a survey is taken, and the following results are obtained:

Number of jobs

	Two or less	More than two
College education	57	22
High school education	37	38

a) What is the null hypothesis?
b) What is the conclusion? Use $\alpha = 0.05$.

Part III

Advanced Data Management

13

Manipulating Your Data

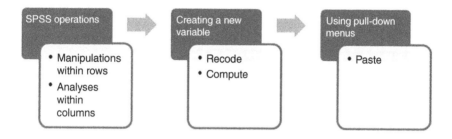

CHAPTER MENU

Chapter Learning Objectives

1. Creating variables
2. Recoding variables
3. Using pull-down menu function with syntax
4. Running syntax file using Ctrl+A

IBM SPSS Essentials: Managing and Analyzing Social Sciences Data, Second Edition.
John Kulas, Renata Garcia Prieto Palacios Roji, and Adam Smith.
© 2021 John Wiley & Sons, Inc. Published 2021 by John Wiley & Sons, Inc.

Creating Scale Scores

Typically, you will want to work not only with the raw, unaltered data, but also with aggregated information – commonly in the form of an average or sum of responses across variables. In psychology, we have traditionally referred to such a summary score as a **scale score**. For example, psychological constructs (such as the personality trait of *extraversion*) are abstract entities. A common technique of psychological measurement is to consider that extraversion drives responses to many different individual inquiries. Personality assessments, therefore, typically ask many extraversion-related questions, even though psychologists are mostly interested in your general standing on the extraversion–introversion continuum.

If you look at the assessment in Appendix A, for example, there are 100 items, but these measure only five different factors of immediate interest to the researcher – extraversion is one of the five. The extraversion scale is an aggregate of responses across 20 individual items.

So, if the researcher is interested in an aggregate or summary score for each respondent, the researcher must *create* that summary score. To do this in SPSS, you will use two very common commands: "**compute**" and "**recode**". Before we discuss scale score creation, however, there is a more general acknowledgement that needs to be made regarding how SPSS "thinks" about data.

How SPSS Thinks About Data

SPSS the *statistical analyst* tends to "prefer" columns to rows. For instance, descriptive statistics (like *means* and *standard deviations*) are reported within columns (collapsing data down rows within the asked-for column). If you request these means and standard deviations for a particular column variable, an output (.spo) file will be created to summarize your request. If you wish to generate means (or standard deviations, or both) *across columns* (for instance, creating a mean score for each individual in your dataset), SPSS does this by creating new variable in your data file. The program will not report these means and standard deviations in an output file – it will just place them at the end of your data file.

We don't think SPSS is particularly biased against rows; the program just "thinks" that manipulations done within a column are important enough to report, whereas manipulations done across columns are generally done for further data analysis purposes. It is appropriate for the program to think this way, in part because your data files generally contain many more rows (people) than they do variables (columns). Reporting statistics for each row in an output file would generally overcrowd your output file with needless information.

It will help your understanding of this tendency if you conceptualize SPSS as having two main purposes: (1) as a **data analyst** – creating summary information (in output files) based on column information, and (2) as a **data organizer** (creating or changing the data you have in your data file). This second SPSS purpose is actually where you will find yourself spending the most time with any data-intensive project.

It is important for you to understand that SPSS thinks this way, otherwise you will be confused by how it handles your manipulation requests. Although the data analyst of SPSS thinks within columns, the data organizer of SPSS most commonly thinks within rows. We'll be utilizing this "data organizing" function in our pursuit of scale scores.

Recoding Your Data

If you look at the 20 items that make up the extraversion scale in Appendix B (items 1, 6, 11, 16, 21, 26, and so on), you will notice that not all 20 measure extraversion – some measure introversion. For example, an extrovert would give a high (Strongly Agree) response to item 1, but an introvert would give a high (Strongly Agree) response to item 6. Before we generate aggregate scores for the extraversion scale (or *any* scale, for that matter), we need to first decide whether high scores (higher numbers) should be indicative of introverts or extraverts. The convention in personality assessment is to give the extroverts the higher scores.

Every time an aggregate score is created, you need to first consider whether any scale component (the items themselves) needs this type of "recoding" (also called response **reflection**). Because we are starting to fiddle with our data (that is, not just defining the data file), it's time to create a new syntax file, as shown in Figures 13.1 and 13.2.

In the syntax statement shown in Figure 13.2, 10 items that were identified as assessing the introversion side of the extraversion continuum were "reverse scored". For example, a response of "Strongly Agree = 5" to item 6 (Often feel uncomfortable around others) was changed to a response consistent with Strongly Disagreeing = 1. Responses of 4 (Agree) were changed to 2's (Disagree) – note that these reciprocal effects also had to be specified in the recode command (1's to 5's and 2's to 4's).

Creating Your Scales

To create one summary extraversion score for each respondent, you'll need to make another decision: what type of summary do you want? Typically, you'll choose from either a **sum** or a **mean**. We advocate choosing the "mean" aggregate scores by default because: (1) they're not as heavily influenced by missing data,

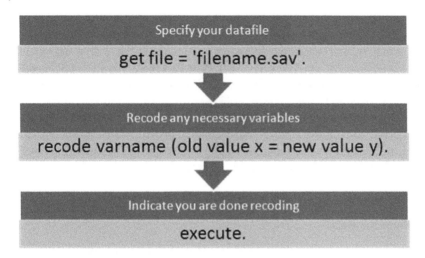

Figure 13.1 Recoding variables.

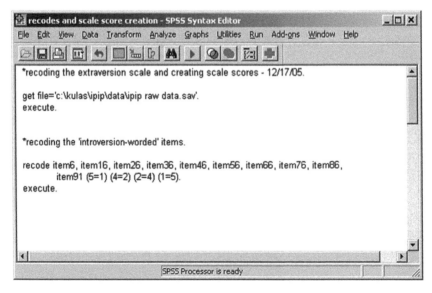

Figure 13.2 Recoding the extraversion scale and creating scale scores.

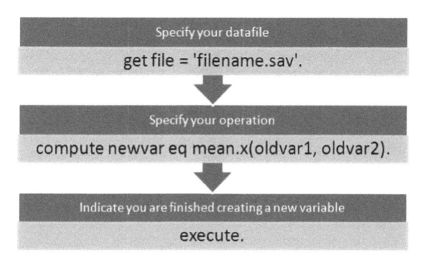

Figure 13.3 Creating new variables.

and (2) they're expressed in the same metric as the scale components (the items; for example, scores of 1–5). To *create* a mean score, we're going to need to specify the name of the variable we're creating (once again, eight characters or fewer, as forecast in Figure 13.3).

Figure 13.4 presents the Figure 13.3 flowchart as applied to our "extraversion" scale score example. Here we've decided to name the new variable "extra". After

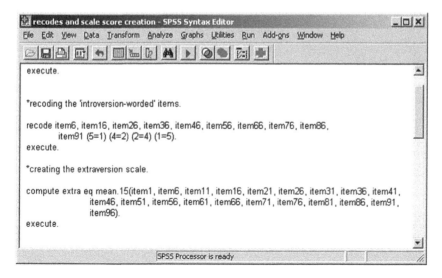

Figure 13.4 Recodes and scale score creation.

choosing a name, we specify which of the 102 variables in our dataset should contribute to the new variable definition (here every fifth item, starting with item 1).

The "**eq**" in "compute extra eq" is a shorthand notation for "="; we could have written "compute extra = mean.15(item1, item6 …)." we use the "eq" notation because it is consistent with these other data manipulation options:

- "**lt**" (less than)
- "**gt**" (greater than)
- "**le**" (less than or equal to)
- "**ge**" (greater than or equal to)

These different commands are very useful; for example, in median/ tertial/ quartile split applications (or more generally **categorization** – an example of this appears just below).

The "0.15" after the mean statement asks SPSS to perform the computation only if there are at least 15 non-missing responses across the 20 items. If the ".xx" wasn't specified after the "mean" command, SPSS would compute a mean even if there was only one valid response across the 20 specified items. The ".xx" therefore allows you to control how many valid responses must be given prior to a scale score being computed – we recommend requiring at least 75% of item responses to be valid, although this convention is rather arbitrary.

Also, it is important to note that parentheses organize your commands for compute statements. The innermost parenthetical command will be initiated first. We could compute our Extraversion scale score as shown in Figure 13.5.

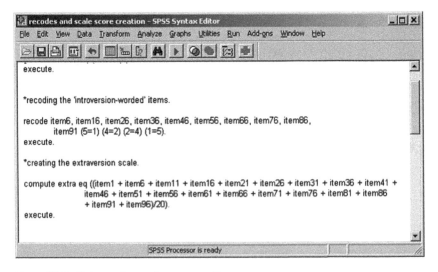

Figure 13.5 Extraversion scale score creation.

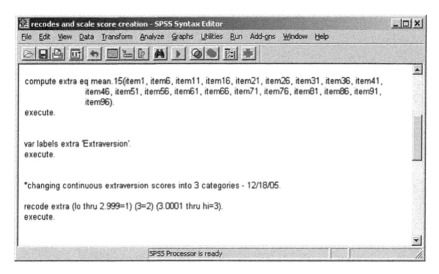

Figure 13.6 Categorizing the extraversion scale.

However, typically we do not do this, because if someone has not responded to item 26, for example, the respondent's score will still be divided by 20. Using the "mean" command, SPSS would more appropriately divide that person's total by 19.

The recode and compute commands can be used in many different applications. For instance, if for some reason we wanted to characterize people as either introverted, extraverted, or firmly on the fence, we could first compute a scale score for each person, then use the recode command on the new scale score to put individuals into one of three categories. First, we give a variable name to our scale score, as shown in Figure 13.6.

Now our scale score "extra" will possess only three values, unless someone scores a 2.9995 or 3.000001 – which is not very likely (actually, it's impossible with only 20 items contributing to the scale score and no data-entry errors). If we wanted to maintain our original continuous extraversion score as well as having this new way of looking at extraversion, we could compute a new variable by using the "into" command with recode. If we do this, it's also necessary to relabel our first extraversion scale score, as shown in Figure 13.7.

The Importance of Selecting All

Regardless of whether we turn our original scale score into three categories or create a new scale score while maintaining our original continuous scale, it's

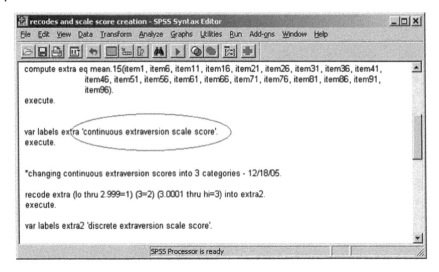

Figure 13.7 Labeling the continuous and categorical extraversion scale scores.

important that when we activate our syntax, *we do it all at once.* If you get into the habit of using your "get file" and "save outfile" commands at the beginnings and ends of your scripts, you can run all of your syntax at once (Ctrl+A and Run) instead of running your commands step-by-step. We hope that you get into the great habit of organizing your diaries by "get file" and "save outfile" commands.

This is so vitally important because if you run syntax one command at a time, it is very easy to "mess up" your data, and it is quite likely that you will not be aware of your mistakes. This really isn't a huge deal as long as you do not "save" what you have done within your datafile, but these sorts of errors can cause unnecessary head-scratching. Let's take a look at what could have happened to our data if we had run the syntax command-by-command.

First, we get our data file, as shown in Figure 13.8.

Next, we recode our identified items, as shown in Figure 13.9.

So far, so good; then we create our extraversion scale, as shown in Figure 13.10.

Still good – the problem now arises with the "change" that we made when we decided to keep the first extraversion scale score continuous and to make a second, discrete extraversion scale score. Figure 13.11 shows the next step we would have taken if we were choosing syntax command-by-command.

Now the decision to make a new variable becomes an issue, because we've already changed the "extra" variable. So what if we now change our mind (decide to create two variables) and run the new command, as shown in Figure 13.12?

We've made a huge mistake (once again, not really a problem as long as we don't go into our Data Editor and "save" the new data). Here's what happened in this

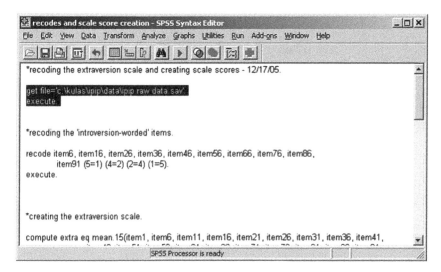

Figure 13.8 One comment at a time (get file).

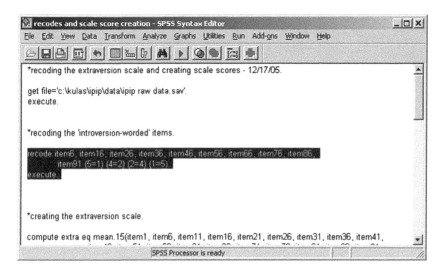

Figure 13.9 One command at a time.

situation – we recoded an already recoded variable. This wouldn't have been an issue if our initial recodes had been: "(lo thru 2.999=1) (3=3) (3.0001 thru hi=4)". Can you see where the error occurred now? Our first recode said, in effect "have fence-sitters be identified by a score of '2' ". Our second recode said "someone with a score of '2' must be an introvert".

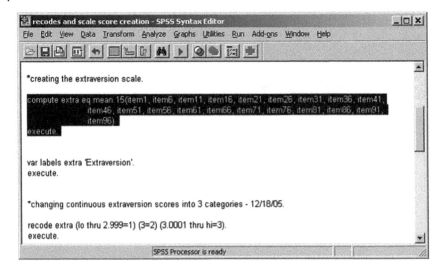

Figure 13.10 One command at a time (scale score).

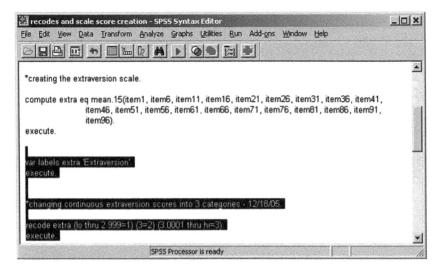

Figure 13.11 One command at a time (categorizing extraversion).

Here's what the mistake did to our data – first, as shown in Figure 13.13, a screenshot of what the data should look like with two scale scores (when we run all of our syntax at one time).

Now Figure 13.14 shows the data if we ran each command separately. You should note that the "extra" column in the dataset is actually categorized correctly,

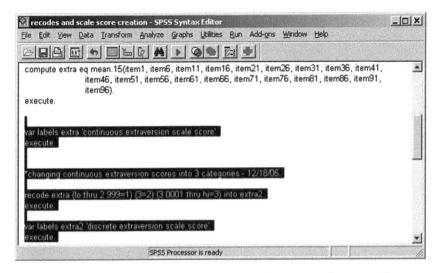

Figure 13.12 One command at a time (new variable through recode command).

but the "extra2" column is now incorrect – this is because, when choosing our transformations command-by-command, we "recoded" a recode. Figure 13.15 shows the proper way to construct a syntax file such that the entire file can be selected and run "at once" instead of command-by-command.

	item95	item96	item97	item98	item99	item100	extra	extra2
1	2.00	2.00	2.00	2.00	4.00	6.00	1.00	1.00
2	3.00	3.00	3.00	3.00	3.00	3.00	2.00	1.00
3	1.00	1.00	2.00	4.00	3.00	4.00	1.00	1.00
4	4.00	4.00	2.00	5.00	1.00	5.00	3.00	2.00
5	5.00	1.00	1.00	2.00	2.00	5.00	3.00	2.00
6	2.00	2.00	3.00	3.00	.	6.00	1.00	1.00
7	1.00	3.00	4.00	2.00	2.00	3.00	1.00	1.00
8	3.00	2.00	5.00	1.00	2.00	2.00	1.00	1.00
9	2.00	1.00	3.00	2.00	3.00	2.00	1.00	1.00
10	4.00	2.00	1.00	3.00	1.00	1.00	1.00	1.00
11	2.00	3.00	2.00	2.00	5.00	2.00	1.00	1.00
12	3.00	1.00	3.00	1.00	5.00	2.00	1.00	1.00
13	1.00	2.00	1.00	1.00	4.00	3.00	1.00	1.00

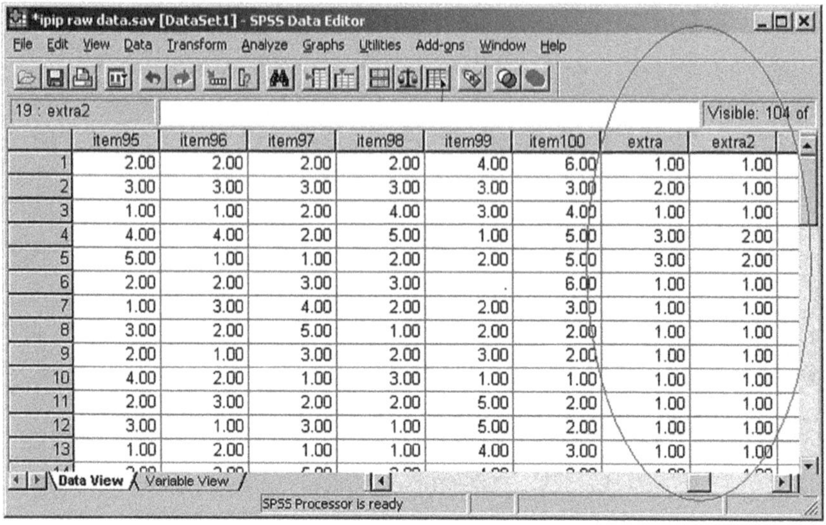

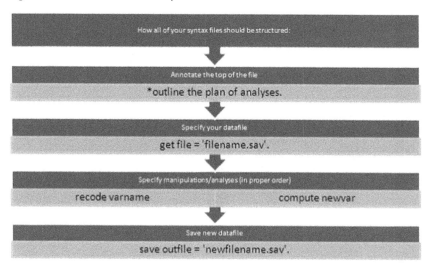

Figure 13.14 Incorrect data manipulations.

Figure 13.15 Recommended structure of all syntax files.

Additionally, it's important that you recode before you create scales. Remember that SPSS always does syntax operations in the order that you specify (starts at the top and goes to the bottom). The take-away message from all of this is that you should use "get file" and "save outfile" and get in the habit of running the entire syntax file at once. You should construct your files with this in mind: "I'm going to run everything all at once".

Summary

Frequently you'll have need to create summary scores that are derivatives of your raw data. Prior to computing these summary scores, it may be necessary to reflect responses. Regardless of what you are attempting to do with SPSS, you should get yourself into the very helpful habit of constructing your syntax files such that you can "select all" and run the entire script from top to bottom. This style of organization will limit your susceptibility to common data management mistakes, and, critically, help you maintain the integrity of your raw datafile.

Key Terms

Categorization – Process of combining ranges of scores.
Compute – Generic command useful for creating scale scores (through, for example, averaging or summing).
Data analyst – One of the two primary functions of SPSS – computations are by default across rows.
Data organizer – One of the two primary functions of SPSS – computations are by default across columns.
eq – SPSS shorthand for the logical expression "equal to".
gt – SPSS shorthand for the logical expression "greater than".
ge – SPSS shorthand for the logical expression "greater than or equal to".
le – SPSS shorthand for the logical expression "less than or equal to".
lt – SPSS shorthand for the logical expression "less than".
Mean – One of two common options for aggregating individual item responses – generally considered more preferred than a sum aggregate.
Recode – Command commonly encountered when also computing scale scores – recode ensures all individual items are scaled consistently.
Reflecting – Process of reversing an item's scoring key – typically done via the "recode" command.
Scale score – Aggregate summary across individual item responses.
Sum – One of two common options for aggregating individual item responses – generally considered less preferred than a mean aggregate.

Discussion Questions

1 Is it ever advisable to not run the entire syntax at once?

2 If I'm going to use drop-down menus, why don't I just skip the "paste" part?

14

Collapsing and Merging Data Files

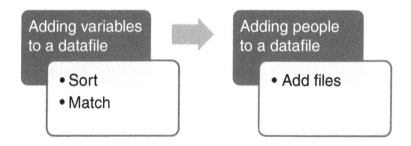

CHAPTER MENU

Chapter Learning Objectives

1. Combining data files: same people, different variables
2. Combining data files: different people, same variables

This chapter is something of an advanced course in the use of the "get file" and "save outfile" commands. Here you will learn more about controlling the constituency of your data files. There are two primary reasons you would use the information in this chapter: (1) you have two or more data files with *different*

IBM SPSS Essentials: Managing and Analyzing Social Sciences Data, Second Edition.
John Kulas, Renata Garcia Prieto Palacios Roji, and Adam Smith.
© 2021 John Wiley & Sons, Inc. Published 2021 by John Wiley & Sons, Inc.

information from the *same individuals,* or (2) you have two or more data files with *similar information* from *different individuals.* In both scenarios you ultimately want to get the files together.

The first situation is exemplified (in our field, for example) by one data file that contains applicant characteristics (typically applicants' scores on selection assessments) and another data file that contains job performance information (collected at a later time from those same applicants, now actual employees). Eventually, you'll need to combine these two files if you want to do anything meaningful with the information.

The second situation is typified by students who we recruit to help us with research projects. Any given semester, these student research assistants enter experimental data into a spreadsheet, such as an SPSS data file. When there are multiple individuals entering data from a stack of, for example, 200 or more completed questionnaires (such as the questionnaire in Appendix A), there are several data entry approaches you can take. One is to have students take turns entering information into one master data file. That's not very efficient – so what we typically do is define multiple duplicate empty data files (one for each student), give each student a stack of questionnaires (and an empty but variable-defined data file), and then when they're done with their data entry, we combine all of the files (with *similar information* from *different experimental participants*) into one master data file.

Same People, Different Information

Using our personality questionnaire example, as part of an experiment, we could have the research assistants, while they are administering the questionnaire to participants, guess which of the five measured personality traits is most dominant for each individual who fills out the hundred-item questionnaire.

This scenario would require not only that the study participants complete the questionnaire, but also that the research assistants record two pieces of information: the "casenum" of the individual they are rating and the trait they believe is most likely to be dominant (Agreeableness, Neuroticism, Extraversion, Openness to Experience, or Conscientiousness).[1]

For these two different sources (research assistants and questionnaire participants) we would construct two different data files. The first data file we've already constructed (100 personality items, 1 casenum, and 1 gender variable). The second data file contains three pieces of information (casenum, rated dimension, and

---

1 Appendix D contains another example of a situation in which you would want to combine files with similar people but different variables.

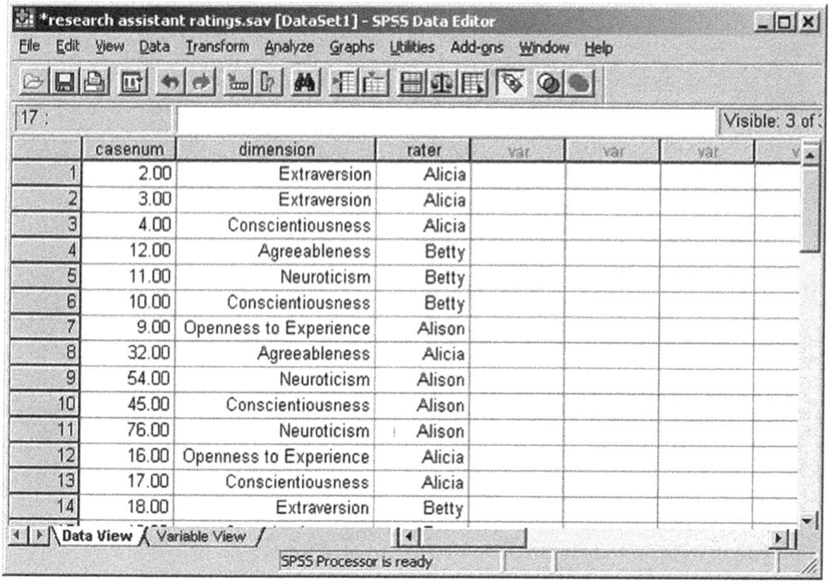

	casenum	dimension	rater
1	2.00	Extraversion	Alicia
2	3.00	Extraversion	Alicia
3	4.00	Conscientiousness	Alicia
4	12.00	Agreeableness	Betty
5	11.00	Neuroticism	Betty
6	10.00	Conscientiousness	Betty
7	9.00	Openness to Experience	Alison
8	32.00	Agreeableness	Alicia
9	54.00	Neuroticism	Alison
10	45.00	Conscientiousness	Alison
11	76.00	Neuroticism	Alison
12	16.00	Openness to Experience	Alicia
13	17.00	Conscientiousness	Alicia
14	18.00	Extraversion	Betty

Figure 14.1 Research assistant ratings.

research assistant who provided the rating). As shown in Figure 14.1, we entered this information as numbers, rather than string variables – the value labels are showing in the data file because we've clicked the Value Labels button (introduced in Chapter 6).

Now, to combine the two data files, we need to know just two things: (1) the names of the data files we want to combine and (2) the variable that identifies individuals in both files (in this situation, casenum).

There is one important requirement when you combine two files with different variables but the same people: you must rearrange your data so the values of your **"matching" variables** are numbered consecutively in both files. This is accomplished quite easily, but it will require a few extra syntax lines, as shown in Figures 14.2 and 14.3. You can also match files based on shared string variables, but just as with numeric variables, you must first organize the string variables alphabetically in both files.

The example shown accesses the original data file and rearranges the data so the smallest casenum is the first row in the file and the largest casenum is the last row in the file. The other option, with the "**sort cases by**" command, is to specify a "d" instead of the "a". Where "d" stands for descending, and "a" represents ascending. It doesn't really matter which we choose, as long as we are consistent (if we pick ascending for one data file, we have to do so for the other as well). Next, we access the file we want to combine with our original data file, then combine

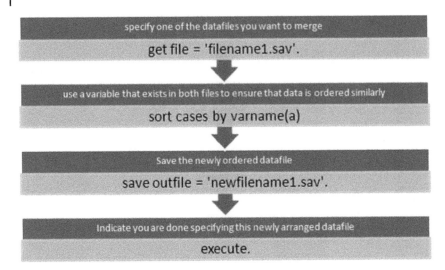

Figure 14.2 Matching variable values consecutively.

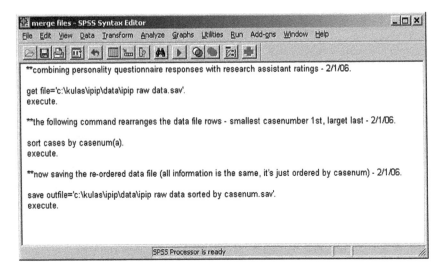

Figure 14.3 Prepping data file to merge data.

the two files as shown in Figures 14.4 and 14.5 and save the new data file as shown in Figure 14.6 (this saved file contains unique information from both files).

The illustrated command specifications indicate that we want to match a file to the open file (that's what the asterisk [*] represents in the **"match files"** command line – here it means whichever data file is open). The second line identifies the file

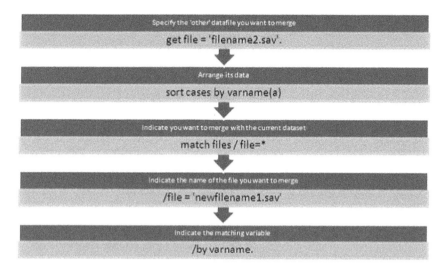

Figure 14.4 Specifying and rearranging data to match values.

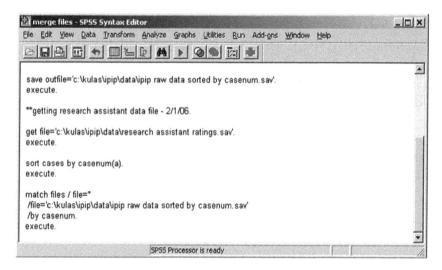

Figure 14.5 Merging data files with matching values.

we want to combine – this file's variables will be added at the end of our open data file (that is, they'll be put to the "right" of the open file's variables). The third line identifies the variable you want to "match" – this is the person identifier. Notice that no period (.) is used until the third line.

If we wanted our information arranged differently in the new data file, we could either switch the order of specification of the original files (this would put

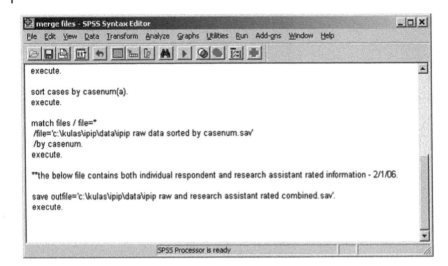

Figure 14.6 Saving merged data file.

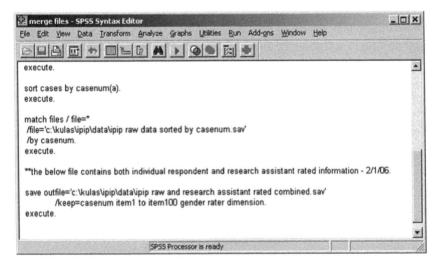

Figure 14.7 Rearranging variable order in merged data file.

the two rater file variables at the end rather than the beginning of our new file) or use the "keep" subcommand on the "save outfile" statement to rearrange the order of our variables (see Chapter 5). As shown in Figure 14.7, we've taken the second approach and moved the "gender" variable more toward the end of the data file.

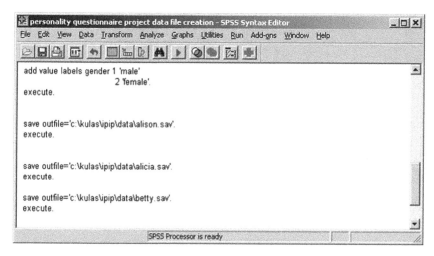

Figure 14.8 Personality questionnaire project data file.

Different People, Same Information

If you have identical data files with different people in them, you can use a similar procedure, although this time you don't have to first do a "sort cases by" command. In the case of multiple research assistants entering data into their own individual data files, as shown in Figure 14.8, we can first use the "save outfile" command at the end of our empty data file creation syntax to create three empty data files (one each for Alison, Alicia, and Betty). First, the data file variables are specified as seen in Figure 14.9, and then the data shells are saved as three separate files (Figure 14.8).

Now we give the three empty (but variable-defined) data files to the three research assistants to work on while we are away for the weekend. When we return, we check our e-mail and save the files they've sent us in the "c:\kulas\ipip \data" folder. Then to merge the files together, we apply the flowchart shown in Figure 14.10 to generate our syntax as shown in Figure 14.11.

You can actually specify multiple files to add with one "**add files**" syntax command, but we recommend doing a separate "add file" command for each file you want to add. At least do this until you're comfortable with the use of the command. The "**in**" **variables** that we specified in Figure 14.11 (coder1 and coder2) are optional. These are the variables that identify who entered the data – Betty has values in the "coder2" variable column, Alicia has values in the "coder1" variable column, and Alison coded the rest of the rows in our merged data file. SPSS enters this information for you if you specify the "in" subcommand.

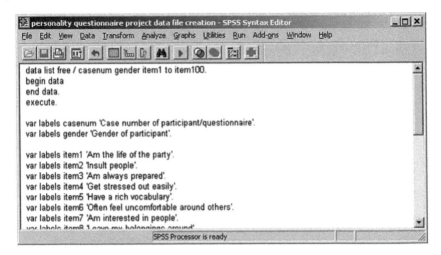

Figure 14.9 Specify data file variables.

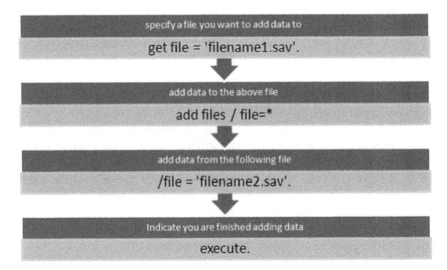

Figure 14.10 Commands to add rows to existing data file.

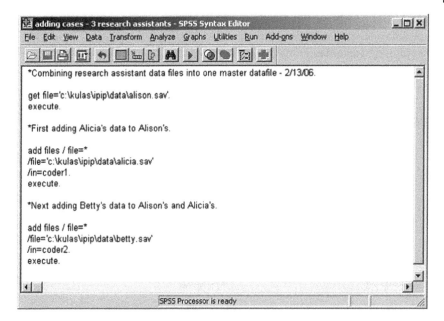

Figure 14.11 Adding cases from three research assistants.

Summary

When you need to combine different data files, you can use one of two different methods. If you have different information or variables from the same people, you need to sort both files first, then merge them together. If you have the same information or variables but different people, you can just add the files to each other without sorting first. Generally, you'll want to save the new, combined file after the merge or add by using the "save outfile" command.

Key Terms

"Add files" – SPSS command for combining files containing the same variables but different individuals.
"In" variables – Variables created by SPSS to identify which original file is associated with each combined file case/row.

Match files – SPSS command for combining files containing the same individuals but different variables.

"Matching" variables – Organizing/identifying variables that exist in more than one data file.

"Sort cases by" – SPSS command for reorganizing data sequentially.

Discussion Questions

1   When matching files, the order of the command specifications indicates what files we want to match (what file's variables will be added at the end of the open file). What do the commands in each command line represent?

2   When matching two sets of data containing string variables, what should you do prior to matching the files based on shared string variables?

15

Differential Treatment of Your Data

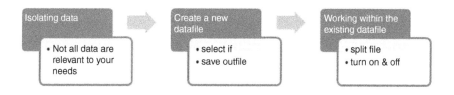

CHAPTER MENU

Chapter Learning Objectives

1. Isolating data: Creating new data files
2. Isolating data: Segregating output and analyses

Occasionally, you'll want to separate "interesting" data from data that you, for whatever reason, find a bit less interesting. This chapter, therefore, focuses on manipulation requests that you can use to segregate your data.

IBM SPSS Essentials: Managing and Analyzing Social Sciences Data, Second Edition.
John Kulas, Renata Garcia Prieto Palacios Roji, and Adam Smith.
© 2021 John Wiley & Sons, Inc. Published 2021 by John Wiley & Sons, Inc.

Isolating Interesting Cases

Consider the following imaginary situation: A train leaves San Francisco for Pittsburgh at 8:00, carrying 150 women, 100 men, and traveling at 100 miles per hour. Another train leaves Pittsburgh for San Francisco at 9:30 (also going really fast). What's the likelihood of the Pittsburgh conductor getting a date from one of the 150 San Francisco women after the two trains collide?

OK, that's a stupid question – we don't even know if the conductor survived the crash – but it raises a point: to answer the question about the likelihood of a date, we'd probably want to isolate information about the 150 San Francisco women from information about other passengers. We don't really care about information from other people in this situation.

Taking this fictional scenario as a case study for the chapter, we will demonstrate how to isolate female San Franciscans from the larger dataset. There are a few different options that facilitate this – we could create a separate data file with only San Francisco women in it, or we could work within the existing data file but somehow identify that particular pieces of data are associated with men or women. Let's first attempt the "create a different data file" option.

Creating a New Data File

As shown in Figure 15.1, this option primarily utilizes commands that you're already familiar with – "get file" and "save outfile". We only need one new command: "**select if**".

You can get fairly intricate with the "select if" command, by specifying multiple conditions that must be met for cases to be identified and retained, although Figure 15.2 only specifies gender. Figure 15.3 is a screenshot of an example data file we've created to mirror the "two train" scenario.

Notice that our variable values are represented by numbers instead of words (they're numeric variables) – because of this, we would need a code sheet for this example, and we would incorporate that code sheet into our "var labels" and "add value labels" commands, as shown in Figure 15.4.

Usually, we place an "execute" after every command (or batches of "var labels" commands). To save space, we've used only one "execute" (you can do this too, but it's not a great habit to develop). As shown in Figure 15.5, if we run the same syntax and revisit the data file (with the Variable Labels button chosen), it looks a little more interpretable.

Now we can get a lot more selective with our data isolation – if we want only women from San Francisco who are single and not too attractive (we don't want the conductor to shoot too high and become discouraged about his dating

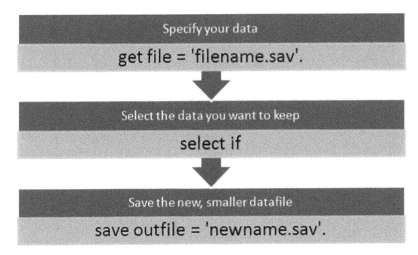

Figure 15.1 Specifying and selecting data and saving the new data file.

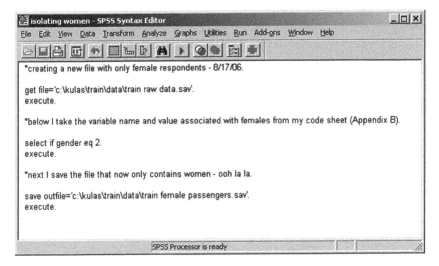

Figure 15.2 Isolating only women – this is regardless of whether they're from Pittsburgh or San Francisco.

prospects – especially after he just crashed his choo-choo), we can specify these multiple conditions with *one* "select if" command. It's important here to note that this command is not constrained just to conditions that are equal (eq) to a particular value (that is, females). Sometimes you'll want to apply the "select if"

	casenum	train	gender	attract	status	var
1	1.00	1.00	1.00	10.00	1.00	
2	2.00	1.00	1.00	9.00	2.00	
3	4.00	2.00	1.00	2.00	1.00	
4	6.00	2.00	1.00	3.00	1.00	
5	10.00	2.00	1.00	7.00	2.00	
6	9.00	2.00	1.00	6.00	1.00	
7	11.00	1.00	1.00	10.00	1.00	
8	12.00	2.00	1.00	9.00	2.00	
9	16.00	2.00	1.00	2.00	1.00	
10	12.00	2.00	1.00	3.00	1.00	

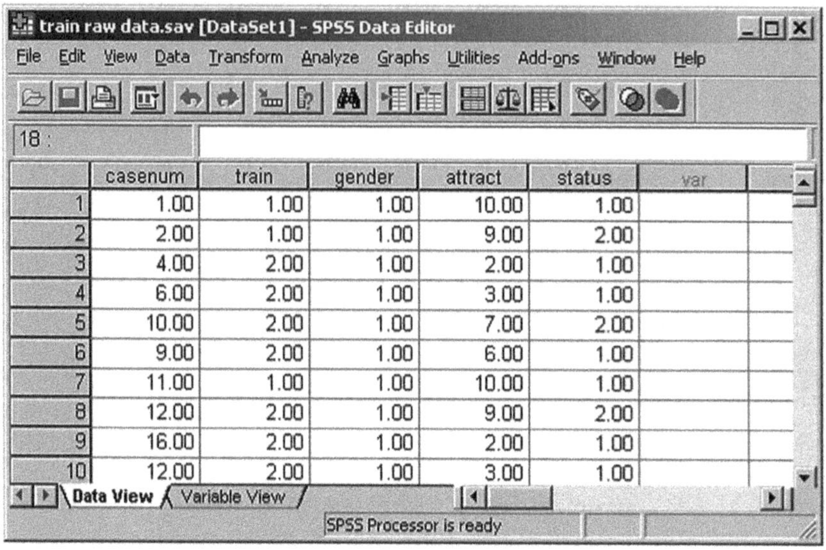

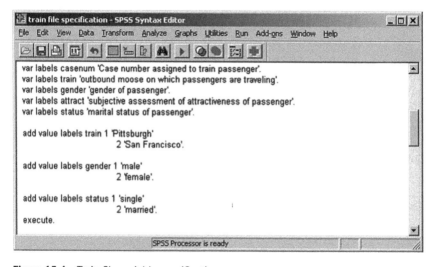

Figure 15.3 Train raw data file snapshot – only men visible.

```
var labels casenum 'Case number assigned to train passenger'.
var labels train 'outbound moose on which passengers are traveling'.
var labels gender 'gender of passenger'.
var labels attract 'subjective assessment of attractiveness of passenger'.
var labels status 'marital status of passenger'.

add value labels train 1 'Pittsburgh'
                       2 'San Francisco'.

add value labels gender 1 'male'
                        2 'female'.

add value labels status 1 'single'
                        2 'married'.
execute.
```

Figure 15.4 Train file variable specification.

command to a range of values, which you can do quite easily because the operations you specify with this command can be less than (lt), less than or equal to (le), equal to (eq), greater than or equal to (ge), or greater than (gt) whatever value you desire, as shown in Figures 15.6 and 15.7.

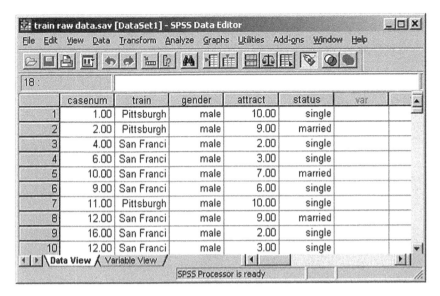

Figure 15.5 Train data file with labels visible.

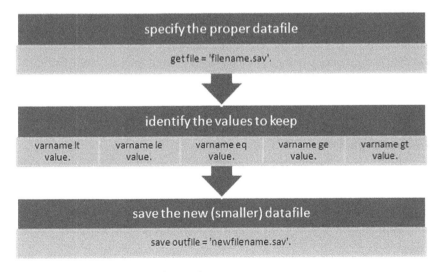

Figure 15.6 Identifying the values to keep.

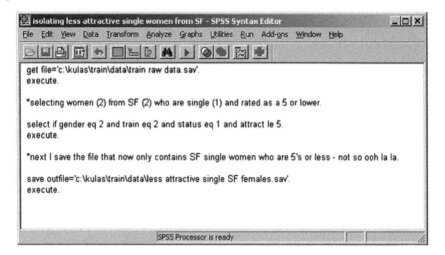

Figure 15.7 Isolating a subgroup.

Splitting Files

Creating separate data files as we have just done means that your new files contain only information from whatever data you have decided is important. You therefore do not have *all* of your data contained in the same location. An alternative approach that accomplishes similar goals is to simply let SPSS know that you're interested in separating your data. You do this through a **"split file"** command. We don't frequently use this command because it's what's we refer to as a **light-switch command** – this means you need to turn it both on and off. If you're someone who tends to forget to turn off a burner when you're done cooking, don't use this command. If you do decide to use this command, remember to turn it off at the end of your syntax file.

Splitting files is considered useful primarily because of what it does to your output (.spv) files. Really, all this command does is organize your analysis and output for you and make it easier to read – it performs analyses and organizes output by your split variable. Using the "two trains" example, if we want to know (for example) how attractive our female passengers are, we first need to sort our data (as discussed in Chapter 14), then we use the "split file" command and request a rudimentary analysis (as we covered in Chapter 7, these analyses are called *descriptives* – they give means, standard deviations, and so on). Examples of this general procedure are highlighted in Figures 15.8 and 15.9.

The output we receive (from the descriptives command) is computed separately for males and females, as shown in Figure 15.10.

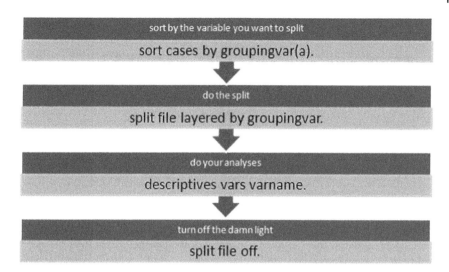

Figure 15.8 Requesting separate reports for different subgroups.

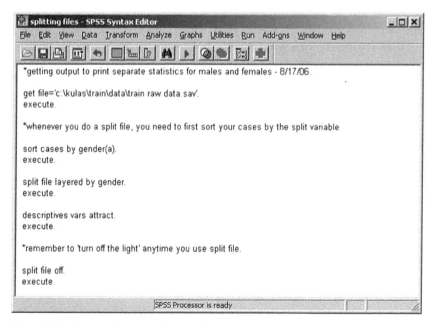

Figure 15.9 Requesting attractiveness data separated by gender.

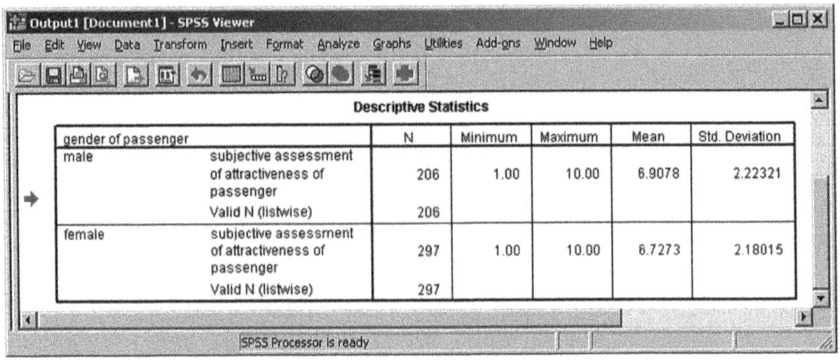

Descriptive Statistics

gender of passenger		N	Minimum	Maximum	Mean	Std. Deviation
male	subjective assessment of attractiveness of passenger	206	1.00	10.00	6.9078	2.22321
	Valid N (listwise)	206				
female	subjective assessment of attractiveness of passenger	297	1.00	10.00	6.7273	2.18015
	Valid N (listwise)	297				

Figure 15.10 Descriptive attractiveness statistics for males and females.

Similarly to using the "select if" command, we can get fairly intricate with "split file" commands – it's important, however, that for every variable you want to split, you also first sort by that variable. If we want to isolate single women from San Francisco, we can do that, but if we do that through the "split file" command, we are also simultaneously isolating married women from San Francisco, single women from Pittsburgh, single men from Pittsburgh, married men from Pittsburgh – the point is, with "split file" you don't truly isolate, you just categorize (while retaining all possible categories). To get attractiveness ratings for single women from Pittsburgh, we can use the split file syntax shown in Figure 15.11 (which will also give us attractiveness ratings for all other possible combinations of Pittsburgh/San Francisco, married/single, and male/female). Regardless of how many categories you use to split a file, you need only one "**split file off**" command. The "split file off" command is your "off" position for the light switch.

Figure 15.12 shows a partial screenshot of what your output request (frequencies) looks like for this particular split file.

To get to the data we're interested in, we have to scroll through the output until we get to the point where it's organized by females from San Francisco who are single. Data from these individuals are shown in Figure 15.13.

Looking at this output, we see that there are seventy single women from San Francisco in our data file. The "Women" label is not visible in this screenshot because of the way SPSS output labels multi-split files. The "attractiveness" label is also not visible (but is present at the top of the output file). The column to the right of the word "valid", however, lists attractiveness ratings (i.e. 2.00, 5.00, 6.00). They range in attractiveness from a couple of 2's to four 10's.

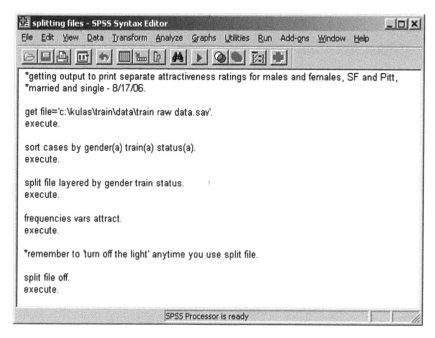

Figure 15.11   Turning the split file on and off.

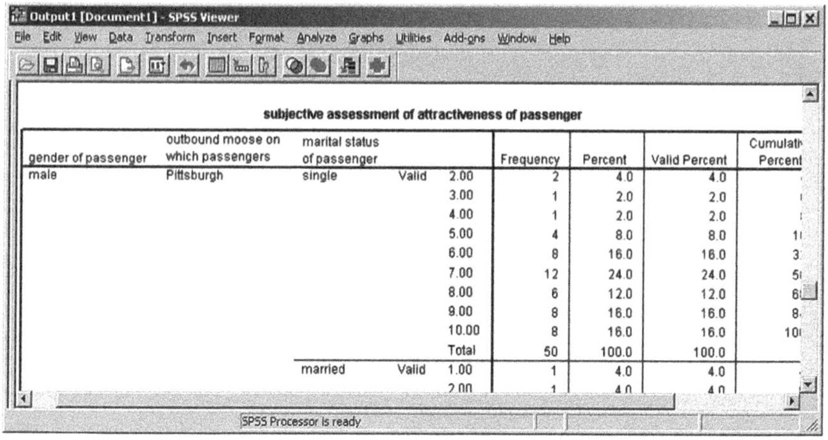

Figure 15.12   Output for the split-file request (single men from Pittsburgh visible).

				7.00	21	31.3	31.3	74.6
				8.00	6	9.0	9.0	83.6
				9.00	5	7.5	7.5	91.0
				10.00	6	9.0	9.0	100.0
				Total	67	100.0	100.0	
San Francisco	single	Valid		2.00	2	2.9	2.9	2.9
				5.00	16	22.9	22.9	25.7
				6.00	6	8.6	8.6	34.3
				7.00	16	22.9	22.9	57.1
				8.00	22	31.4	31.4	88.6
				9.00	4	5.7	5.7	94.3
				10.00	4	5.7	5.7	100.0
				Total	70	100.0	100.0	
	married	Valid		1.00	6	4.4	4.4	4.4
				2.00	6	4.4	4.4	8.8
				3.00	4	2.9	2.9	11.8

Figure 15.13 Output for the split-file request (single women from San Francisco visible).

Summary

If you are interested in only a subset of your data, you have multiple options. You can exclude unwanted cases from your existing dataset ("select if") or you can request that SPSS analyzes and reports information for separate groups ("split file"). The "split file" command is a light-switch command – if you turn it on, you have to remember to also turn it off.

Key Terms

Light-switch command – Command that must be turned off after it's activated.
"Select if" – SPSS command used to identify and retain only certain rows (people) within your data file.
"Split file" – SPSS command to perform analyses and manipulations separately (within groups).
"Split file off" – The "other half" of the "split file" command, it tells SPSS to "stop organizing what you do by group and consider all my data at once".

Discussion Questions

1 "Select if" and "split file" do essentially the same thing; why do I need to learn both?

2 What happens if I forget to turn the "split file" command off?

16

Using Your Output

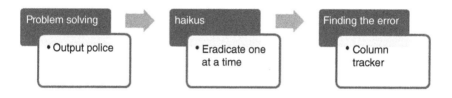

CHAPTER MENU

Chapter Learning Objectives

1. Problem solving with haikus
   a. Offending word
   b. Column location
2. Double-clicking in output files

Congratulations! You're now an SPSS pro – you possess enough knowledge to be truly dangerous. The current chapter further hones your ninja-like skills by teaching you how to maximize the utility of your output files.

IBM SPSS Essentials: Managing and Analyzing Social Sciences Data, Second Edition.
John Kulas, Renata Garcia Prieto Palacios Roji, and Adam Smith.
© 2021 John Wiley & Sons, Inc. Published 2021 by John Wiley & Sons, Inc.

Problem Solving

Output files not only show up when you anticipate – sometimes they appear unexpectedly. This most commonly happens when you make an error with your syntax (say, you miss a period or put a comma where a space should be). When this happens, an output file pops up and reports the indiscretion. Here's what you do with these ".spv" intruders:

1. Take note of these elements:
   a. The offending word.
   b. The column location of the error – if provided (we will say more about this later in the chapter).
2. Close out of the .spv file – *don't* save it when you are prompted to do so.
3. Change your syntax based on the location and offending word.
4. Rerun your syntax and loop back to #1 if another error message pops up.
5. Figure 16.1 provides a handy diagram of the cycle.

Spaces in All the Wrong Places

As shown in Figure 16.2, we've introduced two common errors into the "add value labels" syntax from Chapter 6. Even with the giveaway subhead of this section,

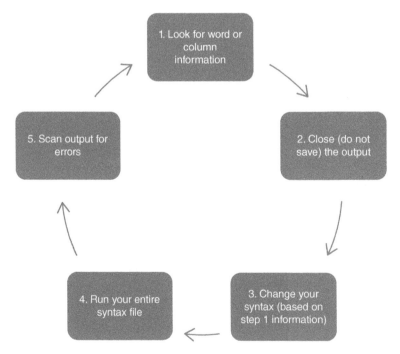

Figure 16.1 Problem-solving cycle.

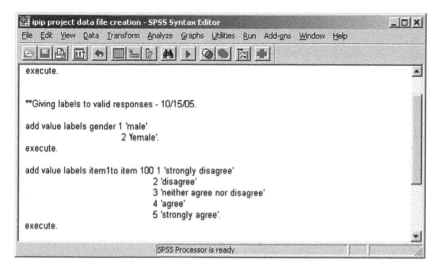

Figure 16.2 Two common errors in syntax.

you'll probably need to read over the commands four or five times before you catch the errors, which is why we included this chapter on problem solving. There's a better way to catch errors than visually scanning your syntax (although you should also generally do a visual check on your syntax before you run it).

When we run the syntax in Figure 16.2, we get the output file shown in Figure 16.3.

When output files (the SPSS police) show up, one of two things have happened. One possibility is that you requested some summary information (such as descriptives or frequencies) or some inferential information (such as a t-test, ANOVA,

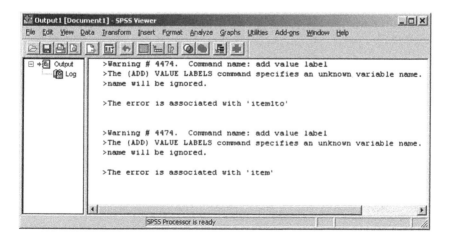

Figure 16.3 Error messages output (aka "haikus").

or correlation). Under these circumstances, you expect to see the police – you essentially called them and they're escorting your information to you. Alternatively, the police might be showing up unexpectedly to let you know about some suspicious activity that they've been noticing around the neighborhood (as seen on Figure 16.3).

This second reason for the police showing up (output file popping up) is actually quite helpful to the syntax writer. SPSS lets you know when this is the case (when you've made an error) by putting the ">" character in the output file. When you see these > characters, you know that something went terribly wrong with your syntax. Think of the > as a big arrow pointing directly at your script, assigning blame to the offending word or character. Using that arrow, you can fix the offender and send the police on their way.

All SPSS errors are called out in three- to seven-line reports that *used to* look to us somewhat like the haiku form of poetry – so we refer to them as **haikus**. Modern versions of SPSS have gotten less poetic in their warning form, but we still refer to these warning messages as haikus.

You should always try to remedy your errors *one at a time*, starting from the first reported error (the one closest to the top of the output file). We advise this because often one initial error will set off a chain of errors, but if you correct the first, it will be as if the other errors never existed.

In the output shown in Figure 16.3, there are two haikus or errors reported, but we're focusing on just the first one. The first and last lines of the haiku are the most important. The first tells us what command SPSS thought we meant to invoke; the last line tells us what part of the command SPSS didn't like. We therefore know that there's a problem in our syntax associated with an "add value labels" command as well as the word "item1to". Now we need to scan our syntax file for an "item1to" associated with an "add value labels" command. Because your syntax files are often quite large, you may want to use the **Find function** (Ctrl+F) in your syntax editor to locate the offending word (whatever is in quotes in the last line of your haiku), as shown in Figure 16.4.

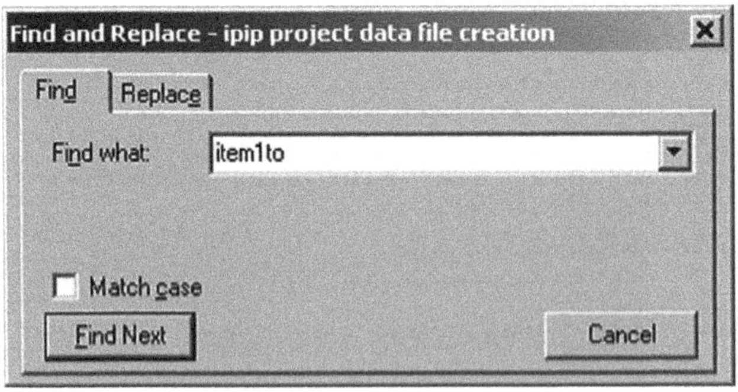

Figure 16.4 Find and replace function (error 1).

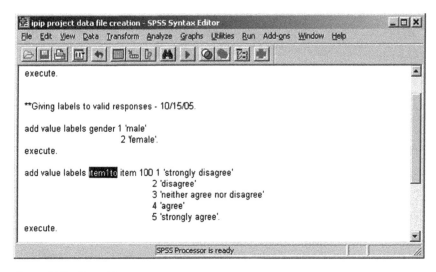

Figure 16.5 Error 1 in syntax.

Using the Find function, we've located a possible offender, as highlighted in Figure 16.5.

Sure enough, the offending word is associated with an "add value labels" command. Good news for the SPSS user, because this is likely the cause of our error. We forgot to put a space between the words "item1" and "to" (see Figure 16.2). This is a very common error. Fixing the error, our revised syntax appears in Figure 16.6.

When we run this new syntax, we get a new warning, shown in Figure 16.7, but now the police have less to report.

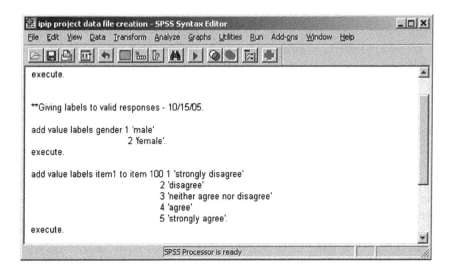

Figure 16.6 Revised syntax after correcting error.

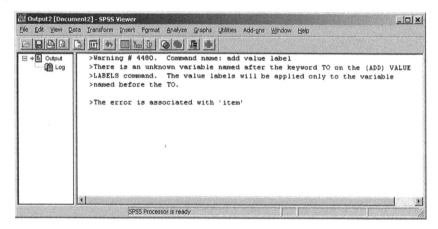

Figure 16.7   Error message (haiku) output.

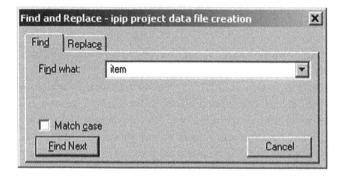

Figure 16.8   Find and replace function (error 2).

Our haiku is now just six lines – an improvement, but we still have work to do. As shown in Figure 16.8, we search for "item" in our syntax.

But the find function is not as useful to us this time. The first possibly offending term that the Find function locates is not associated with an "add value label" command. The offending term actually yields too many hits in this case for the Find function to provide any utility. We have to search visually through the syntax and locate the "item" that is offensive.

It is because of such scenarios that you're best served by constructing your syntax files with similar commands located in similar sections of your syntax files – for example, all of our "var labels" commands are located consecutively. Notice in Figure 16.9 that all of our "add value labels" commands are located toward the bottom of our syntax.

Scanning through our "add value label" commands, we locate an offending space between the word "item" and the number "100". What we *intended* with

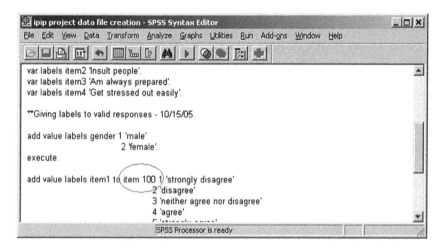

Figure 16.9   Visually locating the offending "item".

the syntax was for all items (item1 through item100) to receive the same value labels. What we *did*, however, was wrongly specify a variable named "item 100". SPSS doesn't like spaces where they're not supposed to be – it believes that a space indicates that you've completed your previous thought and are moving on to the next thought.

If we now delete the space between "item" and "100" and run our syntax (see Figure 16.10), we get no haikus. Spaces are frequently the cause of haikus – keep an eye out for them when you're problem solving.

Let's see what other kinds of haikus we can conjure with different errors. Figure 16.11 offers an example. Running this syntax (only slightly modified from the error-free syntax created in Chapter 13) results in the haiku shown in Figure 16.12.

Notice the additional information located in the first line: *where* SPSS has a problem (column 33). The **column information**, when provided, can be helpful, but it can also sometimes be misleading. The column where SPSS has a problem isn't necessarily the column where the error is, but generally it should be somewhere close. The information contained after the "Text:" is once again very important for our problem-solving efforts; in this case, we are looking for an offending "s".

Column Information

At the bottom right-hand corner of your syntax files is a **column tracker**. It will be hidden if your window is small (as shown, for example, in Figure 16.11), but if you increase the width of your syntax window, it will become visible.

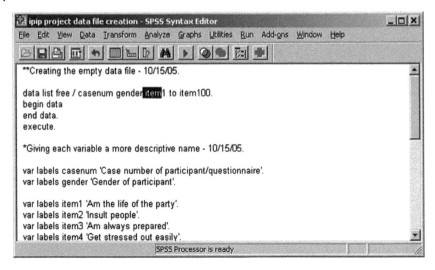

Figure 16.10   The offending "item" fixed.

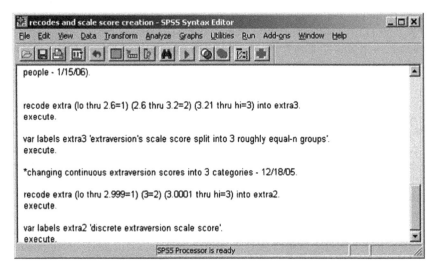

Figure 16.11   Syntax containing error.

The column tracker in Figure 16.13 indicates that our cursor is at line (row) 1 and column 1 in the syntax editor (this is the upper left-hand position). To find the error indicated by the haiku, we need to look around column 33. To do this, we move our cursor until it's at column 33 (right after the word "scale" in our asterisked first-line comment, see Figure 16.14), then scroll down through the syntax file, looking for an offending "s" somewhere around column 33.

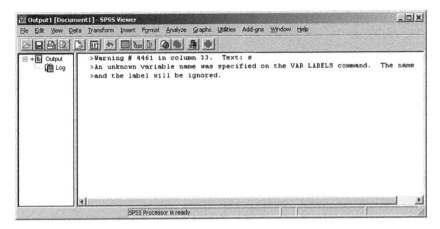

Figure 16.12   Error message (haiku) for column 33.

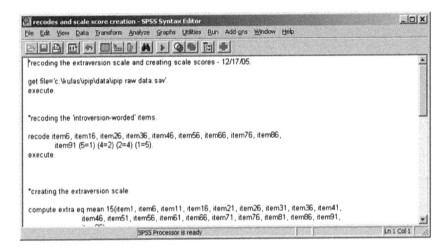

Figure 16.13   Column tracker in syntax.

As we use the arrow key to scroll, our cursor will generally stay within the same column (when possible). If a command or statement is not 33 columns wide (for example, the execute commands), the cursor will place itself at the end of the command (closest to 33) and then typically correct itself at the next opportunity (when a command or statement does possess at least 33 characters). This makes it easier to visually scan the likely locations for your error. Eventually, you'll find a likely culprit for the error, as shown in Figure 16.15.

It turns out that the problem isn't technically the "s" located at column 33, but the unwanted apostrophe in column 32. Along with orphaned spaces, these

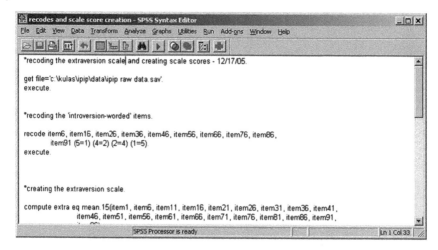

Figure 16.14   Increasing width of window to locate column tracker.

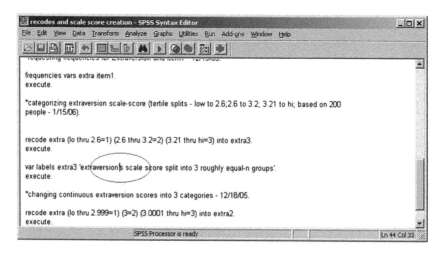

Figure 16.15   Locating error in syntax by column.

apostrophe hooligans are no strangers to the law, and you should always be on the lookout for them when you receive a haiku. Deleting the offending apostrophe and rerunning the full syntax file yields no additional errors. We have successfully eradicated all haikus.

There Is One Little Thing …

A word of warning regarding the use of column information: although the column tracker gives you the location of your cursor, it technically does so by counting characters, not actual columns. This means that if you use the Tab key within your syntax file, as your book authors commonly do, the cursor will occasionally give you *bad* information. Keep in mind that the column number is accurate *as long as there are no tabs*. We really don't know why SPSS works like this – it makes a mess out of problem solving – but we're too attached to tabs not to use them, so we just complain. If you get into a really sticky problem-solving situation, you can always do a find and replace, replacing your tabs with spaces. If you do this, however, you need to rerun your syntax, as the column information contained in the error haiku may change as a result of the new column numbering used in your syntax file.

Maximizing Output Information

Now to our second chapter objective, using the power of double-clicking. The information that is presented when you request output is actually shown in a truncated format. Sometimes you'll need a greater degree of accuracy or precision than what is reported. Fortunately, precise information is available – you just have to know how to ask for it. For instance, if we wanted to know descriptive infor-mation to the millionths place, we would first run our "descriptives" command (introduced in Chapter 7) as shown in Figure 16.16.

From this request we would get the output shown in Figure 16.17.

By double-clicking on the reported numbers, you can see the precise estimate (for the mean, for example) as shown in Figure 16.18.

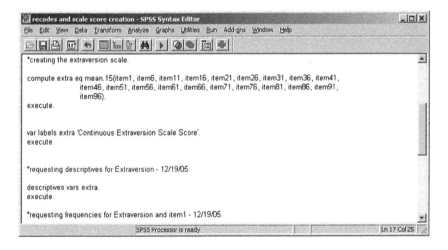

Figure 16.16 Syntax with "descriptives" command.

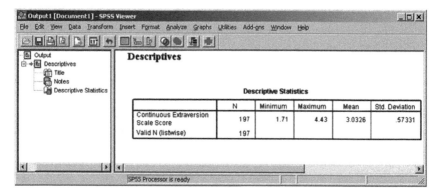

Figure 16.17   Descriptive statistics output.

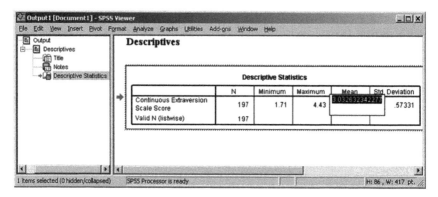

Figure 16.18   Precise estimates in descriptive statistics output.

The point is, even though SPSS reports information in a truncated, digestible format, there is a more precise estimate lurking in SPSS if you go looking for it. SPSS uses these precise estimates for computations and analyses, but when it *reports* the numbers, it uses a convention (generally reporting to the nearest hundredth, thousandth, or ten thousandth).

Summary

You will encounter haikus when you use SPSS. You should eradicate them one at a time, starting with the first reported haiku. If you use the column information to locate the error, remember that column actually refers to *characters*, including the tab character, so the information can be misleading.

Double-clicking in output files gives you more detailed information regarding SPSS estimates. Although truncated numbers are presented visually in output files, SPSS uses nontruncated numbers for calculations and analyses.

Key Terms

> – Indication that the information provided refers to an error – there's been a problem noted with your requested command(s).
Column information – Potentially helpful, potentially misleading problem-solving information (provided in some, but not all haikus).
Column tracker – Number located in the lower right-hand corner of every syntax file, which identifies the location of the cursor (number of characters from the left).
Find function – Useful with haiku information in problem-solving applications.
Haikus – Warning snippets communicating that SPSS has encountered an error.

Discussion Questions

1 Why do I have to start with the first haiku?

2 How can I make the most use out of the column tracker information?

17

Other Tricks of the Trade

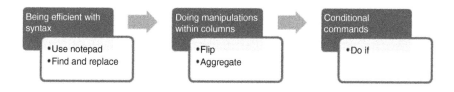

CHAPTER MENU

Chapter Learning Objectives

1. Using Notepad
2. Doing manipulations across rows
3. Scanning for duplicate cases
4. Introducing conditional statements: "do if", "end if"

This chapter contains miscellany that didn't quite fit into the other chapters and continues your progress toward black-belt SPSS status. It basically contains commands and techniques that will make your syntax writing more efficient.

IBM SPSS Essentials: Managing and Analyzing Social Sciences Data, Second Edition.
John Kulas, Renata Garcia Prieto Palacios Roji, and Adam Smith.
© 2021 John Wiley & Sons, Inc. Published 2021 by John Wiley & Sons, Inc.

Salvaging Old Syntax

In Chapter 2, an analogy was made between: (1) syntax files and Microsoft Word, and (2) data files and Microsoft Excel. Excel (and other spreadsheet) files can be directly imported into SPSS (see Chapter 5). Similarly, word processor information can be cut and paste into syntax files (and vice versa).

The Importance of Notepad

Notepad is a stripped-down word processing program that is packaged with Microsoft Windows (you can find it at the Start menu if you search for "notepad"). If you do not have Windows, any standard word processor will do. Notepad is particularly useful because it does not support formatting functions such as tables (syntax files do not support these formatting functions either). Notepad can be used to change variable names or analytical commands from one application to another (for example, salvaging old syntax); it is also useful for creating your variable labels (talked about in Chapter 6).

Using the Appendix A and B example, instead of individually typing variable labels for all one hundred items directly into our syntax file, we can use the information that's already stored in Microsoft Word (as a table). First, we copy the first column of our table from Word, as shown in Figure 17.1.

Then we paste this information into Notepad, as shown in Figure 17.2.

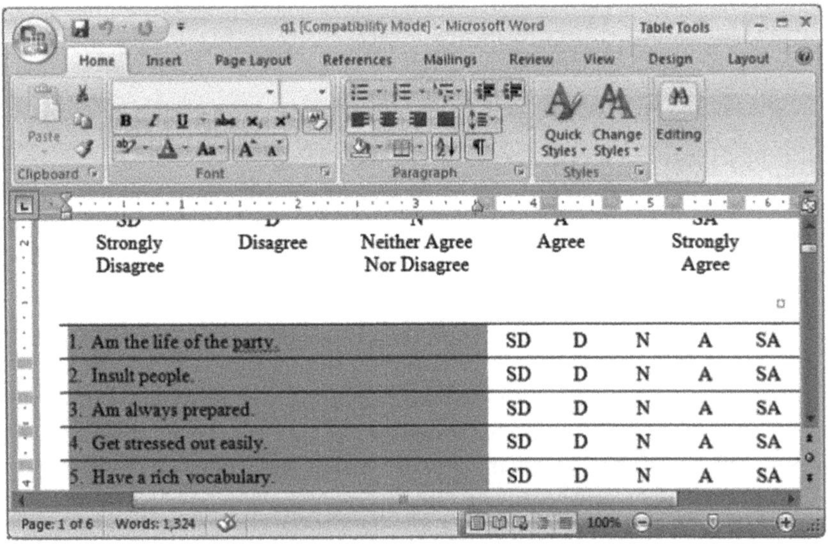

Figure 17.1 Personality questionnaire variables (Word format).

Figure 17.2 Personality questionnaire variables (Notepad format).

Notice that the formatting information (table definitions such as lines/borders) did not transfer to Notepad; this is a good thing. Now we can get creative with the Find and Replace function of Notepad to get our text SPSS-ready. First, we'll get rid of all apostrophes (notice the grammatically correct but potentially SPSS-troublesome apostrophe for items #12 and #17). We do this by searching for an apostrophe and replacing it with nothing (leaving it blank), as shown in Figure 17.3.

Choosing Replace All gets rid of any apostrophes that were in our item prompts and results in the file as shown in Figure 17.4 (notice #12 and #17 again).

Now we need to get rid of the periods after the item numbers – we're doing this by replacing "period, space, space" with "space, space, space, space, space" (see Figure 17.5). This will retain our periods at the *end* of the items while (1) getting rid of our periods after the numbers and (2) allowing us to use the "space, space, space, space, space" for a later Find and Replace. We use five spaces because there may be some accidental spaces at the end of some of our items (if you spaced over for some reason when originally typing the items, Notepad will store the "space" as a character – alternatively we could replace "period, space, space" with a unique character that's not otherwise in our file, such as a "$").

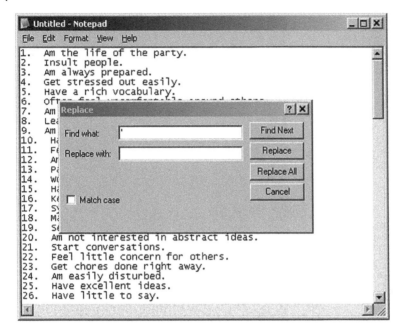

Figure 17.3 Find and replace functions.

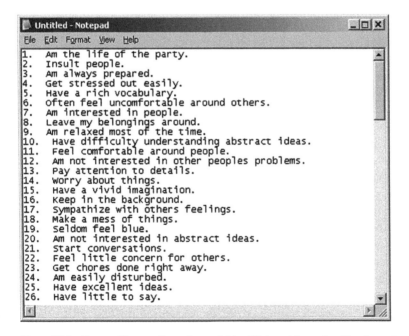

Figure 17.4 Personality questionnaire variables (Notepad format) without apostrophes.

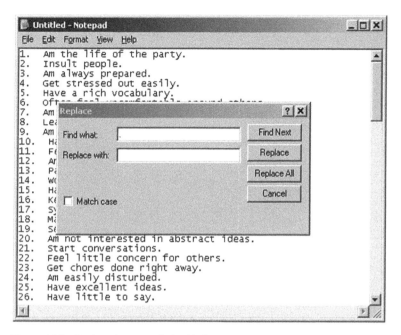

Figure 17.5 Replace box – period with five spaces.

Now, as shown in Figure 17.6, we have a list with five spaces between the item number and the item text.

Now we can replace five spaces with "space, apostrophe" to get an apostrophe at the beginning of my items, as shown in Figure 17.7.

Running that replace as well as a replace "period" with "apostrophe, period" gives us the results shown in Figure 17.8.

Now you've made the most of the usefulness of Notepad and can copy "var labels item" and paste it repetitively down your one hundred rows. Figure 17.9 shows the resulting notepad information at this point.

Now you can copy and paste the whole script into your syntax file, stick one "execute." at the bottom, and you're good to go. Syntax files also contain the Find and Replace option, but it tends to be easier to do this within a separate file (that is, not your main syntax file). If you don't have Notepad, you actually *should* do this in a separate syntax file.

This is just one example of the use of Notepad to facilitate your syntax writing. People who use SPSS frequently could probably fill an entire book with different creative applications of this general technique that they've used. It's very simple and very common but also very useful.

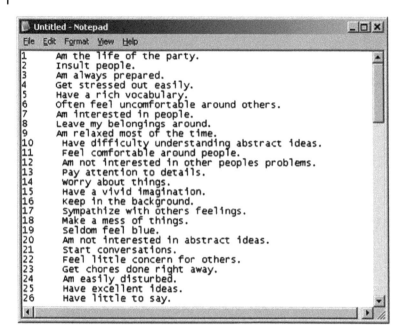

Figure 17.6 Personality questionnaire variables (Notepad format) without periods after numbers.

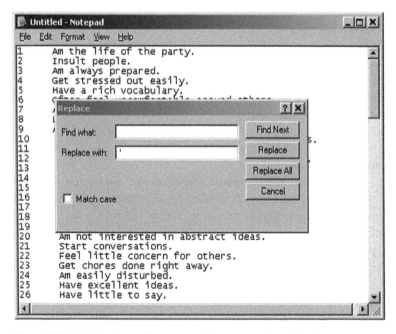

Figure 17.7 Replace box – five spaces with space and apostrophe.

Figure 17.8 Personality questionnaire variables – SPSS-friendly format.

Figure 17.9 Personality questionnaire variable – SPSS ready.

Tricking SPSS To "Think" Across Rows

Chapter 13 focused on SPSS's expectation of acting *across columns* for data manipulations. Occasionally, you will want SPSS to think across rows for manipulations (say, to place a mean variable score in your data matrix instead of just having SPSS's output file report it). There are two main ways to do this: (1) you can transpose your data matrix (turn columns into rows, rows into columns), then do the data manipulation, or (2) you can aggregate the data file. Generally, aggregating is preferred to a matrix transposition.

Transposing Your Matrix

If you've ever had a desire to turn your world (or at least your data) upside down, you can use the **matrix transposition** command. First, you specify "**flip vars=**", then you list all of the variables that you want to transpose, as shown in Figure 17.10. If you exclude some variables from your command, they will be lost from your transposed matrix.

Once again, here we can specify the "to" shortcut or list all variables separately. We could have actually specified "casenum to item100" and every variable would have been transposed – we don't recommend getting into that habit, however, because you may have to backtrack what you have done, and that is easier to do if you specify different variable groups (for example, if we used our "**to**" shortcut, we may forget that gender was included in the transposition).

If we now look at the data file, as shown in Figure 17.11, it will have as many columns as people, plus one – SPSS will create an additional variable called

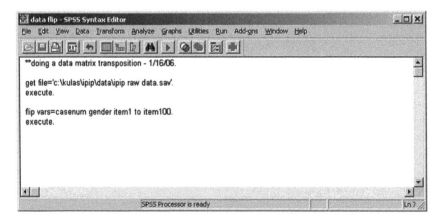

Figure 17.10 Syntax command for matrix transposition.

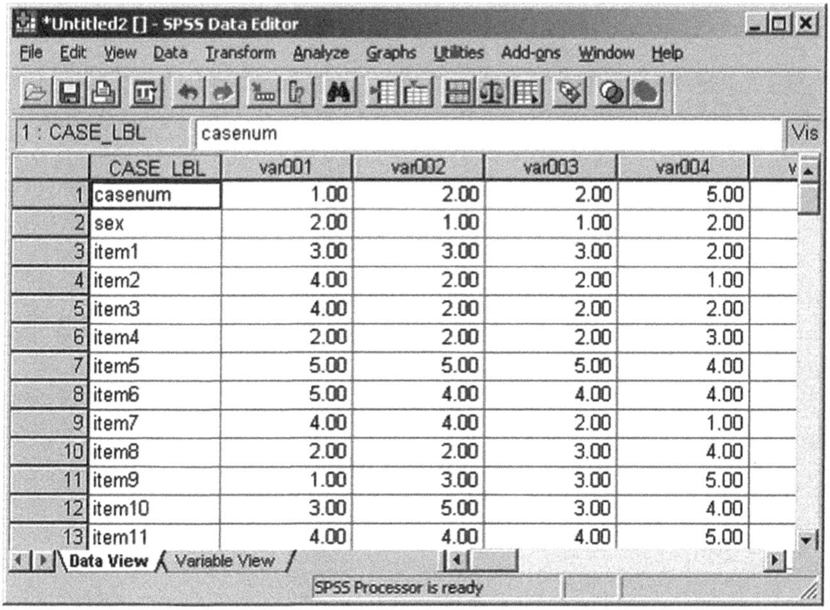

Figure 17.11   Transposed data.

"**CASE_LBL**" that contains all of your variable names – this will be the first column in your newly transposed matrix.

The default is to label your "people" as var001>varXXX (the "X"s represent the number of people in your original file). If we had one thousand people in our data file, SPSS would label the columns "var0001" → "var1000". If we had a few hundred thousand, SPSS would label the columns "var000001">"varXXXXXX". Now if we want to create a mean score for each item (that will be retained in the data file), we simply write a compute statement, as shown in Figure 17.12 (there are 200 people in the original data file, so our compute statement will include var001 through var200).

Now if we want to get the data file back to its original state, we can do a second transposition, as described in Figure 17.13 and shown in Figure 17.14, but now our y last *row* (row #201) will contain item averages.

Aggregating Your Files

As previously mentioned, aggregating data is generally preferred to doing a matrix transposition. A useful example application of aggregating that we have found is the identification and deletion of **duplicate cases**. It is not unusual when dealing with very large datasets to discover that you have duplicate rows of data. There are

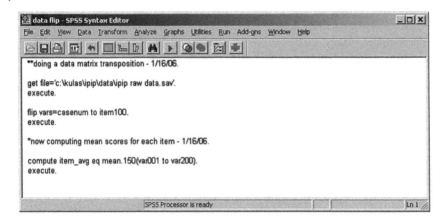

Figure 17.12 Computing item averages to be places in data file.

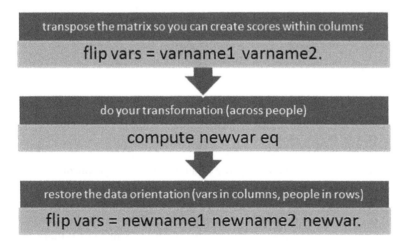

Figure 17.13 Matrix transposition process.

numerous reasons why these things happen – one common cause of data duplication is related to the data storage and retrieval process used by many organizations. It's not unusual to ask for a "data dump" (retrieving stored data) for a particular range of dates. If you later request a second "data dump" and accidentally overlap the date range, you'll likely end up with duplicate information in your data files. It doesn't really matter how it happens if you're staring at a 250,000-person data file and asked to delete duplicate cases. The point is, you need a tool to help identify and delete duplicates.

Figure 17.15 shows an example of a situation in which we have duplicate information in our personality questionnaire data file. This could also happen,

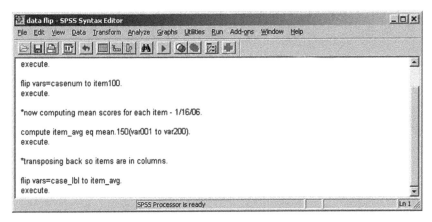

Figure 17.14 Syntax for transposing – restoring data to original configuration.

	casenum	gender	item1	item2	item3	item4
1	1.00	2.00	3.00	4.00	4.00	2.00
2	2.00	1.00	3.00	2.00	2.00	2.00
3	2.00	1.00	3.00	2.00	2.00	2.00
4	5.00	2.00	2.00	1.00	2.00	3.00
5	6.00	2.00	4.00	2.00	3.00	2.00
6	7.00	1.00	2.00	3.00	5.00	2.00
7	23.00	1.00	1.00	2.00	4.00	3.00
8	24.00	2.00	2.00	5.00	3.00	4.00
9	26.00	2.00	1.00	5.00	3.00	1.00
10	28.00	1.00	2.00	3.00	2.00	1.00
11	33.00	2.00	3.00	1.00	2.00	2.00
12	34.00	1.00	1.00	4.00	5.00	3.00
13	35.00	1.00	3.00	5.00	4.00	3.00

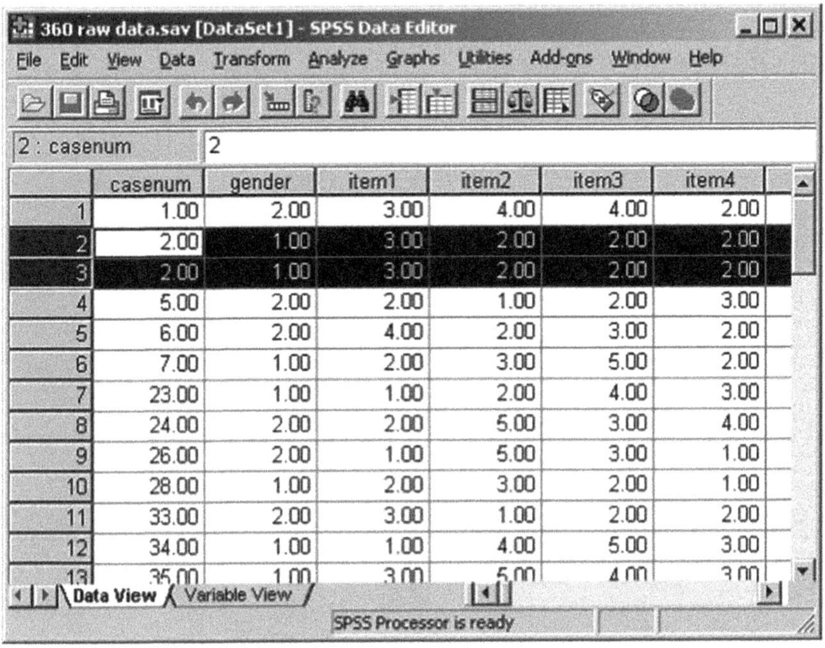

Figure 17.15 Data file with duplicate cases.

for example, if two different research assistants accidentally entered the same questionnaire into the file.

Typically, you do *not* want to visually scroll through your data file and manually delete duplicate cases – that's an inefficient process that is just begging for mistakes to be made – don't do it. Instead, you can control everything through syntax by

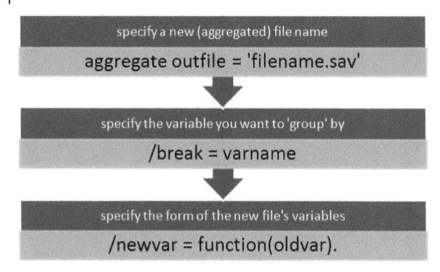

specify a new (aggregated) file name

aggregate outfile = 'filename.sav'

specify the variable you want to 'group' by

/break = varname

specify the form of the new file's variables

/newvar = function(oldvar).

Figure 17.16   Aggregate commands.

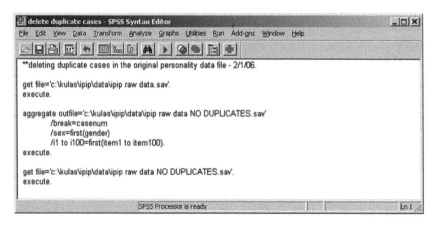

Figure 17.17   Syntax of new datafile without duplicate cases.

using the **"aggregate"** command, as Figure 17.16 describes; Figure 17.17 shows the syntax.

The command **"first"** tells the aggregate function to take the first nonmissing value it finds for each individual "casenum" (the break variable). SPSS will delete the extra rows that contain the same casenum and save the new file wherever you tell the program to put it. The only real drawback to this approach is you'll lose all of your variable and value label information, because you renamed all of your

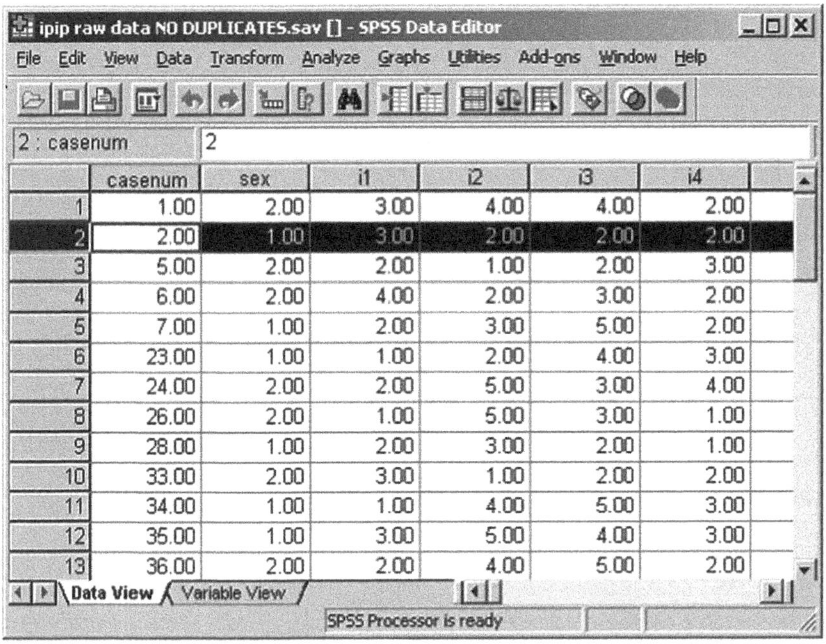

	casenum	sex	i1	i2	i3	i4
1	1.00	2.00	3.00	4.00	4.00	2.00
2	2.00	1.00	3.00	2.00	2.00	2.00
3	5.00	2.00	2.00	1.00	2.00	3.00
4	6.00	2.00	4.00	2.00	3.00	2.00
5	7.00	1.00	2.00	3.00	5.00	2.00
6	23.00	1.00	1.00	2.00	4.00	3.00
7	24.00	2.00	2.00	5.00	3.00	4.00
8	26.00	2.00	1.00	5.00	3.00	1.00
9	28.00	1.00	2.00	3.00	2.00	1.00
10	33.00	2.00	3.00	1.00	2.00	2.00
11	34.00	1.00	1.00	4.00	5.00	3.00
12	35.00	1.00	3.00	5.00	4.00	3.00
13	36.00	2.00	2.00	4.00	5.00	2.00

Figure 17.18 Data file with duplicate cases deleted.

variables in the new data file, so gender is now "sex", item1 is now "i1", and so on). Figure 17.18 shows the data file created by running the Figure 17.17 syntax.

This really isn't a big deal if you know how to use the "rename" command, as shown in Figure 17.19.

Now you're back to your original file format. You can now paste your previously created "var labels" and "add value labels" commands to the end of this syntax (but make sure to place it before the "save outfile" command). You'll notice in the preceding syntax that this is one of the few times we'll actually save an "outfile" using the same file name as the "get file" name. Generally, you should avoid doing this, but similarly you do not want to create *too many* data files that are essentially similar to each other.

"Do If" and "End If"

One of the most *useful* sets of commands you will use is a set of logical statements: "**do if**", "**else if**", and "**end if**". These statements allow you to set up logical parameters around data manipulations. You will likely find yourself having a choice of doing either "recode ... into" or "do if", "end if" statements. They can often be used

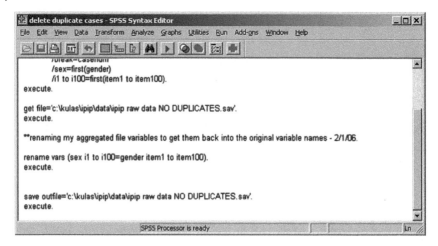

Figure 17.19 Rename command – return variables to original specification.

for the same purpose. For example, in Chapter 13, questionnaire respondents were classified as either introverted, extraverted, or on the fence. To make this classification with the recode statement, we had to pick maximum (2.999) and minimum (3.0001) values for the introverted and extraverted classifications.

The "do if", "end if" command allows you to classify without specifying maximums and minimums. You use the "do if", "end if" commands to enclose a transformation command (usually "compute"), as described in Figure 17.20;

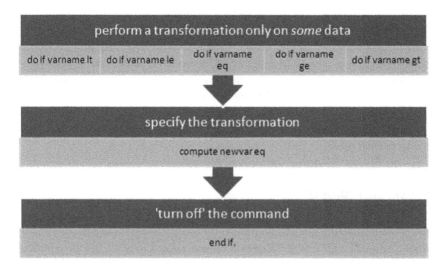

Figure 17.20 Using "do if", "end if" function.

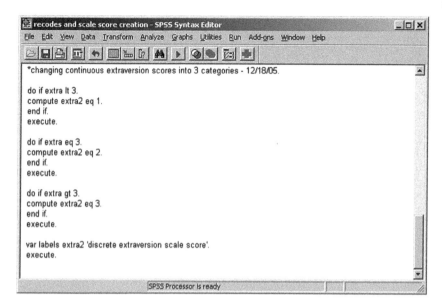

Figure 17.21 Syntax for "do if, "end if" commands – trichotomizing extraversion.

Figure 17.21 shows the syntax. Trichotomizing extraversion with these commands is pretty easy.

It is best to learn the "do if", "end if" commands this way, through using separate four-line commands for each possible "if". Notice that we used the "lt" and "gt" commands – any score less than 3 (i.e. 2.9999 or 2.99999999999) is covered. Just like "split file", the "do if" statement is a light-switch command. You need to remember to turn off the conditional statement by specifying the "end if".

When you get a little more familiar with the "do if", "end if"'s, you can throw a few "else if" commands in there, as shown in Figure 17.22 (this makes your syntax a bit more efficient, but is not necessary).

Appendix D contains an example syntax file that incorporates multiple "advanced-level" data manipulations– we've annotated the file so you should be able to follow along with the procedures. There are many other useful commands that haven't been covered in this book, but if this type of book gets too long, it somewhat defeats the purpose. We've included some of these "also useful" commands along with the commands actually used in the book in Appendix E. It's our hope that at this point you have enough exposure to feel comfortable using SPSS through keeping syntax diaries.

Remember, the main point of this book is to get you used to operating SPSS through the specification of syntax files – never use the Data Editor when doing

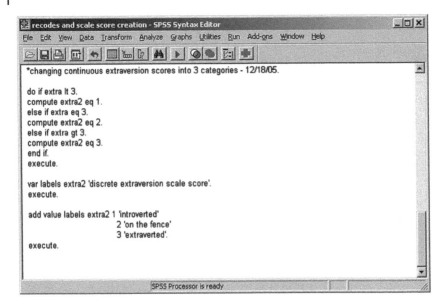

Figure 17.22 Syntax for "else if" command – trichotomizing extraversion.

data manipulations or analyses. The first file you should access *every time* you use SPSS is a syntax file.

Use syntax.
End if.
Execute.

Summary

You can use Notepad to make your monotonous syntax writing a lot more efficient. Develop skill with Notepad and you will benefit within SPSS. If you want to do operations or manipulations across rows, you can either transpose or aggregate the data file. One practical application of aggregating is to "get rid" of duplicate cases. One useful manipulation command that can be used in many different applications is "do if". Using all of the manipulation commands listed in this book, there should be no data manipulation problems that are beyond your capability.

Key Terms

"Aggregate" – SPSS command to collapse across rows; if you use aggregate, you must specify a new outfile name.

CASE_LBL – SPSS creates this variable when you transpose your matrix; old variable names are kept in this SPSS-generated string variable.

"Do if" – Command that tells SPSS there are conditions to be met prior to any transformation or analysis; must be accompanied by an "end if".

Duplicate cases – The same information (from the same person) is repeated within the data file (e.g. two "rows" of information contain identical information).

"Else if" – Optional command to use in a "do if", "end if" sequence.

"End if" – Command that notifies SPSS that your conditional statement has been completed; each "do if" must be followed (eventually) by an "end if".

First – Subcommand to the aggregate function. Many more subcommands can be specified; "first" is useful for deleting duplicate cases.

"Flip" – SPSS command to perform a matrix transposition.

Matrix transposition – Turning columns into rows and rows into columns; flipping a matrix along its diagonal.

Notepad – Standard, simplified PC word processor, very useful for monotonous or repetitive syntax commands.

To – Shortcut word to be used in various syntax commands; you can specify a range of variables by using the "to" command (instead of specifying each individual variable).

Discussion Questions

1   Why can't I do the Notepad Find and Replace function in my syntax file?

2   When would I use the "aggregate" function?

Appendix A

Completed Questionnaire Form Example

IBM SPSS Essentials: Managing and Analyzing Social Sciences Data, Second Edition.
John Kulas, Renata Garcia Prieto Palacios Roji, and Adam Smith.
© 2021 John Wiley & Sons, Inc. Published 2021 by John Wiley & Sons, Inc.

34

Please indicate your gender: Male   Female

On the following pages, there are phrases describing people's behaviors. Please use the rating scale below to describe how accurately each statement describes *you*. Describe yourself as you generally are now, not as you wish to be in the future. Describe yourself as you honestly see yourself, in relation to other people you know of the same sex as you are, and roughly your same age. So that you can describe yourself in an honest manner, your responses will be kept in absolute confidence. Please read each statement carefully, and then indicate to what extent you agree or disagree with each of the statements using the following scale:

SD	D	N	A	SA
Strongly Disagree	Disagree	Neither Agree Nor Disagree	Agree	Strongly Agree

1. Am the life of the party.	SD	(D)	N	A	SA
2. Insult people.	SD	D	N	(A)	SA
3. Am always prepared.	SD	D	N	A	(SA)
4. Get stressed out easily.	SD	D	(N)	A	SA
5. Have a rich vocabulary.	SD	(D)	N	A	SA
6. Often feel uncomfortable around others.	SD	D	(N)	A	SA
7. Am interested in people.	SD	D	N	(A)	SA
8. Leave my belongings around.	SD	D	N	(A)	SA
9. Am relaxed most of the time.	SD	D	N	(A)	SA
10. Have difficulty understanding abstract ideas.	SD	(D)	N	A	SA
11. Feel comfortable around people.	(SD)	D	N	A	SA
12. Am not interested in other people's problems.	SD	(D)	N	A	SA
13. Pay attention to details.	SD	D	N	(A)	SA
14. Worry about things.	SD	D	N	A	(SA)
15. Have a vivid imagination.	SD	D	N	A	(SA)
16. Keep in the background.	SD	D	N	(A)	SA
17. Sympathize with others' feelings.	SD	(D)	N	A	SA
18. Make a mess of things.	SD	D	(N)	A	SA
19. Seldom feel blue.	SD	(D)	N	A	SA
20. Am not interested in abstract ideas.	(SD)	D	N	A	SA
21. Start conversations.	SD	D	(N)	A	SA

22. Feel little concern for others.	SD	D	N	A	**(SA)**
23. Get chores done right away.	SD	D	**(N)**	A	SA
24. Am easily disturbed.	SD	**(D)**	N	A	SA
25. Have excellent ideas.	SD	D	N	**(A)**	SA
26. Have little to say.	SD	D	**(N)**	A	SA
27. Have a soft heart.	SD	D	**(N)**	A	SA
28. Often forget to put things back in their proper place.	SD	D	N	**(A)**	SA
29. Am not easily bothered by things.	SD	D	N	**(A)**	SA
30. Do not have a good imagination.	SD	D	N	**(A)**	SA
31. Talk to a lot of different people at parties.	SD	**(D)**	N	A	SA
32. Am not really interested in others.	SD	**(D)**	N	A	SA
33. Like order.	SD	D	**(N)**	A	SA
34. Get upset easily.	SD	D	N	A	**(SA)**
35. Am quick to understand things.	**(SD)**	D	N	A	SA
36. Don't like to draw attention to myself.	**(SD)**	D	N	A	SA
37. Take time out for others.	SD	D	N	**(A)**	SA
38. Shirk my duties.	SD	D	**(N)**	A	SA
39. Rarely get irritated.	SD	**(D)**	N	A	SA
40. Try to avoid complex people.	SD	**(D)**	N	A	SA
41. Don't mind being the center of attention.	SD	**(D)**	N	A	SA
42. Am hard to get to know.	SD	D	**(N)**	A	SA
43. Follow a schedule.	SD	D	N	**(A)**	SA
44. Change my mood a lot.	SD	D	**(N)**	A	SA
45. Use difficult words.	SD	D	**(N)**	A	SA
46. Am quiet around strangers.	SD	D	N	**(A)**	SA
47. Feel others' emotions.	SD	D	N	**(A)**	SA
48. Neglect my duties.	SD	D	N	**(A)**	SA
49. Seldom get mad.	SD	D	**(N)**	A	SA
50. Have difficulty imagining things.	SD	**(D)**	N	A	SA
51. Make friends easily.	**(SD)**	D	N	A	SA
52. Am indifferent to the feelings of others.	**(SD)**	D	N	A	SA

53. Am exacting in my work.	(SD)	D	N	A	SA
54. Have frequent mood swings.	SD	D	(N)	A	SA
55. Spend time reflecting on things.	SD	D	(N)	A	SA
56. Find it difficult to approach others.	SD	(D)	N	A	SA
57. Make people feel at ease.	SD	(D)	N	A	SA
58. Waste my time.	SD	D	N	(A)	SA
59. Get irritated easily.	SD	D	N	(A)	SA
60. Avoid difficult reading material.	SD	D	(N)	A	SA
61. Take charge.	SD	D	(N)	A	SA
62. Inquire about others' well-being.	(SD)	D	N	A	SA
63. Do things according to a plan.	(SD)	D	N	A	SA
64. Often feel blue.	SD	D	(N)	A	SA
65. Am full of ideas.	SD	D	N	(A)	SA
66. Don't talk a lot.	SD	D	N	(A)	SA
67. Know how to comfort others.	SD	D	N	A	(SA)
68. Do things in a half-way manner.	SD	D	N	(A)	SA
69. Get angry easily.	SD	D	(N)	A	SA
70. Will not probe deeply into a subject.	SD	(D)	N	A	SA
71. Know how to captivate people.	SD	D	(N)	A	SA
72. Love children.	SD	(D)	N	A	SA
73. Continue until everything is perfect.	(SD)	D	N	A	SA
74. Panic easily.	(SD)	D	N	A	SA
75. Carry the conversation to a higher level.	SD	(D)	N	A	SA
76. Bottle up my feelings.	SD	(D)	N	A	SA
77. Am on good terms with nearly everyone.	SD	D	N	(A)	SA
78. Find it difficult to get down to work.	SD	D	N	(A)	SA
79. Feel threatened easily.	SD	D	N	A	(SA)
80. Catch on to things quickly.	SD	D	N	(A)	SA
81. Feel at ease with people.	SD	D	N	(A)	SA
82. Have a good word for everyone.	SD	D	(N)	A	SA
83. Make plans and stick to them.	SD	(D)	N	A	SA

84. Get overwhelmed by emotions.	(SD)	D	N	A	SA
85. Can handle a lot of information.	(SD)	D	N	A	SA
86. Am a very private person.	SD	D	(N)	A	SA
87. Show my gratitude.	SD	(D)	N	A	SA
88. Leave a mess in my room.	SD	(D)	N	A	SA
89. Take offense easily.	SD	D	(N)	A	SA
90. Am good at many things.	SD	D	(N)	A	SA
91. Wait for others to lead the way.	SD	D	N	(A)	SA
92. Think of others first.	SD	D	N	A	(SA)
93. Love order and regularity.	SD	D	(N)	A	SA
94. Get caught up in my problems.	SD	(D)	N	A	SA
95. Love to read challenging material.	SD	(D)	N	A	SA
96. Am skilled in handling social situations.	SD	D	(N)	A	SA
97. Love to help others.	SD	D	N	(A)	SA
98. Like to tidy up.	(SD)	D	N	A	SA
99. Grumble about things.	SD	D	N	A	(SA)
100. Love to think up new ways of doing things.	SD	D	N	(A)	SA

Appendix B

Example Code Sheet for Questionnaire

IBM SPSS Essentials: Managing and Analyzing Social Sciences Data, Second Edition.
John Kulas, Renata Garcia Prieto Palacios Roji, and Adam Smith.

gender

Casenum

Please indicate your gender: Male 1   Female 2

On the following pages, there are phrases describing people's behaviors. Please use the rating scale below to describe how accurately each statement describes *you*. Describe yourself as you generally are now, not as you wish to be in the future. Describe yourself as you honestly see yourself, in relation to other people you know of the same sex as you are, and roughly your same age. So that you can describe yourself in an honest manner, your responses will be kept in absolute confidence. Please read each statement carefully, and then indicate to what extent you agree or disagree with each of the statements using the following scale:

SD	D	N	A	SA
Strongly Disagree	Disagree	Neither Agree Nor Disagree	Agree	Strongly Agree

item 1

	1	2	3	4	5
1. Am the life of the party.	SD	D	N	A	SA
2. Insult people.	SD	D	N	A	SA
3. Am always prepared.	SD	D	N	A	SA
4. Get stressed out easily.	SD	D	N	A	SA
5. Have a rich vocabulary.	SD	D	N	A	SA
6. Often feel uncomfortable around others.	SD	D	N	A	SA
7. Am interested in people.	SD	D	N	A	SA
8. Leave my belongings around.	SD	D	N	A	SA
9. Am relaxed most of the time.	SD	D	N	A	SA
10. Have difficulty understanding abstract ideas.	SD	D	N	A	SA
11. Feel comfortable around people.	SD	D	N	A	SA
12. Am not interested in other people's problems.	SD	D	N	A	SA
13. Pay attention to details.	SD	D	N	A	SA
14. Worry about things.	SD	D	N	A	SA
15. Have a vivid imagination.	SD	D	N	A	SA
16. Keep in the background.	SD	D	N	A	SA
17. Sympathize with others' feelings.	SD	D	N	A	SA
18. Make a mess of things.	SD	D	N	A	SA
19. Seldom feel blue.	SD	D	N	A	SA
20. Am not interested in abstract ideas.	SD	D	N	A	SA
21. Start conversations.	SD	D	N	A	SA

item 21

Item 22

		1	2	3	4	8
22.	Feel little concern for others.	SD	D	N	A	SA
23.	Get chores done right away.	SD	D	N	A	SA
24.	Am easily disturbed.	SD	D	N	A	SA
25.	Have excellent ideas.	SD	D	N	A	SA
26.	Have little to say.	SD	D	N	A	SA
27.	Have a soft heart.	SD	D	N	A	SA
28.	Often forget to put things back in their proper place.	SD	D	N	A	SA
29.	Am not easily bothered by things.	SD	D	N	A	SA
30.	Do not have a good imagination.	SD	D	N	A	SA
31.	Talk to a lot of different people at parties.	SD	D	N	A	SA
32.	Am not really interested in others.	SD	D	N	A	SA
33.	Like order.	SD	D	N	A	SA
34.	Get upset easily.	SD	D	N	A	SA
35.	Am quick to understand things.	SD	D	N	A	SA
36.	Don't like to draw attention to myself.	SD	D	N	A	SA
37.	Take time out for others.	SD	D	N	A	SA
38.	Shirk my duties.	SD	D	N	A	SA
39.	Rarely get irritated.	SD	D	N	A	SA
40.	Try to avoid complex people.	SD	D	N	A	SA
41.	Don't mind being the center of attention.	SD	D	N	A	SA
42.	Am hard to get to know.	SD	D	N	A	SA
43.	Follow a schedule.	SD	D	N	A	SA
44.	Change my mood a lot.	SD	D	N	A	SA
45.	Use difficult words.	SD	D	N	A	SA
46.	Am quiet around strangers.	SD	D	N	A	SA
47.	Feel others' emotions.	SD	D	N	A	SA
48.	Neglect my duties.	SD	D	N	A	SA
49.	Seldom get mad.	SD	D	N	A	SA
50.	Have difficulty imagining things.	SD	D	N	A	SA
51.	Make friends easily.	SD	D	N	A	SA
52.	Am indifferent to the feelings of others.	SD	D	N	A	SA

Item 52

Item 53

		1	2	3	4	5
53.	Am exacting in my work.	SD	D	N	A	SA
54.	Have frequent mood swings.	SD	D	N	A	SA
55.	Spend time reflecting on things.	SD	D	N	A	SA
56.	Find it difficult to approach others.	SD	D	N	A	SA
57.	Make people feel at ease.	SD	D	N	A	SA
58.	Waste my time.	SD	D	N	A	SA
59.	Get irritated easily.	SD	D	N	A	SA
60.	Avoid difficult reading material.	SD	D	N	A	SA
61.	Take charge.	SD	D	N	A	SA
62.	Inquire about others' well-being.	SD	D	N	A	SA
63.	Do things according to a plan.	SD	D	N	A	SA
64.	Often feel blue.	SD	D	N	A	SA
65.	Am full of ideas.	SD	D	N	A	SA
66.	Don't talk a lot.	SD	D	N	A	SA
67.	Know how to comfort others.	SD	D	N	A	SA
68.	Do things in a half-way manner.	SD	D	N	A	SA
69.	Get angry easily.	SD	D	N	A	SA
70.	Will not probe deeply into a subject.	SD	D	N	A	SA
71.	Know how to captivate people.	SD	D	N	A	SA
72.	Love children.	SD	D	N	A	SA
73.	Continue until everything is perfect.	SD	D	N	A	SA
74.	Panic easily.	SD	D	N	A	SA
75.	Carry the conversation to a higher level.	SD	D	N	A	SA
76.	Bottle up my feelings.	SD	D	N	A	SA
77.	Am on good terms with nearly everyone.	SD	D	N	A	SA
78.	Find it difficult to get down to work.	SD	D	N	A	SA
79.	Feel threatened easily.	SD	D	N	A	SA
80.	Catch on to things quickly.	SD	D	N	A	SA
81.	Feel at ease with people.	SD	D	N	A	SA
82.	Have a good word for everyone.	SD	D	N	A	SA
83.	Make plans and stick to them.	SD	D	N	A	SA

Item 83

item 84

	1	2	3	4	5
84. Get overwhelmed by emotions.	SD	D	N	A	SA
85. Can handle a lot of information.	SD	D	N	A	SA
86. Am a very private person.	SD	D	N	A	SA
87. Show my gratitude.	SD	D	N	A	SA
88. Leave a mess in my room.	SD	D	N	A	SA
89. Take offense easily.	SD	D	N	A	SA
90. Am good at many things.	SD	D	N	A	SA
91. Wait for others to lead the way.	SD	D	N	A	SA
92. Think of others first.	SD	D	N	A	SA
93. Love order and regularity.	SD	D	N	A	SA
94. Get caught up in my problems.	SD	D	N	A	SA
95. Love to read challenging material.	SD	D	N	A	SA
96. Am skilled in handling social situations.	SD	D	N	A	SA
97. Love to help others.	SD	D	N	A	SA
98. Like to tidy up.	SD	D	N	A	SA
99. Grumble about things.	SD	D	N	A	SA
100. Love to think up new ways of doing things.	SD	D	N	A	SA

item 100

Appendix C

Summary of Creating and Defining a Data File

1. Determine what information should be stored as words (usually not much) and what information should be stored as numbers (the majority of your information).
2. Develop a "code sheet" identifying how your information will look in SPSS.
3. Activate SPSS and immediately open a "new syntax file" as shown in Figure C.1.
4. Specify your code-sheet variables in your new syntax file (these will create your empty [but defined] data file) as shown in Figure C.2.
5. Save your syntax file within your organized file system as shown in Figure C.3.
6. Add your variable and value labels as shown in Figures C.4 and C.5.
7. Save your empty data file within your organized file system as shown in Figure C.6.
8. Select all (Ctrl+A) as shown in Figure C.7 and run (with the Play button) your syntax to create an empty (but defined) data file.
9. Enter data into your empty but defined data shell as shown in Figure C.8.
10. Go ahead and save your data file after you've entered data into the empty cells (*this is the only time you'll save a data file without doing it within a syntax file – when you have physically entered data*).

IBM SPSS Essentials: Managing and Analyzing Social Sciences Data, Second Edition.
John Kulas, Renata Garcia Prieto Palacios Roji, and Adam Smith.
© 2021 John Wiley & Sons, Inc. Published 2021 by John Wiley & Sons, Inc.

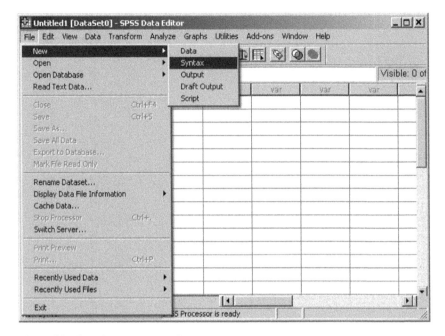

Figure C.1   Opening new syntax file.

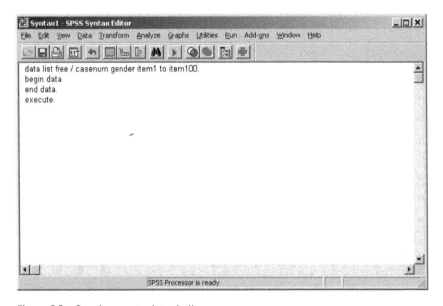

Figure C.2   Creating empty data shell.

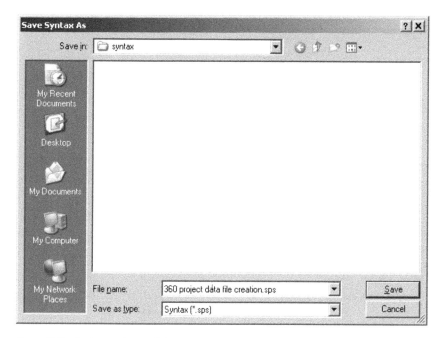

Figure C.3 Saving syntax script.

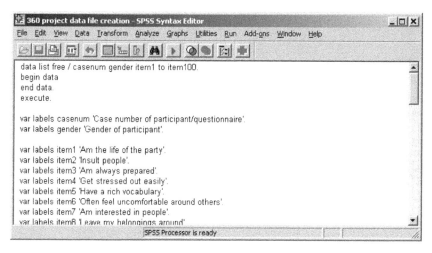

Figure C.4 Adding variable labels.

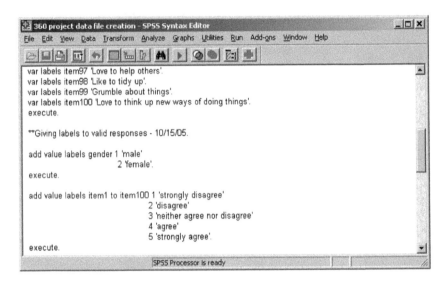

Figure C.5 Adding value labels.

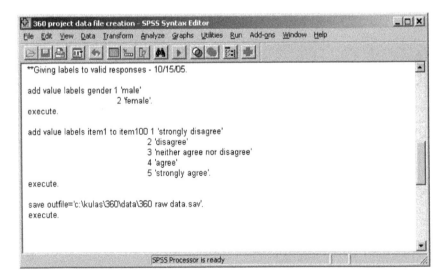

Figure C.6 Saving data shell.

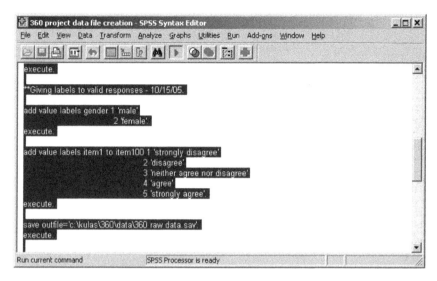

Figure C.7   Activating and running syntax.

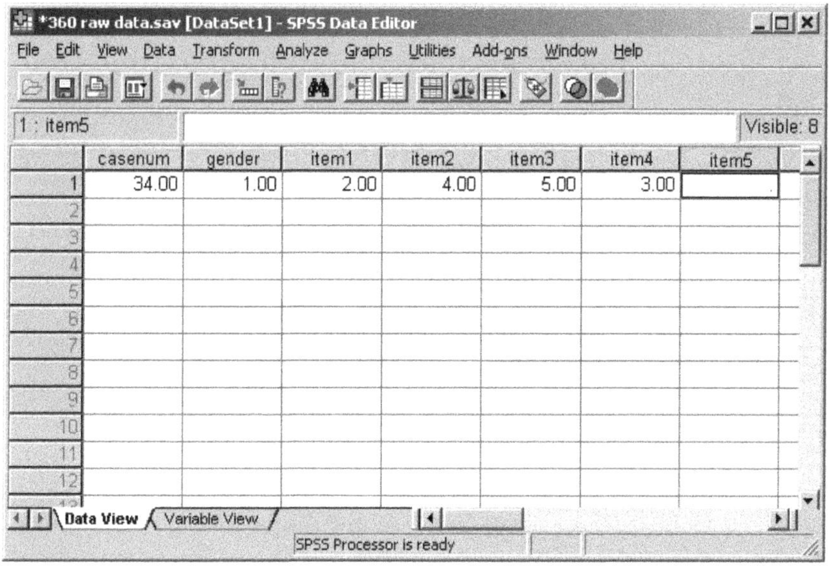

Figure C.8   Entering data via the data editor.

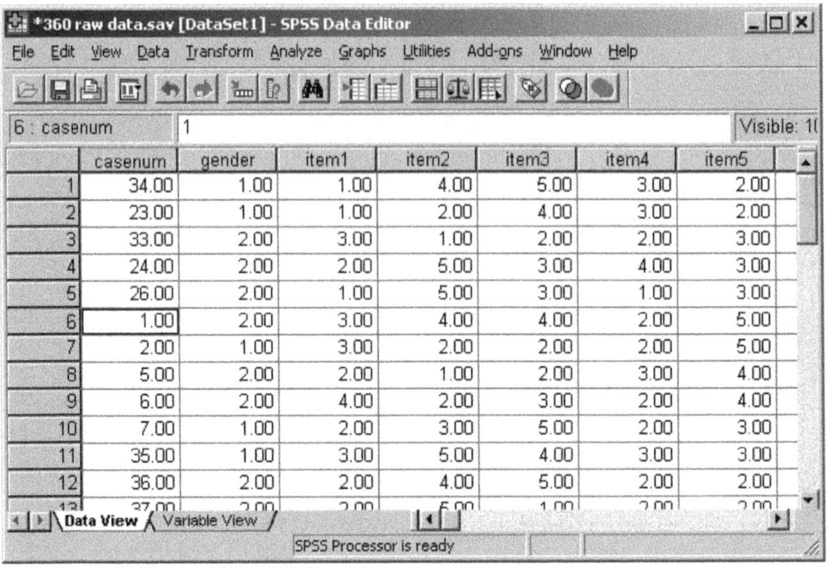

Figure C.9   Saving raw data.

Appendix D

Example Syntax File Integrating Multiple Commands (Fulfilling Multiple Purposes)

The following example demonstrates how to combine two initially separate (and quite different) datasets. One dataset contains employee personality information; the other contains performance ratings from employees' supervisors, subordinates, and peers. In the personality dataset, each row represents one rated employee. The performance rating file contains several rows per rated employee (the different rows reflect supervisor, subordinate, or peer ratings of the rated employee). Additionally, these performance rating files typically contain different numbers of raters per rated individual. The goal of the syntax is to create a new data file in which one row contains (1) employee personality information, (2) one supervisor rating, (3) one peer rating, and (4) one subordinate rating. To start this example, we bring up the employee personality information, as shown in Figure D.1.

This brings up the original data file (personality.sav) and saves it as an ordered and sorted file (sorted personality.sav), as shown in Figure D.2.

Next, we grab the performance file and do the same sort procedure, as shown in Figure D.3.

IBM SPSS Essentials: Managing and Analyzing Social Sciences Data, Second Edition.
John Kulas, Renata Garcia Prieto Palacios Roji, and Adam Smith.
© 2021 John Wiley & Sons, Inc. Published 2021 by John Wiley & Sons, Inc.

```
**combining personality and performance rating files with one sup, one sub, and one peer - 9/29/06.

get file='c:\kulas\360\data\personality.sav'.
execute.

**sorting the file by casenumber so I can later match with performance data.

sort cases by casenum(a).
execute.

save outfile='c:\kulas\360\data\sorted personality.sav'.
execute.
```

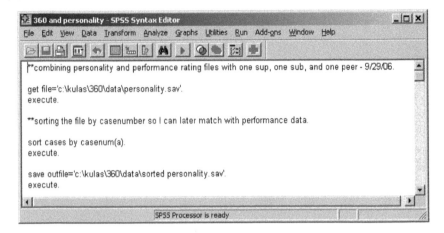

Figure D.1 Retrieve, sort, and save the personality data.

	casenum	open	cons	extra	agree	neuro
1	1234.00	2.54	2.65	2.11	4.84	2.54
2	1235.00	1.55	1.54	2.11	3.55	2.65
3	1253.00	4.52	3.55	3.12	2.10	2.11
4	1645.00	1.64	4.55	4.52	1.22	3.42
5	2135.00	3.42	3.42	1.22	3.42	1.54
6	2153.00	3.55	2.11	1.44	3.42	3.84
7	2164.00	3.12	2.00	3.55	4.22	1.22
8	2213.00	1.22	4.54	3.42	3.22	1.33
9	3151.00	2.52	3.55	2.65	4.52	3.42
10	4651.00	2.65	2.54	3.12	4.54	1.44
11	6512.00	2.11	2.65	1.55	3.12	3.55
12	6554.00	4.03	2.01	2.65	2.54	2.55
13	6845.00	4.65	4.52	3.55	2.11	1.55

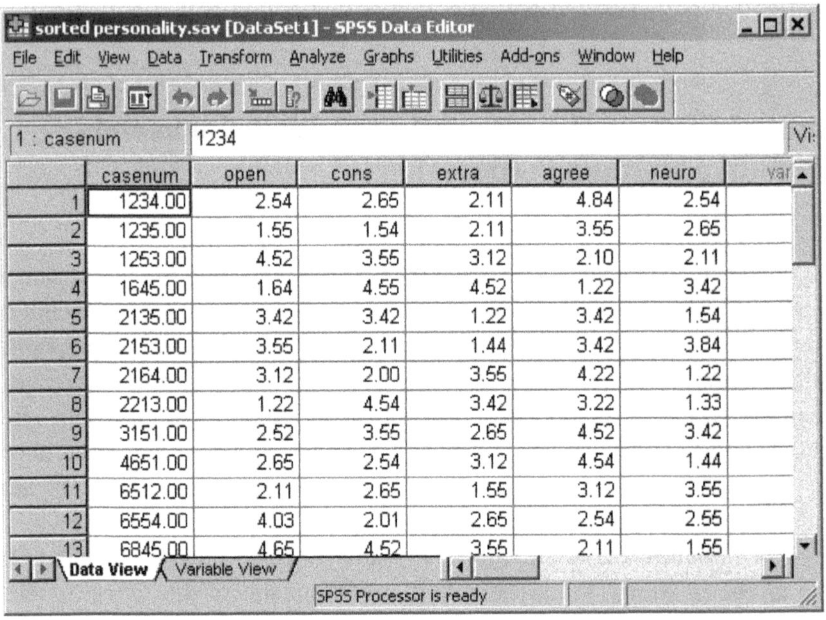

Figure D.2 Personality data file.

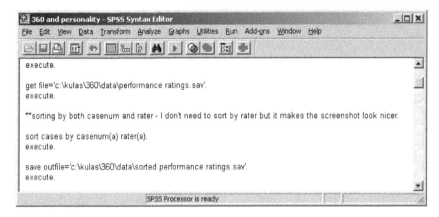

Figure D.3 Retrieve, sort, and save the performance rating data.

	casenum	rater	perf_1	perf_2	perf_3
1	1234.00	self	1.00	2.00	1.00
2	1234.00	subordinate	5.00	5.00	5.00
3	1234.00	subordinate	1.00	2.00	1.00
4	1234.00	subordinate	1.00	2.00	1.00
5	1234.00	subordinate	5.00	5.00	5.00
6	1234.00	subordinate	1.00	2.00	1.00
7	1234.00	peer	3.00	3.00	3.00
8	1234.00	peer	3.00	3.00	3.00
9	1234.00	peer	3.00	3.00	3.00
10	1234.00	peer	3.00	3.00	3.00
11	1234.00	peer	3.00	3.00	3.00
12	1234.00	supervisor	1.00	2.00	1.00
13	1234.00	supervisor	5.00	5.00	5.00
14	1235.00	self	2.00	2.00	3.00
15	1235.00	subordinate	4.00	4.00	4.00
16	1235.00	subordinate	2.00	2.00	3.00

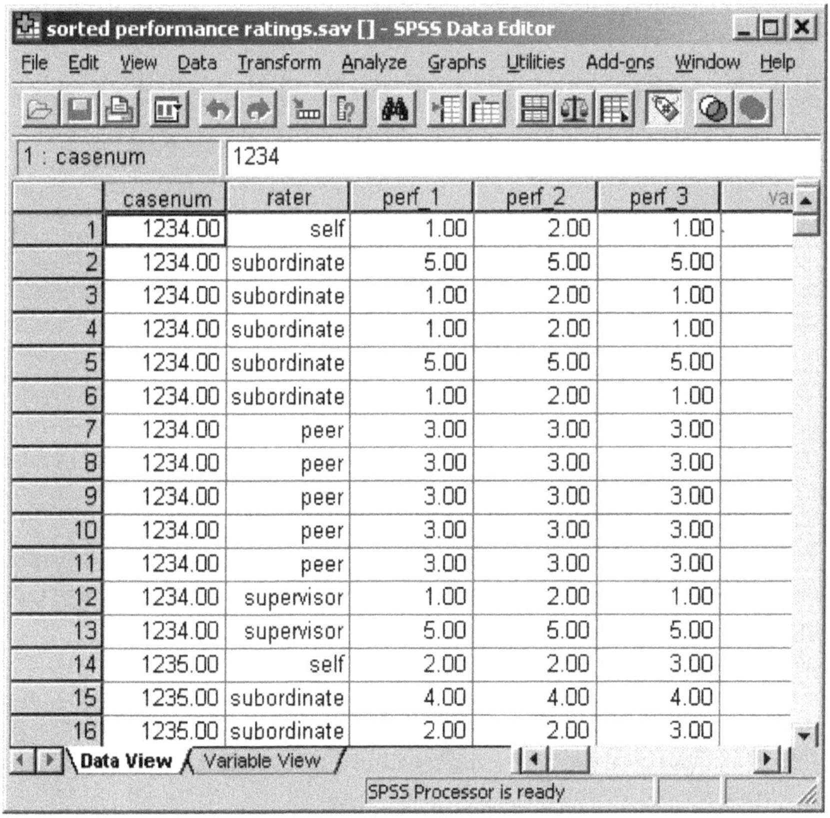

Figure D.4 Performance rating data file (value labels shown).

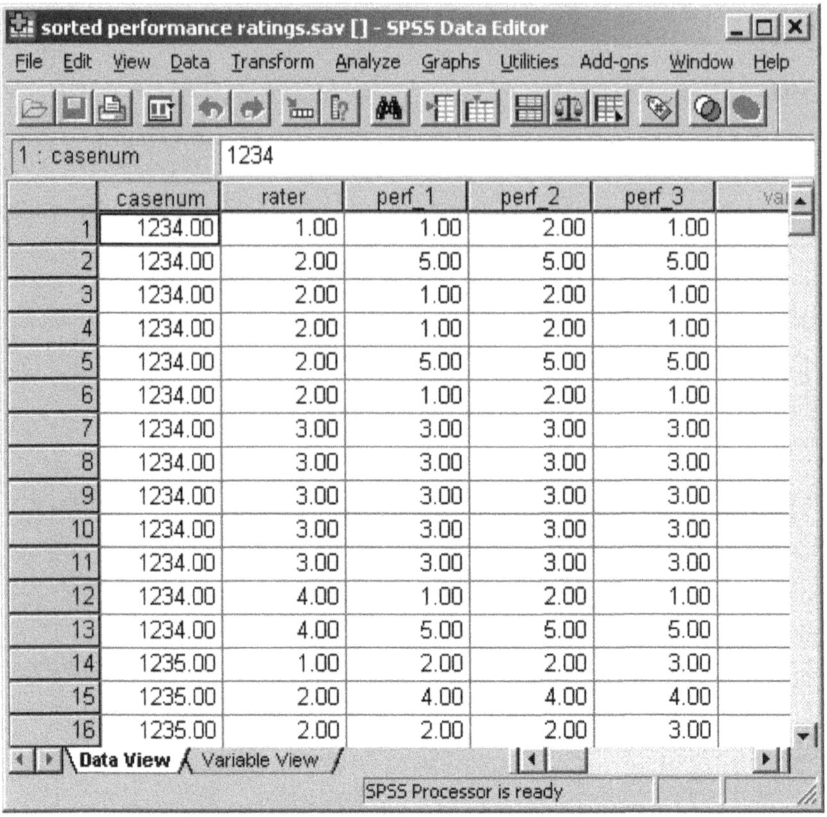

	casenum	rater	perf_1	perf_2	perf_3	var
1	1234.00	1.00	1.00	2.00	1.00	
2	1234.00	2.00	5.00	5.00	5.00	
3	1234.00	2.00	1.00	2.00	1.00	
4	1234.00	2.00	1.00	2.00	1.00	
5	1234.00	2.00	5.00	5.00	5.00	
6	1234.00	2.00	1.00	2.00	1.00	
7	1234.00	3.00	3.00	3.00	3.00	
8	1234.00	3.00	3.00	3.00	3.00	
9	1234.00	3.00	3.00	3.00	3.00	
10	1234.00	3.00	3.00	3.00	3.00	
11	1234.00	3.00	3.00	3.00	3.00	
12	1234.00	4.00	1.00	2.00	1.00	
13	1234.00	4.00	5.00	5.00	5.00	
14	1235.00	1.00	2.00	2.00	3.00	
15	1235.00	2.00	4.00	4.00	4.00	
16	1235.00	2.00	2.00	2.00	3.00	

Figure D.5 Performance rating data file (value labels hidden).

The performance rating file has three performance rating items, as well as rater and ratee (that is, casenum) information. Figure D.4 shows the result.

Figure D.5 shows the result with the Value Labels function off.

Prior to combining the two files, we need to select one subordinate, one supervisor, and one peer for each rated individual. First, we create data files with only subordinates, supervisors, and peers, as shown in Figure D.6.

Within each of these three data files (sorted subordinates, sorted peers, and sorted supervisors), we now need to "count" the number of raters per rated individual (number the raters within each rated employee) (Figure D.7).

This command creates a new column within our supervisor data file, as shown in Figure D.8.

Now we can save each supervisor, subordinate, and peer file with either one or two raters per rated individual. To later combine the files, however, we'll need to

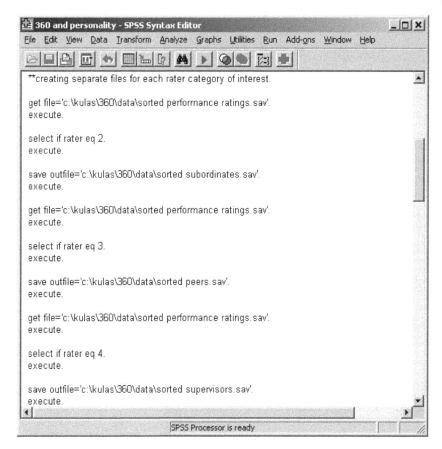

Figure D.6 Creating performance rating data files each containing only subordinates, supervisors, or peers.

rename the variables (other than casenum – we're going to use casenum to match files, so this variable needs the same name across files), as shown in Figure D.9.

The new data file has one supervisor rating per rated individual; we dropped the "rater" variable because we identified who is doing the rating in the new performance rating names (sup_1, sup_2, and sup_3), as shown in Figure D.10.

The syntax to repeat this with the subordinate and peer files is shown in Figures D.11 and D.12.

Now we have four files ready to be combined. First, as shown in Figure D.13, we call up our original personality file and then add each "other" rating file separately.

```
save outfile='c:\kulas\360\data\sorted supervisors.sav'.
execute.

**now numbering each rater category within each casenum.

get file='c:\kulas\360\data\sorted supervisors.sav'.
execute.

do if $casenum=1.
compute num_sup=1.
else.
compute num_sup=(lag(casenum)=casenum)*lag(num_sup)+1.
end if.
execute.
```

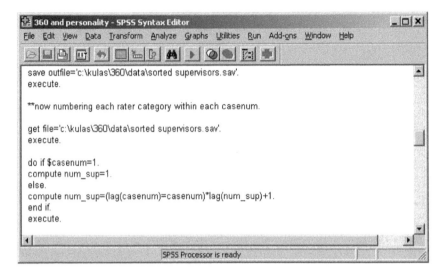

Figure D.7 Asking SPSS to number each supervisor within rated individuals.

	casenum	rater	perf_1	perf_2	perf_3	num_sup
1	1234.00	4.00	1.00	2.00	1.00	1.00
2	1234.00	4.00	5.00	5.00	5.00	2.00
3	1235.00	4.00	2.00	2.00	3.00	1.00
4	1235.00	4.00	4.00	4.00	4.00	2.00
5	1253.00	4.00	4.00	4.00	5.00	1.00
6	1253.00	4.00	1.00	2.00	2.00	2.00
7	1645.00	4.00	5.00	5.00	5.00	1.00
8	2135.00	4.00	5.00	5.00	5.00	1.00
9	2135.00	4.00	1.00	2.00	3.00	2.00
10	2135.00	4.00	5.00	5.00	5.00	3.00
11	2135.00	4.00	5.00	5.00	5.00	4.00
12	2135.00	4.00	5.00	5.00	5.00	5.00
13	2153.00	4.00	4.00	4.00	4.00	1.00
14	2153.00	4.00	3.00	3.00	3.00	2.00
15	2153.00	4.00	4.00	4.00	4.00	3.00

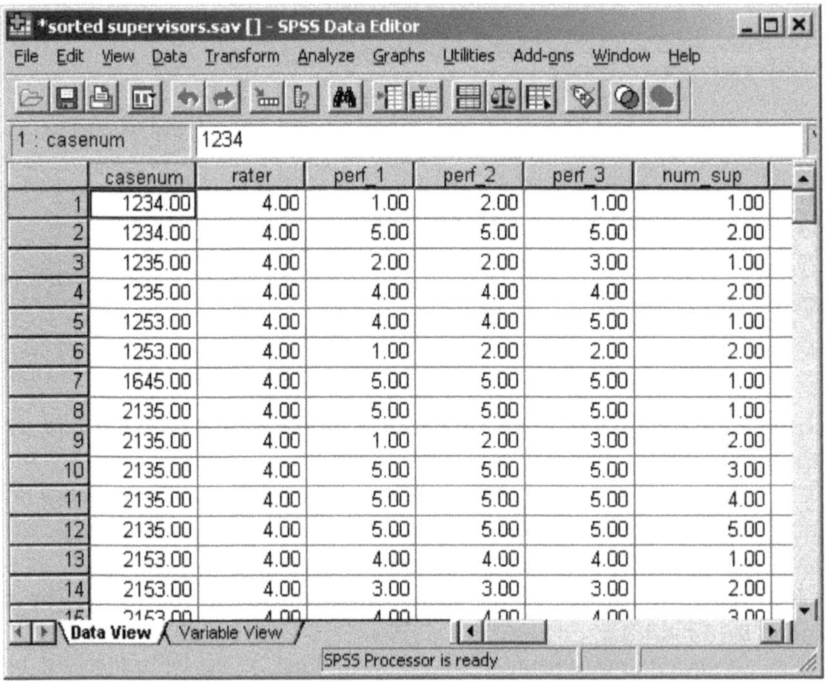

Figure D.8 Supervisor performance ratings with different supervisors identified.

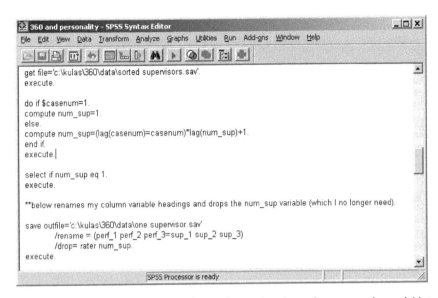

Figure D.9 Selecting the first supervisor and renaming the performance rating variables.

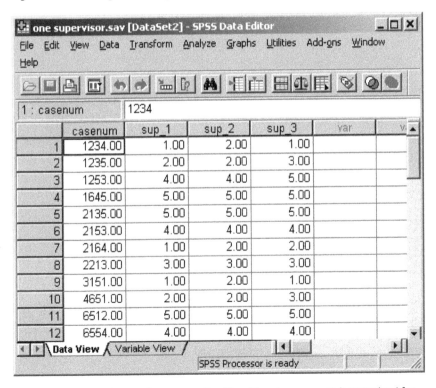

Figure D.10 Supervisor performance rating file with only one supervisor retained for each rated individual.

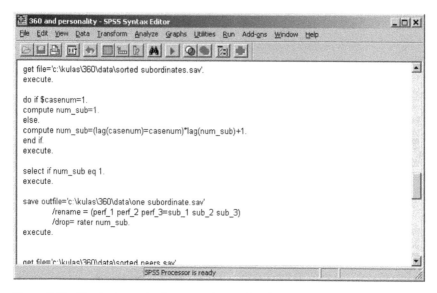

Figure D.11 Numbering, selecting, renaming, and saving one subordinate rating per rated individual.

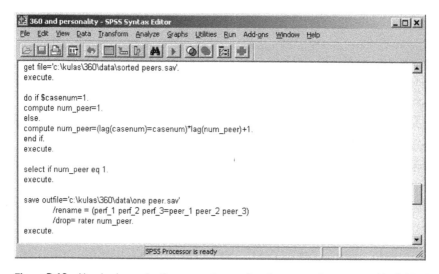

Figure D.12 Numbering, selecting, renaming, and saving one rating per rated individual.

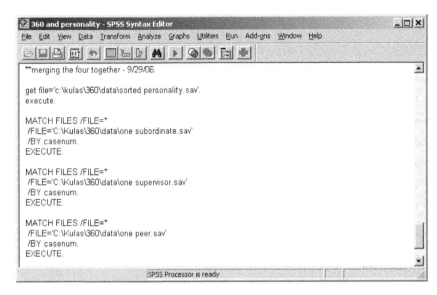

Figure D.13 Retrieving the rated individual data file and adding one subordinate, one supervisor, and one peer rating to each rated individual.

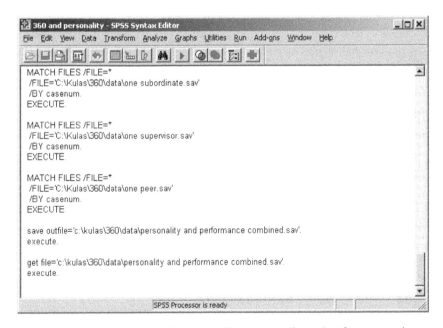

Figure D.14 Saving and retrieving the combined personality and performance rating data file.

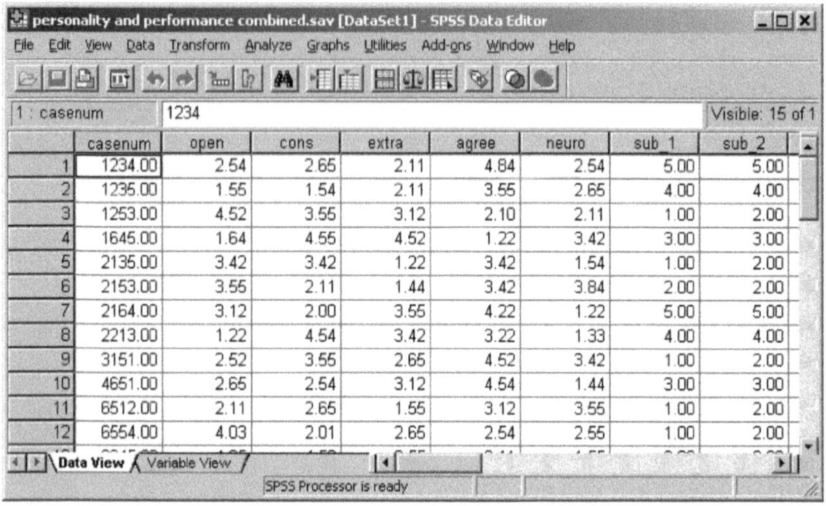

	casenum	open	cons	extra	agree	neuro	sub_1	sub_2
1	1234.00	2.54	2.65	2.11	4.84	2.54	5.00	5.00
2	1235.00	1.55	1.54	2.11	3.55	2.65	4.00	4.00
3	1253.00	4.52	3.55	3.12	2.10	2.11	1.00	2.00
4	1645.00	1.64	4.55	4.52	1.22	3.42	3.00	3.00
5	2135.00	3.42	3.42	1.22	3.42	1.54	1.00	2.00
6	2153.00	3.55	2.11	1.44	3.42	3.84	2.00	2.00
7	2164.00	3.12	2.00	3.55	4.22	1.22	5.00	5.00
8	2213.00	1.22	4.54	3.42	3.22	1.33	4.00	4.00
9	3151.00	2.52	3.55	2.65	4.52	3.42	1.00	2.00
10	4651.00	2.65	2.54	3.12	4.54	1.44	3.00	3.00
11	6512.00	2.11	2.65	1.55	3.12	3.55	1.00	2.00
12	6554.00	4.03	2.01	2.65	2.54	2.55	1.00	2.00

Figure D.15 Combined data file (first few variables shown).

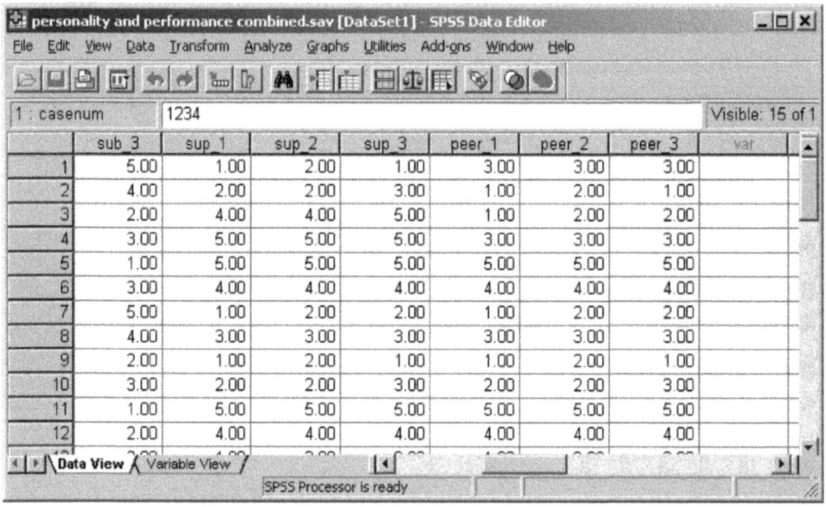

	sub_3	sup_1	sup_2	sup_3	peer_1	peer_2	peer_3	var
1	5.00	1.00	2.00	1.00	3.00	3.00	3.00	
2	4.00	2.00	2.00	3.00	1.00	2.00	1.00	
3	2.00	4.00	4.00	5.00	1.00	2.00	2.00	
4	3.00	5.00	5.00	5.00	3.00	3.00	3.00	
5	1.00	5.00	5.00	5.00	5.00	5.00	5.00	
6	3.00	4.00	4.00	4.00	4.00	4.00	4.00	
7	5.00	1.00	2.00	2.00	1.00	2.00	2.00	
8	4.00	3.00	3.00	3.00	3.00	3.00	3.00	
9	2.00	1.00	2.00	1.00	1.00	2.00	1.00	
10	3.00	2.00	2.00	3.00	2.00	2.00	3.00	
11	1.00	5.00	5.00	5.00	5.00	5.00	5.00	
12	2.00	4.00	4.00	4.00	4.00	4.00	4.00	

Figure D.16 Combined data file (more variables).

Now we save the new file and take a look. Figures D.14 and D.15 show the results. Figure D.16 shows the view after scrolling to the right.

There are alternatives to this method, but if you can get in the habit of compulsively using "get file" and "save outfile" commands, you can pretty much apply this general procedure to any major manipulation you wish to accomplish.

Appendix E

Commands To Know, Organized By Importance

The following essential SPSS syntax terms (ones you should know how to use) are organized by their importance.

IBM SPSS Essentials: Managing and Analyzing Social Sciences Data, Second Edition.
John Kulas, Renata Garcia Prieto Palacios Roji, and Adam Smith.

Command	Importance	Pages (or explanation)
get file	Very, very important	[insert pg. 36]
save outfile		[insert pg. 33]
compute		[insert pg. 156]
eq, gt, lt, ge, le		[insert pg. 160]
recode		[insert pg. 156]
descriptives		[insert pg. 65]
frequencies		[insert pg. 60]
var labels		[insert pg. 51]
add value labels		[insert pg. 52]
match files		[insert pg. 172]
add files		[insert pg. 175]
sort cases		[insert pg. 171]
split file		[insert pg. 184]
do if, else if, end if		[insert pg. 215]
formats		Changes the format of variables (for example, f8.2→f1.0)
write outfile		Changes your data to ASCII format (no grids/cells)
$casenum		Numbers cases in your datafile (number of nonempty rows); use this with compute
select if		[insert pg. 180]
aggregate		[insert pg. 214]
flip	Very important	[insert pg. 210]

Answers to Chapter Discussion Questions

Chapter 1

Questions

1 Why is SPSS superior to Excel?

2 What are some advantages and disadvantages associated with SPSS's evolution toward an Excel–Word hybrid?

Answers

1 You can keep a record of what you've done and what you're going to do. Formulas don't "run automatically" – they run only when you tell them to run.

2 The data file interface is nice for data entry and organization, but there is too much capability in the data file. Ideally you should not be able to run analyses straight from your data file.

Chapter 2

Questions

1 In the text it is mentioned that _____ files look similar to a spreadsheet such as the ones you would find in Excel. On the other hand, there are _____ files which look similar to a Word Document, and are to be used as diaries to keep track of where your data came from, what analysis you have done, etc.

2 Why is it important to maintain your raw data "untouched"?

IBM SPSS Essentials: Managing and Analyzing Social Sciences Data, Second Edition.
John Kulas, Renata Garcia Prieto Palacios Roji, and Adam Smith.

Answers

1 Data files, Syntax files

2 Maintaining the unadulterated status of your original raw data file is key to using SPSS correctly, this is what will enable you to redo and undo any errors that you make.

Chapter 3

Questions

1 What numbers can be used to code the following values?
   a. Gender
   b. Military rank
   c. Height

2 Why would anyone include covariates in a data file?

3 Data represented by numbers are known as _____ variables, while data represented by words are known as _____ variables.

Answers

1 Gender doesn't matter (nominal value), military rank needs to follow a sequence (ordinal value), and height needs *real* numbers (ratio value).
   a. Many possibilities
      Male (1) Female (2)
      Male (100) Female (−1)
      Male (0.24) Female (0.6)
   b. Fewer possibilities
      Private (1) Corporal (2) Sergeant (3)
      Private (−1) Corporal (0) Sergeant (1)
      Private (10) Corporal (8) Sergeant (6)
   c. Very few possibilities (you have no options other than the metric [inches, mm, cm] with ratio-level variables)
      1 inch = 1, 1 and 1/2 inches = 1.5
   d. Many possibilities
      Male (1) Female (2)
      Male (100) Female (−1)
      Male (0.24) Female (0.6)

e. Fewer possibilities
Private (1) Corporal (2) Sergeant (3)
Private (–1) Corporal (0) Sergeant (1)
Private (10) Corporal (8) Sergeant (6)
f. Very few possibilities (you have no options other than the metric [inches, mm, cm] with ratio-level variables)
1 inch = 1, 1 and 1/2 inches = 1.5

2 You include covariates when you do not have an experimental design (these situations are either classified as quasi-experimental or nonexperimental). They allow for control to be exerted analytically instead of methodologically (as is the case with experimental designs).

3 Numeric, String

Chapter 4

Questions

1 What is the importance of the case number?

2 Why are the "get file" and "save outfile" commands so important?

Answers

1 If you find a mistake in your electronic data file (for example, an out-of-range value), it's helpful to know what person or data is associated with that mistake. Instead of looking through many hardcopies for a possible match, you can go directly to the associated hardcopy.

2 Especially with newer versions of SPSS, in which multiple data files can be open at the same time, it's *critical* that the user specifies which data file he or she is dealing with. You can *avoid* having more than one data file open at a time by religiously using the "get file" and "save outfile" commands.

Chapter 5

Questions

1 Why is it important to save a new data file every time you make changes to the data?

2   When would you want to create a subset of data, and what command should you use?

Answers

1   You create a new data file when making changes to the raw data file in order to preserve the integrity of the raw data file. The original raw data file should always remain unaltered, and any changes made should be saved in a new data file under a different name.

2   You can create a subset of data if your original data set is too large, or if you want to analyze specific information within your data file. You would use the "save outfile/" and specify what you do want to keep with the "keep" command, or omit what you don't want with the "drop" command.

Chapter 6

Questions

1   If my variable names are self-explanatory, do I still need to give them labels?

2   Does the coding scheme make a difference if I add value labels?

Answers

1   Yes, output will report labels, so even if your label is the same as your variable name (that is, gender), go ahead and get in the habit of giving every variable a label.

2   The coding scheme could potentially make a difference depending on the measurement of your variables (see Chapter 3 discussion questions). If you have a nominal variable, the coding scheme does not matter. If you have an ordinal variable, the coding scheme should match the variable sequence.

Chapter 7

Questions

1   What are some applications of the "descriptives" information?

2   What are some applications of the "frequencies" information?

Answers

1 Some possible uses
   a. Computing z-scores
   b. Reporting means and standard deviations

2 Some possible uses
   a. Determining tertial, median, quartile, and so on split locations
   b. Scanning for out-of-range values – these are usually data entry errors

Chapter 8

Questions

1 What is the goal when computing an inferential statistic?

2 Explain the differences between Type I and Type II errors.

3 What would you conclude (Step 6) if your obtained value is equal to 0.027, while your critical value is equal you 0.05?

Answers

1 To make the statistical decision of either rejecting or failing to reject the null hypothesis.

2 Your Type I error rate is your willingness to reject the null hypothesis when in fact you "shouldn't do so". Your Type II error rate is your willingness to fail to reject the null hypothesis when in fact you "should do so".

3 You reject the null hypothesis.

Chapter 9

Questions

1 What would happen to my obtained t if I ran a paired-samples t-test situation as an independent-samples t-test?

2 How practical is the one-sample t-test?

3 Your parents claim college students sleep too much. They claim the average amount of sleep "normal" people get is eight hours. You survey seven of your classmates, who sleep 9, 11, 7, 8, 13, 12, and 10 hours per night. Do college students sleep more than what your parents claim is "average"?

4 You believe llamas from Peru are able to spit farther than llamas from Australia. You travel to Peru to measure the distance llamas are able to spit and obtain the following: 22, 26, 28, 19, 24 cm. You catch a flight to Auburn, Australia, and find a llama farm where you are able to measure the distance to which those llamas are able to spit: 20, 15, 40, 23, and 18 cm. Are llamas from Peru able to spit (on average) further than the llamas from Auburn, Australia?

5 You want to know the effect of caffeine on reaction time. You recruit your friends on two different occasions. Once you have them drink five cups of coffee before you throw foam-tipped darts at them; on the second occasion you have them drink five cups of water before trying to hit them with darts. You record the following number of hits (out of 20 throws):

	Caffeine	Water
Bob	5	10
Sally	15	16
Persephone	12	15
June	4	6
Eunice	8	12

Does caffeine affect reaction time?

Answers

1 I would obtain a "lower" t-value (closer to zero) with the independent samples t-test – try it.

2 Not very – it's not usual to be given a value to compare a sample against.

3 One-sample t-test situation: $t = 2.45$, $p < 0.05$ (one-tailed). Yes, college students sleep more than average.

4 Two independent-samples situations: $t = -0.13$, $p > 0.05$. The mean for llamas in Peru resulted in 23.8, while the mean for llamas in Auburn resulted in 23.2.

Even though there was a slight difference between the means, our two independent samples t-test shows that the difference is not statistically significant.

5   Two paired-samples situation: t = 4.24, p < 0.05 (two-tailed). Caffeine does help reaction time.

Chapter 10

Questions

1   Why does SPSS use different terms than the terms that social science students learn?

2   Why is the repeated measures output so over-the-top?

3   Thirty chronic headache sufferers were assigned to one of three conditions: watch cartoons, go for a walk, or eat ice cubes. The researcher hopes that one of these treatments may help their suffering. Over the course of one month, the thirty people record the following number of reported headaches:

Cartoon watchers	Walkers	Ice-eaters
5	20	5
2	16	6
13	25	20
8	8	25
20	6	6
25	9	30
15	11	11
11	15	5
6	5	15
8	6	8

Are any of these treatments more or less effective than the others?

4   Maybe the effectiveness of these treatments depends on the gender of the headache sufferer. Organizing the data a little bit differently we want to know if there is a difference in number of headaches across treatments for men and women.

	Cartoon watchers	Walkers	Ice-eaters
Men	5	20	5
	2	16	6
	13	25	20
	8	8	25
	20	6	6
Women	25	9	30
	15	11	11
	11	15	5
	6	5	15
	8	6	8

5   Run the appropriate t-test as well as the appropriate ANOVA for the caffeine example from Chapter 10. What's the relationship between your obtained F and t?

Answers

1   Social science fields use statistics, but statistics does not serve only the social sciences. Some of the terms used by statisticians make more sense to physicists and astronomers than they do to psychologists, geographers, or economists.

2   Because it is such a flexible analysis – you can run this procedure or command for many reasons other than doing a repeated-measures ANOVA.

3   No, there is no difference among treatments: $F = 0.14$, $p > 0.05$.

4   It still doesn't matter; the interaction effect is nonsignificant ($F = 0.95$, $p > 0.05$).

5   Two (paired samples) t ($t = 4.24$, $p < 0.05$) and repeated measures ANOVA ($F = 18$, $p < 0.05$). Your t is the square-root of your F (alternatively, your F is your t squared). This is true for any t situation (between or within subjects) for which you specify an ANOVA rather than the simpler t.

Chapter 11

Questions

1   Why is there an ANOVA table in my regression output?

2   Why doesn't SPSS include R^2 change as a default reported statistic?

3 Based on the following data, is there a relationship between shoe size and height? Number of siblings and height? Shoe size and number of siblings?

	Shoe size	Height	Number of siblings
Hector	12	68	2
Sue	7	66	10
Sally	17	75	9
Eugene	14	70	8
Valencia	8	64	7
Penelope	9.5	60	3
Fernando	5	63	2
Norbert	15	74	10

4 If I wanted to predict how tall someone might be, given their shoe size and number of siblings, how would I go about doing that?

Answers

1 This is the statistic (F) used to report the significance of your overall regression equation (Multiple R/R^2), so you need it.

2 Probably because a straight regression (in which you have only one step) is so common. Putting an R^2 change column in the default output table would be confusing in this situation. It is informative only in a hierarchical or stepwise regression (these are less common regression procedures than the straight regression).

3 Correlation is appropriate here. Shoe size and height are related ($r = 0.85$, $p < 0.05$), but shoe size and number of siblings ($r = 0.44$, $p > 0.05$) and height and number of siblings ($r = 0.64$, $p > 0.05$) are unrelated. Note that we have pretty high correlations (0.44 and 0.64) that are nonsignificant – this means that there is a relationship in our sample, but it's not strong enough (and our sample's too small) for us to say that these sample relationships reflect meaningful associations in the larger population.

4 Regression: height $= 54.66 + 0.89$*height $+ 0.49$* number of siblings. This could also be written generally as: $Y' = 54.66 + 0.89(X1) + 0.49(X2)$.

Chapter 12

Questions

1. When a population parameter is estimated, or assumptions are made about the underlying population, you have a _____ analysis. On the other hand, when you conduct an analysis where there is no estimation of the parameter, and no assumptions are made, you have a _____ analysis.
2. An industrial psychologist is interested in determining whether there is a relationship between the education level of employees and the number of jobs they currently have. Accordingly, a survey is taken, and the following results are obtained:

	Number of Jobs	
	Two or less	More than less
College Education	53	22
High school Education	37	38

1 What is the null hypothesis?

2 What is the conclusion? Use $\alpha = 0.05$.

Answers

1 Null hypothesis: The educational level of parents and the number of jobs they have are independent. The frequency obtained in each cell is due to random sampling from a population where the proportions of college-educated and only high-school-educated people have (a) two or fewer and (b) more than two jobs are equal.

2 Conclusion, using $\alpha = 0.05$:
$X^2 = 3.841$
Since $X^2 > 3.841$, we reject the null hypothesis. The educational level of employees and the number of jobs they have are related.

Chapter 13

Questions

1 Is it ever advisable to not run the entire syntax at once?

2 If I'm going to use drop-down menus, why don't I just skip the "paste" part?

Answers

1   If you are testing out a command (for example, to see if it works), you can highlight and run a small part of your syntax file. Even in this situation, however, after you have determined that your syntax works, you need to close any open output file and run the entire syntax file at once prior to interpreting your results.

2   One of the primary reasons you are using syntax is to keep a record of everything that you have done to your data. You paste so you have such a record.

Chapter 14

Questions

1   When matching files, the order of the command specifications indicates what files we want to match (what file's variables will be added at the end of the open file). What do the commands in each command line represent?

2   When matching two sets of data containing string variables, what should you do prior to matching the files based on shared string variables?

Answers

1   The first line with the * represents the file that is currently open. The second line identifies the file we want to combine to the open file (this file's variables will be added to the open file). The third line identifies the variables you want to "match" from both files.

2   You must first organize the string variables alphabetically in both files.

Chapter 15

Questions

1   "Select if" and "split file" do essentially the same thing; why do I need to learn both?

2   What happens if I forget to turn the "split file" command off?

Answers

1 "Select if" creates a smaller data file; "split file" keeps all of your data but organizes analyses, manipulations, and output. They have similar effects, but they actually do different things.

2 All of your manipulations, analyses, and output will be done separately for your split. This can really screw up manipulation and transformation requests that you write.

Chapter 16

Questions

1 Why do I have to start with the first haiku?

2 How can I make the most use out of the column tracker information?

Answers

1 Later errors may actually be consequences of the first error. Once you correct the first one, the others may be resolved.

2 If you're going to rely heavily on the column tracker, don't use tabs in your syntax file. If you do use tabs, remember that the column tracker reflects characters, not actual columns.

Chapter 17

Questions

1 Why can't I do the Notepad Find and Replace function in my syntax file?

2 When would I use the "aggregate" function?

Answers

1 You *can* do this within a syntax file; it's just important that you don't do it within the same syntax file that you're going to use the information in. If you do this within the syntax file that you want to eventually use, the Find and Replace is too broad; it will find and replace stuff that you don't want to replace.

2 In addition to deleting duplicate cases, anytime you want to collapse across rows to create a new data file, you need to use this command; it's actually very flexible and you'll use it for reasons that I haven't yet thought of.

Index

IBM SPSS Essentials: Managing and Analyzing Social Sciences Data, Second Edition.
John Kulas, Renata Garcia Prieto Palacios Roji, and Adam Smith.
© 2021 John Wiley & Sons, Inc. Published 2021 by John Wiley & Sons, Inc.